SO-BAK-229

Jonathan Harley is a reporter and producer with the Australian Broadcasting Corporation. He was the ABC's New Delhi-based South Asia Correspondent from 1998 to 2002, during which time he covered coups, cricket corruption scandals, earthquakes and a royal family massacre. Jonathan reported from Taliban-ruled Afghanistan and was the only Australian journalist in Kabul on September 11, 2001. He covered the ensuing war, post-Taliban Afghanistan and the 2003 conflict in Iraq. Jonathan lives in Sydney with his wife and daughter.

Lost in Transmission

Jonathan Harley

BANTAM
SYDNEY • AUCKLAND • TORONTO • NEW YORK • LONDON

LOST IN TRANSMISSION
A BANTAM BOOK

First published in Australia and New Zealand in 2004
by Bantam

Copyright © Jonathan Harley, 2004

All rights reserved. No part of this publication may be reproduced, stored
in a retrieval system, transmitted in any form or by any means, electronic,
mechanical, photocopying, recording or otherwise, without the prior
written permission of the publisher.

National Library of Australia
Cataloguing-in-Publication Entry

Harley, Jonathan.
Lost in transmission.

ISBN 1 86325 399 8.

1. Harley, Jonathan. 2. Foreign correspondents – Australia
– Biography. 3. Television journalists – Australia –
Biography. I. Title

070.4332092

Transworld Publishers,
a division of Random House Australia Pty Ltd
20 Alfred Street, Milsons Point, NSW 2061
http://www.randomhouse.com.au

Random House New Zealand Limited
18 Poland Road, Glenfield, Auckland

Transworld Publishers,
a division of The Random House Group Ltd
61–63 Uxbridge Road, London W5 5SA

Random House Inc
1745 Broadway, New York, New York 10036

Typeset in 11/14 Sabon by Midland Typesetters, Maryborough, Victoria
Printed and bound by Griffin Press, Netley, South Australia

10 9 8 7 6 5 4 3 2 1

To Mum,
To Sarah
And
To Harry, Matt, Malakai and Muza

AUTHOR'S NOTE

This book is a personal look at a time of upheaval in India, Pakistan, Afghanistan and Nepal, beyond to Iraq and around the entire world. Generally, events appear in chronological order, but in some cases, there have been slight shifts for the purposes of narrative. Names of some characters have been changed, either on their request or to protect them. The transliteration of foreign words remains the subject of endless debate; and I have tried to balance personal preference and expert advice with what is widely accessible to readers.

CONTENTS

PROLOGUE

DEATH BY BUFFET

20 March 2003
US Central Command, Doha, Qatar
Operation Iraqi Freedom
Day One

The war is a thousand kilometres away. No, really: the war *is* a thousand kilometres away. I'm on the outskirts of a synthetic city, in a cavernous khaki hangar on a soulless expanse of desert. Welcome to Coalition Central Command. In an age of acronymphomania, it is known as CENTCOM.

'More like CENT-CON!' a British journalist growls into his coffee, glaring at the bank of TVs with their smorgasbord of satellite networks. The televisions all show us the same pictures and the same information – that the war has begun – but we're getting more information from these screens than the commanders here in our midst who are supposed to brief us.

Our pens are poised, our pads prepared, our brows are good and furrowed. We've come to write history's first draft of this war but the halls are not humming with briefings; corners are not crowded with colonels chatting with correspondents. In the conference hall, the quarter-million-US-dollar, Hollywood-designed stage set has lights, cameras and sparkling plasma screens, but no action. More than 700 registered journalists have congregated only to be deafened by the din of military silence.

After twelve years of diplomatic wrangling and wrong-footing, breast-beating and military mobilising, the push to putsch Saddam Hussein has begun. American warplanes have walloped what US President George W. Bush calls a 'target of opportunity'. We, the media, have been panting for the opportunity to declare the war started, working ourselves into a flurry of speculation and analysis. 'Shock and awe'. 'Precise munitions'. 'Softening up the enemy'. The retired colonels and armchair generals wore out their jargon before the first shot was fired, and now, armed with only a smattering of hard facts, we have little more to add.

The ABC, like almost every news broadcaster around the world, has moved to rolling coverage, and I'm on the phone, waiting to do a live cross with *PM*'s Mark Colvin. Despite CENTCOM's shortcomings, I am revved with the buzz of a big, moving story. I hear Mark's voice down the line.

'Jonathan,' he begins, 'what exactly are the Americans telling the world about what they've done?'

I glance down at my notepad. The page is blank.

'Well, from here in the middle of the desert in Qatar, just on the outskirts of Doha, Mark, they are telling us absolutely nothing . . .'

When I finish, *PM*'s producer, quite rightly, gently suggests I take a slightly different tack: to outline what we *do* know from other sources before citing CENTCOM's cone of silence.

As if to make up for the military's muteness, the air is thick with journalists yelling down phones, the frantic tap of fingers on laptops, the stench of egos burning. It feels more like a Wall Street trading floor than the start of a war. We are in full flight but there's barely a soldier in sight. A battalion of military media officers hide in their operations room, though just inches away on the opposite side of a common wall. Knock on the door and no-one will answer. Instead, we must go through the ridiculous charade of phoning whenever we seek any sort of update or clarification. If we're very lucky, they'll agree to speak with us in person. Mostly, I'm not sure why we bother: on the phone or in person, by appointment or random appearance, they have little of substance to say.

Outside, under a gritty Gulf sky, grinds the chatter of correspondents, staring sternly down cameras to New York, Tokyo or Madrid. A Humvee has been thoughtfully placed as a backdrop to the camera positions to make it look like we're in a war zone.

And since Saddam Hussein is supposed to have weapons of mass destruction poised – that's what this war is apparently about, after all – most of us carry gas masks or chemical suits. But the only danger here is to be had in the five-star hotels that dot Doha, a city that has morphed Islamabad with Sanctuary Cove. At the end of each day, when we retire to our towers of marble and brass, where smoked salmon and fine French wines await, our greatest threat is death by buffet.

Day three of the war and the man in charge, American Combat Commander General Tommy Franks, strides on stage. We sit abuzz with anticipation, herded into strict social classes – the American networks get nametagged front-row seats, while behind them are us lesser media beings. General Franks is folksy, forceful and euphemistic. His military campaign is a 'mosiac', delivering 'decisive precision shock' and 'at places and times of our choosing'. And there will be truth in war. 'This platform is not a platform for propaganda,' he promises, 'this is a platform for truth.'

We lap it up because it's all we've got. General Franks has provided fodder for filing, which is all that matters when life is a continuous live cross, punctuated by hourly news bulletins and snippets of sleep.

I turn to a colleague for reassurance. 'Is this journalism?' I plead.

'God, no!' he replies with not so much as a bat of the eyelids. 'But if we're lucky, it might just pass as reporting.'

Don't tell that to the boys from Rupert Murdoch's Fox News Channel. With its shameless sloganeering and non-stop Stars and Stripes fluttering on its screen, Fox's reporters refer to Coalition troops as 'we', 'ours' and 'liberators'. Off air, these young guns are appropriately gung-ho, with thunderous high fives and shouts of 'LET'S GO!' I despise their so-called journalism but I smile at their bravado. They ooze ambition and testosterone, enthusiasm and arrogance.

But I shall not judge them.

I have been there myself. Almost.

CHAPTER 1

OPTION OVERLOAD

1998

Don't think me ungrateful. I'm just no longer sure I want the job. Those wiser and more worldly might say that becoming the ABC's New Delhi-based South Asia corre-spondent is a three-year sentence to dysentery, delays and clichés buried at the bottom of the weekend news bulletin. But in my innocence, or ignorance, I had imagined roaming around India, Pakistan and Afghanistan, not to mention the half-dozen smaller nations of South Asia, as adventure itself.

How a little love and lust can change your view.

For the last two weeks I have been falling for an old friend, forgetting about the job bid and falling out of love with the idea of India.

Now the boss is on the phone and I don't know what to say. 'Congratulations,' he chirps. 'I'm just about to put your appointment out on email.'

My mind is racing: Sarah, a presenter at the ABC's youth network, Triple J, will read that her new boyfriend is about to leave town. You'd at least want to hear it from the horse's mouth so you could whack him there and then.

'I need to think about it over the weekend,' I blurt. 'I need to think it through.'

Friday afternoon. There goes the weekend.

By Saturday lunch, my fingernails are gnawed to stubs; staring at the peeling ceiling above the bath has never been so arresting. My mental jukebox is on high rotation with The Clash: should I stay or should I go? If I stay and say no to the job, my career ends before it begins. And it is the job I've been desperately wanting. If I say yes and go, it's in the knowledge that long-distance love never lasts long. I want it all – love life, work life, a life. Such is the bane of my privileged generation: the quandary of option overload.

Sarah is attempting a brave face, which only amplifies her look of bemusement.

'Oh no! Not India! *Anywhere* but India!'

'I'm getting too comfortable.'

'What's wrong with comfortable?'

'I need a challenge.'

I know she won't leave Sydney – she has her perfect job presenting the *Morning Show* across Australia; she has success and an ocean-view apartment. For a fleeting moment she had a little love, but now she's just got an abandoning boyfriend, and I've got the guilts.

Monday morning, I take the job. Friends knew I would.

Amid the maze of packing boxes littering my living room, Sarah and I try to find our way to some sort of 'real' relationship. We are on accelerated affection. My boss insists I be in India 'by Christmas', so I book the flight for a few days before, and the closer it gets, the greater our denial. Silently, behind Sarah's resigned smile and my excited apprehension, we count the days. A last long night is spent cursing my decision, until Sarah finally falls asleep as a screaming December sun washes the sky pink and orange.

Strips of clouds hang inky blue, the ocean is glassy flat and, like a man on death row ordering his last meal, I go for one last swim. Tomorrow I will be soaking in diesel fumes and dust, so I dive in with boyish joy. Small fish whisk through strands of seaweed, sand washes in graceful, silent swells; my skin records every tingle. Lingering in this underwater wonderland, I say my goodbyes and prepare for more fraught farewells.

I can't bring myself to shower away the sea, so with salt still thick in my hair and caked on my skin, I check in at the Singapore Airlines desk with a trolley full of gear and a head crammed with ideas. I used to think of Sydney's Kingsford Smith Airport as an exciting exit for new adventures but today it feels sombre and uncertain. Sarah looks fantastic, already tanned by the first weeks of summer, her hair spraying in lawless coils. Mum and friends are full of Christmas love and optimism; hugs last forever, yet never long enough. I hold Sarah for an eternity, or rather she holds me up. Then I am gone. And so is she.

'Where ya headin'?' the immigration officer drawls.

'To India,' I reply, a bit coyly, 'Pakistan . . . Afghanistan . . . that part of the world.'

'India? Christ, mate, that's another bloody universe over there. Good luck. You'll need it.'

The only immediate luck I need is with the in-flight entertainment. I can't work out how to change channels with the handset. It's a bad technological omen: I am about to face an endless array of technical challenges from satellite phones to digicams and here I am struggling just to organise a rerun of *Friends*. Truth be known, I am a TV virgin. I mean, I love watching it but have never had to make it. Radio has been my passion but in the brave new world of 'bi-media' reporting, where my filming skills will be as important as my words, all is about to change: I have a tiny, shiny digicam with an impossible instruction manual and a wobbly tripod. With no cameraman awaiting me in New Delhi, I will be a one-man band, a lab rat in a new multimedia experiment. Given I can barely use a box brownie and am already defeated by this handset, my hopes are not high. Too embarrassed to ask the stewards for help, I stare out the window.

Australia's scorched patchwork of scrub and soil provides the best in-flight entertainment in the world. Even from thirty thousand feet (*especially* at thirty thousand feet) my country vibrates – a chorus of ancient Aboriginal songlines and a young nation's enthusiasm. Its expanse reminds me how little I know about my own home but also how much it has moulded me. The Australian outback always seemed like a vast runway to an even wider world beyond. I am a Sydney boy who grew up with families from the far off battlegrounds of the 1970s – Cambodia, Vietnam and Lebanon. They sought sanctuary in suburban sterility and provided first glimpses of lands beyond redbrick views and barbecues; while the streets' concrete footpaths were mercifully brightened by Indian mothers in brilliant saris and subdued by Mediterranean widows draped in black. Now, as the edge of northern Australia slides beneath me, the rust red and electric green of Arnhem Land dissolving into the cobalt Gulf of Carpentaria, I feel quietly, incurably Australian. Pressing my face against the glass, like a kid not wanting to say goodbye, I catch a last glimpse of home.

The new home awaiting me feels remote and daunting as I ponder how little I know about South Asia. The Indian Prime Minister is a seventy-year-old bachelor-cum-poet called Vajpayee, whose first and second names I am yet to commit to memory. A billion people live in India – eighty-two per cent of them Hindu – and growing by the equivalent of Australia's population every year. Muslim Pakistan is run by a billionaire called Nawaz Sharif, whose name I remember because it sounds like 'sheriff'. India and Pakistan are dysfunctional siblings who waste countless time, money and lives fighting for the Himalayan territory of Kashmir. Adding fuel to the furore, when Prime Minister Vajpayee's Hindu-Nationalist coalition won office in May 1998, it celebrated with a cracker-bag of nuclear tests in the Rajasthan desert. Not to be outdone, Pakistan returned the fireworks soon after, blasting itself into the world's craziest military club, giving birth to a new regional arms race.

But wait, there's more.

Pakistan's friend and neighbour, Afghanistan, under the notorious Taliban regime, is conducting a medieval social experiment to create a seventh-century Islamic utopia. The militia also harbours 'honoured guest' Osama bin Laden, along with his several wives, more than a dozen children and his thousands of loyal, battle-hardened foreign fighters. That's about the sum total of my knowledge, suspended in a head sizzling with romantic notions of being a so-called roving reporter on the Indian subcontinent – dreams stewed on Kipling's India, Hemingway's war stories and journalistic idealism.

The silent assumption among family and friends is that this whole adventure will end my teen-creep: the phenomenon of prolonging adolescence into your twenties and even thirties. In the words of an older journalist, the assignment will 'put chalk on ya bones'. I think he meant it will make me a man. I think I need a drink.

The stupid red watch I bought in a rash of retail therapy during a short stopover in Singapore says it is eleven at night. The clock on the wall says it's six; but it's been saying that for the last hour, which is how long New Delhi airport officials have been contemplating my passport. Well, contemplating their navels. I have been shunted into a side room furnished with a dozen men sipping tea and that stinks of jetlag and cigarettes. The fat man with shiny epaulets and a greasy comb-over is clearly top dog: his every word meets a roar of laboured laughter or knowing head wobbles from fawning inferiors. These guys are nestling in for a night of adulation.

'Mr Jonathan . . .' fat official man finally begins.

'Yes, sir.' I adopt my most flattering tone, trying to mask my Australian contempt for bureaucracy, hierarchy and plain old wankers.

'Have you met Shane Warne?'

'Ummm, no.'

'Shane Warne is verrrry good cricketer.'

A round of knowing wobbles from the chorus line of lads.

'BUT HE IS A MATCH-FIXER!' he booms, and even the chorus line looks rattled.

'Well, sir . . .' I offer, not sure what to say. He saves me by interrupting.

'Mr Jonathan, you are a journalist?'

'Yes, sir.'

'You work for Channel 9?'

'Um, no sir, I work for the ABC, the Australian Broadcasting Corporation. You can see there on my papers . . .'

'Channel 9 verrrrry good cricket network!'

I won't tell him it's the ABC's news rival.

'Your papers say you are the South Asia Chief of Bureau,' he condescends with a smile. 'I think you are far too young for such a job but I am telling you . . . you are most welcome in India!'

And with a thunderous stamp of my passport, fat man waves me into the abyss, having proven nothing except his power to waste my time – a display not for my benefit but for his minions'. The first volley in my three-year battle with India's notorious bureaucracy has been fired.

'AND MR JONATHAN!' fat man repeats as I walk out the door. 'You are most welcome!'

Angry, amused, relieved, I head for the exit with my trolley of boxes and bags, to be greeted by a heaving wall of humanity: Indians waiting for family and friends are pinned to a high cyclone fence opposite the exit. Columns of steam rise from this reception ruck into the cold, pungent air. It's after midnight but this airport is alive with activity – I'd hate to see it at peak hour. As I step beyond the safety of the barrier, I am suddenly swept into an unstoppable current of hawkers, porters and nonstop talkers. Amid the din, one voice persists – one I don't notice at first.

'Sir! Sir!' the man is almost whispering to me.

'No thank you.'

'Sir! Sir!'

'Look, no thanks.'

'Sir! Sir!'

'Look, mate. I DON'T NEED TAXI!'

'Sir! Sir! I am Abraham, sir. I am driver.' He speaks so quietly I barely make out his words but soon realise this is the man I've been told to meet: Abraham, the ABC's man of the road for more than twenty years. He smiles warmly through his obvious nervousness at meeting his new boss (is that *me*?), takes my trolley and sets off through the throng. While Abraham may be softly spoken, he is no soft touch and he cuts a sharp path through the airport anarchy.

'No, sir! I will do!' Abraham gasps when I try to throw the gear into the back of the car. It would seem 'sir' does not lift luggage. A bony boy asks for money to help us but Abraham sweeps him away, bundles me into the car and roars off in a pall of fumes and horns, the boy left coughing in our cloud of smog.

The damp New Delhi night is grey and dense – the thick wintry haze makes it impossible to see beyond the bonnet. Abraham feels his way through this soup, packed with blurting trucks, farting auto-rickshaws and doddering cows. When a cyclist spins out of a side street into our path, he swerves, unfazed, and barely seems to notice the towering truck almost scraping my side. Thankfully, it's not long before we pull into the ABC compound, where I am greeted by a wide-smiling man who opens my door and offers a compromise between a wave and a salute. I go to shake his hand only to cause untold confusion and embarrassment to the both of us.

'Hi, my name is Jonathan.'

'Yes, sir,' comes the reply, with no less than a little bow.

Perhaps this is not the time to be forging new friend-ships, so I step straight up to the first floor, to find a shell of an apartment. There's a sofa and table, some chairs and a bed, but otherwise it's empty. The bare walls are blotchy with black crud from pollution, the freezing marble floor is naked; my footsteps greet me in melancholy echoes. I walk from room to room, up and down the hall, I kick around the kitchen and try to imagine this as home. It will take some imagination.

I didn't expect a maharajah's palace or a welcoming parade of elephants and dancing girls, but I did expect hot water.

I walk into the bathroom and turn on the shower tap to be greeted by a cold, rust-coloured dribble. Crusty and jet-lagged, I collapse on the bed, clothes and all.

Now I'm sure: I definitely don't want the job.

CHAPTER 2

TO SIR WITH LOVE

So this is Christmas: cold, damp and anonymous. It's not the humid madness of an Australian family Christmas and it's certainly not the scorching heat for which India is infamous. In fact, I've never been so bone-chillingly cold. A dank fog has squatted on New Delhi – carrying a cocktail of diesel and the acrid smoke from millions of people burning cow dung to cook and keep warm. The smoky windows of the apartment look out on a crowded intersection of waddling auto-rickshaws and Toontown taxis. Dust seems to grow on trees, their leaves thick with orange muck. This city, among the most polluted in the world, needs a serious scrub and so does this apartment.

Thankfully, serious help is at hand.

My domestic loneliness ends with an invasion of staff returning from their Christmas break. The front line in this small army of workers is Rachel, the cook. She is matronly, twenty-three, and has twice as much sense as I do. She starts my day with steaming sweet tea, firm homemade curd and a cheerful 'Good morning, sir'. My Australian upbringing makes me allergic to being called 'sir' at any time of the day and first thing in the morning it is driving me insane – more like being on a parade ground than in my living room.

'Rachel,' I implore, 'please don't call me "sir".'

'Yes, sir,' she replies, scurrying off to the kitchen.

Returning with a pad, pencil and purposeful look on her face, Rachel is ready to take orders. 'What would sir like for lunch and dinner?'

'Ummmm, I don't even know what I want for the rest of breakfast.' But Rachel's day must be planned. She is efficient, caring and constant in a city that is none of the above. This lass from Madras knows where to get the best fresh fish in from Bombay and can dig out Delhi's last slice of ricotta. Her fish curries are to die for and her *masala dosa* – a huge, thin southern Indian pancake filled with spicy delights – is sublime.

However, such culinary wonders need forethought. The *dosa* mix must foment overnight and the fruit and vegetables need to be soaked and scrubbed in a strange disinfectant that looks too much like the purplish potassium permanganate we used in school science experiments. Even the water itself needs industrial purifying and then boiling, thanks to New Delhi's deadly blend of pesticides, poisons and heavy metals. The water filter sings a ditzy rendition of 'Jingle Bells' every morning when it's turned on, and it's fast becoming the maddening soundtrack to my new domestic life.

Rachel flips through my cookbooks, suggesting recipes and asking after others.

'What is it, sir?' Pointing at a photo of quiche.

'That's quiche. It's like a fluffy egg pie.'

'Kweeesh? Good, isn't it? I will make.'

As Rachel scuttles out, a much smaller figure silently shuffles in. Mary, the cleaner, is a diminutive woman who seems to slide along the floor in an endless sweeping motion, uttering only the rudiments of service-class English. 'Hello, sir. Fine, thank you, sir,' seems to be on endless loop. There must be millions in this city who spend their working day saying little else. Even when I ask her to do something, Mary's stock reply is 'Thank you, sir' – and Rachel translates my request into their native Tamil tongue. But Mary's slightness and whispered patter hide a steely resolve to change my world in her image.

After I unpack my books and clothes, she moves them all from one cupboard to another. Apparently I put them in the 'wrong place'. Mary is cleaning my life into chaos and we embark on a silent, daily battle of nerves.

Our most bitter battleground will be in the office. Directly above the apartment for round-the-clock access, it's as crowded with junk as my new home is sparse: old newspapers are piled in corners, dog-eared, yellow and horribly dusty. The cabinet is a mess of old files not maintained in years. Opening a cupboard, a tangled mess of cords, old tape recorders and cassettes tumble onto the floor in a puff of dust. It's the accumulated crap of a decade of predecessors; Mary can do no more than clean around it. I am dreading sorting through it all but start by trying to bring a little order and function to my desk. I have skewed it at an angle from the wall, so I can see out the window and the TV in the corner.

Slowly, insidiously, the desk develops a mind of its own. The next day it is edged back square with the window. So I slide it back to where it was, only to discover the next day that it has crept back again. I am wondering if there is not some poltergeist hiding in the studio – a ghost of a former correspondent who never made it out of India. Part investigation, part brewing obsession, I even mark out the desk corners on the floor, so as to measure the drift. Eventually, I realise Mary has been waging a silent campaign for symmetry. As if to create an island of order in the most disorderly place on earth, she is squeezing me into her template. Correspondents come and go but the staff is constant. Mary gets her way.

With such determined domestic help, my Australian instinct for equality and self-sufficiency is being eroded by the day, encouraged by a healthy streak of laziness. Raising three boys, my mother's mantra was 'Just because you're male doesn't mean you have to be useless!' She cracked a tough whip, so by the time my two brothers and I left home, we were a small step up from useless. That is fast disappearing. Rachel's cooking is turning me into such a dunce in the kitchen, I can barely boil water. Mary is making my cleaner's elbow go to mush and Moolchand, the ever-smiling, pear-shaped laundry man, or *dobhiwallah*, has made me horrified by the mere sight of ironing.

My business card may say Chief of Bureau but the man really running the show is the office manager, John Peter. Like many Indians, he drops his first name and is known as Peter, which causes initial confusion. But after the few days it takes to work out what to call him, there is nothing confusing about the man – Peter is smart, hardworking and straightforward in a job demanding patience and deftness.

'*Sahib*,' he says, 'we must get your press pass from PIB.'

'What's PIB?' I ask, already drunk with India's love of abbreviations and acronyms.

'Press Information Bureau. They control your life.'

I thought the ABC controlled my life, which can only mean I am now sandwiched between two bureaucratic masters – the ABC's *and* India's. So, we head into central New Delhi with Abraham, a picture of concentration behind the wheel. Outside my window is a scene that defies my stereotypical image of a squalid, crowded India. New Delhi's carefully planned inner sanctum boasts wide, tree-lined boulevards and cosy bungalows occupied by India's political classes. This is the heart of a synthetic capital, cast in the image of the British Crown Raj, and built after King George V announced in 1911 that the central seat of power would move from the original colonial capital of Calcutta to New Delhi. At its centre, like a buxom wench, sits the Presidential Palace in pink Rajasthan stone, offset by India's answer to the Champs Elysées – a thrusting boulevard crowned by India Gate. Less spectacular is the nearby Press Information Bureau, with its seemingly endless maze of dark corridors and big-moustached men.

Fortunately, I have Peter, who darts in and out of dingy offices, introducing me to countless bureaucrats, getting me to sign four thousand pieces of paper, handing out copies of my passport photos, presenting letters from Sydney, and generally working a system designed to do anything but work. He even manages to laugh at the bureaucrats' jokes in a way that pleases them but doesn't demean him. All this from a low-caste, southern Indian, who should not normally be given the time of day by these northerner, New Delhi power paunches. Perhaps it's because he knows the fine line between greasing the wheels and an unashamed bribe.

'*Sahib*, see that man there,' he points to a thin, self-satisfied looking guy lounging behind a desk piled high with papers. 'Last time, he say "my trouser length is this and my jacket size is that".'

'He wants a new suit? That's corruption.'

'*Sahib*, that is New Delhi. It is city of money and madness. But he is not so powerful right now, so it is okay. One day, he may be strong, then may be problem.'

A senior bureaucrat, apparently his star rising rapidly through the system, pulls me aside.

'Jonathan, any time you need me to lean on someone, just call.' He hands me his card as he shakes my hand. I don't know whether to thank him or report him.

'Peter, do we . . . um, pay, um . . . inducements?' I can't believe my naivety in even asking the question.

'*Saaahhhiib*,' Peter flashes a brilliant smile beneath his greying moustache, 'a little gift here and a little present there, just to say thank you.' Peter is sage against the machine.

Before I know it, I have a freshly laminated press pass in my hand and Peter is sliding me out to the car. The trip back is quiet with Peter and Abraham doing their best to ignore each other, perhaps not wanting to appear informal or overly chatty around their new *sahib*. The only smile I see for the whole journey comes from Lakhan, the gate-keeper, as he offers his comical salute, which could just as easily be him scratching his head. He and his junior brother-in-guard, Amar, work a twelve-hour day each, opening the gate, keeping the place safe and keeping Peter in a constant supply of tea. India's legendary love for hierarchy is well entrenched even in the ABC's little empire, not that I have begun to understand it. I am grateful, though, that ours seems to be a peaceful realm. Many of the guards in the street have rifles and dogs but Lakhan and Amar look as if they would melt if they had to deal with any security accessory. Neither looks like they would say boo to a cockroach and that's fine by me.

As I get out of the car and Peter walks upstairs, Abraham whispers his first words for the whole journey. I think he says, 'Sir, may I show you, please?' He nervously ushers me into his 'quarters' above the garage – a tiny two-room bedsit where he, his wife and their three children live, sleep and study. The whole space reminds me of a small squat I had as a broke university student and is smaller than my living room in the three-bedroom, three-bathroom bachelor pad in which I now rattle around. Realising that half his family sleeps on the floor, for a split second I consider suggesting we swap houses, but think better of it. This is my first glimpse of working-class New Delhi and, while I have been in and out of more shocking places from Brazil to Benin, it comes as a bleak reminder of how tightly people live. Especially when it's on a salary and in conditions I am providing. No doubt millions are living in much worse ways but they are not my responsibility. Just the same, this home is littered with middle-class symbols of success: a colour TV in the corner, a stereo next to the sofa and a 'cooler' – a cheap form of airconditioner – filling in the window. But in the miniscule bathroom there is no washbasin. Which is why Abraham has brought me here.

'Sir, my family need to wash,' he whispers.

'No problem,' I declare benevolently, 'we can organise a washbasin for you. Sounds reasonable to me.'

Abraham beams and utters endless 'thank yous' as I tip-toe down his narrow stairs. I feel good and wonder why this was not done earlier: Abraham has worked as the ABC driver for more than two decades and lives on site, so that he is available all hours. The least we can do is provide him with a washbasin. I should be so naive.

It does not take long for the 'washbasin scandal' to rip through the staff like wildfire. I hear whispers in the hallway and on the stairwell in Tamil and Hindi, punctuated by the words 'washbasin' and 'Abraham'. Staff sulk around the place, until they see me and flash fake smiles. Finally, Peter broaches the subject.

'*Sahib*, Abraham has told me to organise a washbasin for his quarters, isn't it?'

I confirm it is.

'*Sahib*, this is problem,' he begins in very measured tones, as if giving me fatherly advice. 'All staff very upset. Abraham already has free quarters, no-one else has, and now he has washbasin, isn't it. Nobody has washbasin, very luxury item.'

I thank Peter for his advice, tell him to arrange a washbasin for Abraham, close my office door and slump into my chair with my head in my hands. I came to India to report, not mediate staff rivalries. Maybe fat man at the airport was right: perhaps I am too young for this job. I have been dropped into a world of secret resentments and petty competitions for the bosses' approval and favour. I have authority in a society where power is usually the preserve of elders. I feel like a boy playing grownups, entangled in this compound controversy over whether I approve a washbasin for a man nearly twice my age and with children not much younger than I am.

Rather than engage in a pointless conversation with myself about my predicament, I call for a staff get-together with coffee and cake to try to break the ice. It's a disastrous idea: everyone is too shy to say anything, and the lingering resentment over Abraham's washbasin is not helping. I am left to fill the void with words, any words. The guards, Lakhan and Amar, look like stunned mullets at being in the same room as the boss. Everyone gingerly sips their coffee, too coy to say they would rather have tea. I try a few jokes, which meet blank stares. I thank everyone for their warm welcome to India, which meets bemusement. In a desperate attempt to connect, to reveal there's more to their new boss than just journalism, I show some photos of Sarah, which meet nervous titters. When I ask if there are any questions, complaints or comments, I'm surrounded by giggles. No-one complains. Not directly, at least. The awkward silence is broken only by Moolchand, the *dhobiwallah*, who's wearing a toothy grin.

'Noooo, sir, noooo problems. Verrrryyy happy, sir!'

'And another thing,' I add. 'Can everyone please stop calling me "sir"?'

Everyone replies in chorus: 'YEESSS, SIR!'

I give up.

CHAPTER 3

BOYS DON'T CRY

I'm rescued from my office minefield by a story. But the news is brutal: reports are emerging of a horrible murder in India's eastern state of Orissa. A gang of Hindu zealots has burnt to death an Australian missionary, Graham Staines, and his two young sons – the boys, Timothy and Philip, were only six and ten years old, asleep with their dad in the family jeep when the mob locked them in, doused the vehicle in petrol and set the lot ablaze. It's terrible to feel strangely excited in the face of such horror, but I finally have a story. Bad news is news, and news is what correspondents do. Bad is good. Good is bad. I may be as green as can be, but I do know this will be a big story back home. A mix of instinct, ego and adrenalin kick in, dulling any sense of revulsion at what has happened and allowing me to focus on the task at hand. Revved up, all I have to do is get there.

Peter books me a dawn flight to Calcutta. The ageing plane is packed and groans off the ground with all the power of a lawn mower. Breakfast is a choice between vegetarian curry and chicken curry, so I just have a little tea. I must have dozed off because I am jolted awake by the crunch of plane on tarmac. In the midst of a screaming match at the taxi rank, involving a dozen men pulling my bags in as many directions, I hook up with Irish freelance journalist, Ian MacKinnon, who writes for the *Australian* newspaper, and we grab the one driver who is not hassling us – a half-blind man with a rusting Ambassador sedan. The three of us head off for a potholed, bandit-controlled road littered with the mangled carcasses of deadly car accidents.

Orissa is one of India's poorest states, a rural backwater ignored by New Delhi and forgotten by time. We chug through fields that look idyllic but the swaying crops of rice and maize hide a grinding poverty. Women hunch their way through the fields in thin, simple saris, which are more toga than dress – just a long, single strip of cloth, without the midriff blouse worn almost everywhere else in India. The blouse was introduced by the prudish English to cover the breasts but even the mighty British Empire did not stamp its influence on this remote area.

The roads are so bad the two-hundred kilometre journey from Calcutta takes ten hours, flattening my bum to a pancake and spinning my head with the petrol fumes that fill the car. The taxi putters into Baripada at dusk. It looks like the countless other towns we've passed today – everything made with string and tin; shaky stalls sell cigarettes and sachets of chewing *paan*; my nose stings with strong smells of spice, sweat and stale urine blended with diesel and cow dung. As darkness envelops the town, people are packing up; their working day may be finished but mine has only begun. With Sydney's time zone five hours ahead of India, I have only till midnight to find and file the story, and already I am twelve hours behind the eight-ball: the *Sydney Morning Herald*'s Christopher Kremmer, a legend for his decade of reporting throughout the region, arrived in Baripada *this morning*. Chris has been welcoming since I arrived in New Delhi but he is also my fiercest Australian competitor and I don't want to be shown up on my first story. I send the taxi to the hotel and follow a crowd towards the church.

The closer I get, the thicker the crowd. There are those who have come to grieve, others to stare and, hanging back in the evening shadows, a few lepers. Graham Staines came to Baripada from Queensland thirty-four years ago to treat society's most detested and rejected; he was the only person who showed these outcasts any affection and offered them any dignity. To his murderers, youths claiming to champion Hindu truths, he was a dangerous Christian soldier in a western conspiracy to convert Hindus and take over their country. In their madness, they not only torched the missionary but his sleeping sons.

Mourners' low moans and sobs line my path and I shudder at the thought of the boys' final, terrifying moments trapped in their jeep one hundred and seventy kilometres west of here. Their remains, burnt beyond recognition, are expected to come home later this evening. I step up to the rectory, which is overrun by friends, officials and the media but linger at the front door, nervously waiting to be invited in and rather embarrassed to be contributing to the swelling mayhem. I always thought a 'death knock' was the preserve of commercial TV; I've never done one and I have no desire to start now, but my awkwardness is thrust aside by an Indian camera crew rushing through the door. I follow to find a mass of media racing around the house as if it were theirs.

Beyond huddles of people weeping and praying, an arc of camera lights glare on Gladys Staines. India's latest widow sits calmly, almost serenely, patiently fielding reporters' questions. Perhaps she has not had time to cry or she's waiting for some privacy. She'll wait forever. Like most things in India, grieving is a public event. The rectory, a rambling colonial home behind the church, is overrun with those who come to comfort and condole, and those who come to gawk. We, the media, have come so the whole world can peek into Gladys Staines' suffering. I feel ashamed to be part of the invading rabble but that does not stop me edging to the front of the circle, to secure an interview. I guess one more journalist won't change her day. I press record on my minidisc and ask the most predictable, ridiculous question in journalism: 'How do you feel?' But her response is far from ordinary.

'God called them to him and I believe they were willing to die. This is how my husband would have wanted to die. I feel proud that he was willing to die,' she says with a measured smile, as if reciting lines in a play to an audience of journalists. Her thick Queensland accent is the only hint of home. My mind reels at what I hear, unsure whether I believe her, ashamed at judging her sincerity. On the wall, a poster tells the uninvited assembly: 'The Lord is my rock, and my fortress.' Gladys's only remaining child, her thirteen-year-old daughter Esther, sits in the adjacent room, dressed in a lime-green sari, clutching a Bible, staring awkwardly at the passing parade. Gladys explains that she delivered the impossible news to Esther in the softest language she could find: 'We've been left alone.' Esther apparently replied that she's glad her brothers and father are now in heaven. My interview with Gladys lasts just a few minutes, before the next imposter distracts her. I speak to a few mourners and officials before tumbling out of this invaded home and head for the hotel.

Walking against the tide of mourners still heading for the rectory, I realise I have a good story, a strong interview with the widow, and I am on track to meet the deadline for the morning programs. I should be embarrassed by my self-satisfaction but I am running on a steady stream of adrenalin. I step up to Baripada's best hotel: it's a smoky, soulless place; the room is mouldy and the phone line looks dodgy. Still, I am pumped up, so what does it matter? There is no desk, so I dump myself on the lumpy bed to play back the Gladys interview.

Nothing.

The volume must be down, so I turn it up. Still nothing. I take out the minidisc, check it, rewind, skip tracks. Not a word. I have not used the minidisc much and am suspicious of them because you can't monitor the recording levels like an old-school tape recorder. Now, less than two hours to deadline, those suspicions are confirmed. Australia will soon wake up to the morning news and I have lost *the* interview with *the* key person, the widow. I've cocked up my first big story as a foreign correspondent.

I try to focus on the task at hand: making do with what I have. I tap my laptop furiously, trying to make a diamond out of dust. An imperfect story is better than none and, as I work through the words, it is looking bearable. But the god of journalism – an occasionally benign but mostly bitter, vindictive force – seems determined to baptise me with fire. My laptop battery dies. No problem, I'll just plug in the power cord. I rummage through my kitbag, only to find I've left the cord back in New Delhi. And I thought things were going badly. My nearly complete story is trapped in a computer I cannot turn on. With just forty minutes to deadline, I scramble up and down the hall, banging on other journalists' doors. No-one has the same laptop as I do and, besides, they've got their own stories to worry about. My brain pumping with panic, I start from scratch with pen and paper.

Keep calm.

My stomach is a knot of nervous energy.

Breathe.

My throat is as tight as a drum.

I ring Sydney with a half truth: the story's 'on the way'. I adopt the correspondent's mantra: never explain, never complain – just deliver. I take the phone off the hook; there is no time for distractions. The winter night is cool but I am sweating as if it were high summer. Having already written the story once, it is relatively quick to rewrite, so I take some deep breaths and lay down my voice track into my other, working tape recorder.

There's a knock on the door; I ignore it. No time to deal with anyone. I return to my voice track. Another knock and I persist. So does the knocking. Suddenly the hotel night manager walks straight into my room, looking like an Indian Manuel from *Fawlty Towers*.

'Excuse me, *sahib* . . .'

But Indian Manuel gets no further.

'WHAT THE FUUUUCCKK DO YOU THINK YOU'RE DOING?'

'Excuse me, *sahib* . . .'

'WHAT THE FUUUUCCKK GIVES YOU THE RIGHT?'

Indian Manuel will not be deterred.

'Excuse me, *sahib* . . .'

'WHAT!?! WHAT COULD IT POSSIBLY BE AT 11.30 AT NIGHT!?!? WHAT!?!?'

'*Sahib*, phone is off hook.'

'IT'S OFF THE HOOK SO PRICKS LIKE YOU DON'T DISTURB ME. FUUUUCCKKK OFF!'

Deadpan stare. Slack jaw. The silent shock of a man who knows he has been abused but is not sure of the exact words slung at him. He appears to be waiting for me to translate the abuse into Hindi or his local Oriya language.

'GEEETTTT OUT!!!!!'

Finally, he makes a slow, broken reverse, his well-meaning gesture of service shot down in a barrage of anger and foreign contempt.

Anyone who has ever been to India knows its unique ability to infuriate; but there is no excuse for my outburst. Especially when Indian Manuel was going out of his way to *help* me. Whether you've lived here for years or spent a few hours in a Bombay transit lounge, India can scrape away your norms of behaviour like a sandblaster. And the place has sent more than one journalist over the edge. On my first visit to New Delhi's rickety Foreign Correspondent Club, old hands warned me of the madness that can consume even the most mild-mannered hacks. Working to constant and rigid deadlines in a country infamous for its unreliability is a volatile combination. I vowed never to turn into a media monster. It has taken me all of one day on the road.

Ashamed and out of time, I file a mess of unedited material for Sydney to assemble into a story. It's not the usual practice but I swallow my pride and make the *AM* deadline. Just. Strung out, I must now do a fresh version of the story for the lunchtime program, *The World Today*. Finally, at three in the morning, I am done. I am also grimy and need a shower. There is no hot water and the 'shower' is the traditional Indian bucket and ladle, so I pour freezing water over myself, biting against the cold air. Drained, confused, I collapse on the bed, only to stare at a ceiling dripping with mosquitoes waiting for me to sleep.

Boys don't cry. And foreign correspondents certainly don't. Yet, tears are threatening to erupt into a full-blown weep. I should not be the one losing it: a woman has lost her husband and two young sons to mob madness. My mind is a blur of images: a father and his sons' desperate last moments trapped in their burning van; Gladys Staines' extraordinary response; my own pumped-up excitement blinding me to the suffering of others. And, crowning it all, my outburst at Indian Manuel, the night manager.

Once it starts, there is no stopping the flow pouring down my cheeks in thick, wet, salty bursts of exhaustion and anguish. I'm not sure if I am bawling for two murdered boys, their father, or their mother and sister. Or, more likely, for my own, inconsequential failure to get the best story to Sydney. Perhaps I am also finally face-to-face with the algebra of tragedy which states that white skin has so much more news currency than dark; I am only here because the victims are

Australian and one of our own. I may even be weeping for the way I dealt with Gladys and the other mourners: I was too psyched to be sensitive. I always thought I would respond to people as a person first, correspondent second, but I have failed on all scores – professionally and personally. I fall asleep in a haze of tears and tiredness, wondering what ever possessed me to take this job.

I creak my eyes open after an hour of shallow sleep broken by noisy thoughts and kamikaze mosquitoes. I ring Sydney to do some blurry live crosses with the lunchtime programs. I brace myself for the jeers of colleagues, who must still be rolling their eyes at my disastrous early file. 'What disasters?' they ask. 'Sounded fine to me.' If anyone had noticed problems in the morning stories, they seem to have already forgotten. The fickle world of news has a short memory. And whatever they may have thought of the stories, they definitely had no idea about the hassles I was having. Their day was running as normal as ever: no late-night knocks on the door, power cord problems, feeble phone lines. They don't get it and they won't ever. Suddenly, I realise these are *my* problems to handle as best I can. In India no-one can hear you scream.

I haul myself out of bed, climbing over a spaghetti mess of leads, microphones, tapes and bags. The place looks like a crazed ape was let loose in here. I clean up a bit and head back to the rectory for the funeral. It is still early but mourners are already arriving, their numbers even greater than last night. Some never left, holding a vigil in the dirt outside the family home. There are many lepers, forming a tearful, fearful congregation, unsure of who will care for them now.

Three coffins are draped in rose petals and chains of marigolds, shaded by an elaborate cloth pagoda. The boys' coffins look too small to seem true; more like toy boxes. Tribal people from surrounding villages stand shoulder to shoulder with Christian clergy, as Gladys Staines kneels at the coffins and tries to comfort her daughter. I wonder how Gladys can seem so stoic, only to remember being asked the same of me after my father's funeral. When he died just over a year ago, I was more struck by guilt than mourning, having rushed home from Mexico when his cancer suddenly worsened, to find him barely conscious. I missed his final articulate moments by hours, leaving unsaid final goodbyes, regrets and resentments. It was an early lesson in the price of travel: when it really matters you're really not there. No-one could read such things beneath my mask on that sparkling Sydney winter's funeral day, so I won't begin to try to read Gladys Staines'.

In a green sari, she again urges forgiveness, and shares her faith in Christ: 'Because He lives, I can face tomorrow. Because He lives, all fear is gone. Because I know He holds the future and life is worth living just because He lives.'

I've not sought comfort or guidance in God since I was thirteen, and now wonder how Gladys reconciles her love for God with what seems to be his blatant disregard for her. She has been dealt one of fate's cruellest cards: for a parent to bury their children.

'Don't be ashamed to call yourself Christian,' the officiating pastor tells the crowd, trying to reassure India's tiny Christian minority. 'And forgive those who have done this, for they know not what they have done.'

India's Christians may not feel ashamed but they've good reason to feel afraid. Making up less than three per cent of the population, they've come under increasingly violent attack since Prime Minister Vajpayee's Hindu nationalist-led government came to power less than a year ago. Hinduism's message of peace, tolerance and many paths to enlightenment should make the idea of 'Hindu militants' or 'Hindu fundamentalists' impossible. And in a country that fiercely prides itself on its astonishing diversity, 'Hindu nationalism' might also seem a bit rich, but it's as real as the coffins in front of me.

A procession slithers to the cemetery, through streets lined with genuine mourners and the merely curious. Maybe I am just one of the curious, a distant onlooker turning up for the spectacle. The only difference is I am paid for the pleasure and then tell the story for TV and radio audiences. When all this is over, we will all go home. Except for Gladys and Esther. Their home, their lives, will never be the same.

I leave the mourners to their misery, the gawkers to their curiosity and scab a ride back to Calcutta with an Australian diplomat who has the unenviable task of providing consular assistance to Gladys. It's a tough job and hardly fits with my image of diplomats skipping from golf course to cocktail party. He's full of morbid tales of Australian travellers claimed by India's roads, rip-off merchants or bad acid, but at least his taxi is comfortable and quick. I am only half-listening to his stories. Preoccupied with the events of the last two days, I am reminded how much there is to learn about India's religious and political mix.

India may be officially secular but religious tensions lurk close to the surface, made all the more flammable by a surging new idealogical movement. The Staines' murders represent the ugliest side of Hindu nationalism, a front emboldened by the surging popularity of the ruling Bharatiya Janata Party (BJP), or India People's Party. Its more hard-core supporters don't want a secular India but a Hindu state: India's one hundred and forty million Muslims should move to Pakistan while other minorities such as Christians, Parsis and Jews should simply mind their own business and be grateful to live in India at all. The once mighty Congress Party, which fought for independence under Mahatma Gandhi and Jawaharlal Nehru, still claims to be the champion of secularism but after ruling unchallenged for most of the first fifty years of independent India, it has been weakened by corruption scandals and complacency. Adding to an already complex picture is the raft of regional parties, some of which have been essential to the BJP forming government. As we bounce along the potholes to Calcutta two things are clear: I have a lot of swotting to do and the inclusive India envisaged by Gandhi seems dangerously threatened.

In a relatively speedy eight hours we are in the cacophony that is Calcutta, crawling through gridlock towards the airport – just in time to catch a flight to New Delhi. However, there'll be little time to rest at home because, while inter-religious war may be threatening Orissa, regional peace is about to break out in the eastern Pakistani city of Lahore.

It must be the first bus in Indian history to arrive on time. Right on four o'clock, the Indian Prime Minister is at the Wagah border gates, waving and smiling from his coach as he enters Pakistan. The crowd is cheering and waving in return – even though it consists almost entirely of members of the media. The New Delhi-based press has been flown *en masse* to Lahore, then bussed twenty-five kilometres east to the Wagah border gates, ahead of what is already being dubbed an historic summit between the leaders of India and Pakistan. For most of the Indian media, it is their first visit to Pakistan and many feel the journey is a daring dash into enemy territory. Which is probably how their Prime Minister is feeling as his bus rolls through the gates.

But all is bathed in the golden spring Punjabi sun, and it feels more like a traditional wedding than the meeting of rival nuclear leaders. Ahead of Mr Vajpayee, a pair of Indian soldiers strides across the border with baskets of celebratory sweets and lays them at the feet of waiting Pakistani Prime Minister Nawaz Sharif. On any other day at dusk, both nations' tallest and most ferocious-looking soldiers prance and stomp in a carefully choreographed gate-slamming and flag-lowering spectacle, which defies the region's disorderly reputation. It's a ritual show of military precision and mimicked threats, in which towering, moustached Indians scowl and snort at identikit towering, moustached Pakistanis, punctuated by shoulder-high goose-steps and thunderous stomps to the cheers of crowds that come to barrack for their side. The soldiers puff up like peacocks, spin on their shining boots and appear to parody pomp itself – in fact, Monty Python would be jealous.

But today is different. The message is love, not war and Wagah is stomping to a different tune. Punjabi *bangra* dancers herald Mr Vajpayee's bus, swirling as military bands play hits from Bollywood classics. And in Bollywood style, the leaders don't just smile and shake hands. They embrace.

Under intense diplomatic and economic pressure from Washington, the two leaders have been pushed to meet, greet and smile like old friends. It may be a shotgun wedding but they are promising to embark on a new relationship. It is enshrined in their new Lahore Declaration and symbolised by the shiny new 'Friendship' bus that brought Mr Vajpayee here today and will ferry people between New Delhi and Lahore more easily than the train and more cheaply than the plane. The Lahore Declaration is vague, though some overexcited Indian commentators will compare the summit to the fall of the Berlin Wall. It's an absurd comparison and the western journalists are more skeptical, but there can be no doubting a thawing of sorts. It's a good news story and I try to enjoy it, knowing that peace in the region is the enemy of journalistic opportunity – too much peace will mean too few stories

Even Pakistan's cricket team is touring India for the first time in twelve years, which is as likely as anything to ease tensions between the historical rivals. However, there is one thing to challenge the passions stirred by cricket. It is the one matter noticeably papered over by the Lahore Declaration; something able to spark Indians' and Pakistanis' darkest passions. A place described as heaven on earth.

The Himalayan kingdom of Kashmir.

CHAPTER 4

LOVE IN THE TIME OF MILITANCY

I am radiating an aroma I have never smelt before, at least not from me. New Delhi is still only officially in spring, but already the heat is searing and my armpits seep a salty, sticky mix of masala, curry and curd. I had been warned that India 'gets under your skin' but this insurgency is incredibly aggressive: India is the victor, my deodorant the vanquished, and Rachel's spicy cooking keeps giving all day long. So it's just as well I am heading for the cooler climes of Kashmir. I want to see this mythologised mountain land first-hand and find out whether the newborn Lahore Declaration has tempered last year's nuclear testing tensions.

The trip to the airport is agonising – the airconditioning is the latest part of the ABC car to give up. This rusty wagon-cum-camel cart has broken down almost every week since I arrived, and though only six years old, it's ready for the scrap heap. A common scam is for drivers to fleece their bosses with nonsense car problems only to split the phoney repair bill with a colluding mechanic, but a quick look at this vehicle tells you the sham began back on the designer's drawing board. Poor Abraham, ball bearings of sweat gathering on his brow, stays characteristically quiet. Until we pull into the car park.

'Sir . . .' Abraham whispers.

'Yes?'

'Can I please use the car for my family while sir is away?'

I feel like a father being asked for the keys by his teenage son on a first date. My private chuckle is instantly doused by flashbacks to the notorious washbasin affair.

'No. Sorry. Gotta go!'

I hurriedly gather my bags and head for the hills.

Northern India's sandpapered plains fall behind as purple, pregnant clouds hug mountain peaks. They promise rain – something I've not seen since leaving home. Srinagar looks snug, nestled into the Kashmir Valley, lakes twinkling in the early afternoon sun. From the air it hardly looks like the hotbed of violence that, depending on whose figures you accept, has claimed between thirty thousand and seventy thousand lives over the last decade. Conservatively, that's about ten deaths a day. This place may be dubbed heaven on earth but since 1989, the only link to heaven has been the stream of soldiers, militants and civilians sent to their early death.

'BRRRRUUUDDER! BRRRRUUUDDER!' roars a low nasal drone across the car park, shaking me from thoughts of death tolls. A man I've never met before bounds up like an excited dog and slams me with a spine-crushing hug.

'BRRRRUUUDDER! It is soooo good to see you,' he shouts in his heavy Kashmiri accent, with its rolling 'Rs' and elusive 'TH' sounds that I have already got used to in our phone conversations.

'Come, brudder, come. Much to do.'

While Mukhtar's diction could be better, his spirit could not. He is a jewel of Srinagar, a quiet survivor where there is no quiet. His cherub face wears a childish smile but inky rings beneath his eyes betray years of sleepless nights spent working or worrying. Mukhtar is my 'fixer', my eyes and ears in Kashmir. He helps arrange interviews, does legwork and is a living history of the insurgency. Correspondents love the public to see them as romantic, resourceful loners – cowboys who tread where no-one else does. But the reality is you depend heavily on your local guides. You are only as good as your fixer.

Mukhtar's instant adoption of me as his 'brudder' is a tender gesture born of Kashmir's gentle, hospitable nature. But brotherly love brings responsibility and, although ten years his junior, I am cast in the elder sibling role. I am not just boss but provider and patron – Mukhtar's kin.

'Brudder, I know you will not forget us,' he smiles as we drive into town, past nervous-looking Indian soldiers puffed up by the bulk of their flak jackets. 'Did you bring some medicines?'

Mukhtar's father, who presumably is now also my own, is ill. I don't know what is wrong with him but thanks to Mukhtar's polite pleas over the phone, I did know to bring my supply of Australian pain relievers and vitamins. Getting reliable medicines in India can be something of a lottery, so I hand over the stash of pills from Sydney kept for a rainy day.

If this is paradise, I'd hate to see hell. Armoured personnel carriers crawl like steel cockroaches along Srinagar's crowded streets. Paramilitary troops press the pavements, peek from behind sandbags or inside pillboxes. Timber houses teeter with frailty, while others have been saved the indignity of slow decay: fighting has already reduced them to charcoal carcasses. Rickety houseboats squat on the Jhelum River that coils through the city, while ritzier ones with names like 'New Australia' and 'Kashmir Hilton' bob on beautiful Dal Lake. They're empty of tourists. Indian authorities say relative calm has returned to Srinagar, proudly declaring a 'return to normalcy', but to Australian eyes there is nothing normal about these streets. The only hint of happiness is the smattering of Indian honeymooners walking along the promenade – at least some have been persuaded that this once most popular of places for newlyweds is again safe.

Don't tell Ghulam Nabi Butt that life is normal, let alone beautiful. As we roll through his discreet, green gates the proprietor of Clermont Houseboats charges forward, a lanky figure in a finely cut suit.

'My dear! My dear!' he declares. 'Welcome! Welcome!'

Wide arms wrap me up as if I were a long lost son, then his spindly legs make a manic march towards the water's edge. I have come to stay at one of his famous houseboats and it's clear from the outset Mr Butt is no quiet, retiring host. If the hapless hotel night manager in Baripada was India's answer to Manuel, then I have found Kashmir's version of Basil Fawlty and, like the Fawlty Towers hotelier, he can't help but mention the war.

'Terrible situation, my dear. Only journalists visit these days.'

Ramazan, the porter-cum-manservant, a tiny, middle-aged man with a gentle demeanour and a moustache oddly reminiscent of Hitler's, scurries behind with the bags. Then, with a spray of rose petals, a clap of hands and the cutting of a bow, Mr Butt opens the door to the houseboat with a grand grin. This display is as pathetic as it is touching: I feel too welcome, too loved. My only virtue is having turned up. In these days of trouble, those who venture to Kashmir are instantly adored; there is little competition for the great affections of its people.

Mr Butt's Clermont Houseboats are the grandest example of one of the British Empire's better legacies. The Raj would flee to Kashmir's cool valley climes from the blistering heat of the plains and, banned from buying land, the foreign fun-lovers had the Kashmiris build impressive floating cottages. Mr Butt's boats may groan for want of care but the delicate carpets, embroidered sofas and sculptured cedar ceilings speak of luxurious lost days of Empire. Tourists fuelled a houseboat revival through the 1970s and 1980s, but today the Clermont fleet has shrunk from nine boats to just four. Half-sunken vessels squat amid the lotus leaves like old men too tired to lift themselves from their favourite armchair, as if deciding it is easier to die where they are.

Ghulam Butt plays out his practised role but his stiff smile betrays a decade of lost profits and absent guests. Behind his tidy necktie and neat, knitted vest, he looks desperate to break the calm by screaming 'FUCK THIS!' across the glassy water. His staff, including Ramazan, who survive mainly on the generosity of guests, have lived on practically nothing for ten years. It's not just loss of income crippling them, but pride. The office, just inside the front gate, is wallpapered with framed photos of famous guests – film stars and ambassadors have signed across their airbrushed smiles for the Butts. Stacks of guest books pay tribute to the houseboats and hospitality, reading as a who's who of the sixties and seventies. Beneath the four-hundred-year-old chinar trees in this dappled, secret universe, George Harrison and Ravi Shankar played their sitars in a private performance for a lucky few. Today, a return to Kashmir's famed tranquillity feels as likely as a reunion of the Fab Four.

'It is still beautiful, my dear,' Mr Butt half mumbles to himself staring across the water, 'but not like it was. No, my dear, it is not like it was.'

Even for those who have never been there, Indians know Kashmir, with its dramatic peaks and fertile valleys, as a perennial backdrop to Bollywood song and dance numbers. Kashmir is deeply romanticised; an ideal offering escape from the drudgery of everyday life. And like all romances, it is clouded with emotion.

When British India was partitioned in 1947, it was assumed Kashmir's overwhelming Muslim majority would join the new Islamic state of Pakistan. But, in a bad omen for democracy, the decision did not rest with the people. Instead, it was down to the Maharajah of Kashmir who, as a Hindu, sided with India. So began the two new independent nations' first war over Kashmir. A promised plebiscite is yet to be held, and makes no mention of a third option of autonomy – one that is attractive to many Kashmiris disillusioned with both squabbling nations. Since that first stoush in 1947, India and Pakistan have officially gone to war twice more over Kashmir, and after half a century of tensions, temper tantrums and arms racing, it remains their cradle of contention. Roughly two-thirds of the strategically important territory is administered by New Delhi, a third is in Islamabad's hands, and a tiny north-eastern tip is claimed by China.

In the late 1980s, a fierce insurgency rocked Srinagar's rambling alley ways and the idyllic villages that dot the Valley. Outraged by brazenly rigged state elections in 1987, Kashmiri separatists began launching brutal assaults against the minority Hindu and Sikh communities, driving them from their homes. The Indian military responded with vengeance, and fighting slid into a bitter test of cruelty by both sides. Sons vanished, daughters were raped, houses were torched, people were kidnapped and tortured. As the original Kashmiri fighters were killed off, they replaced by growing numbers of foreign fighters, bolstered by all-important support from Pakistan. These battle-hardened 'guest *mujahideen*' came from as far afield as

Africa and the Philippines; some were Arabs on Osama bin Laden's payroll who had fought against the Soviets in Afghanistan. The global *jihad* had come to Kashmir.

I have come primarily to visit the Line of Control, the ceasefire line that carves up Kashmir, and the place to watch India and Pakistan's eyeball-to-eyeball standoff. It is only a few hours' drive from Srinagar but days will pass before I get there, as India's glacially paced bureaucracy processes my travel permit. The delay is frustrating but on Mukhtar's calming advice, we search for stories in Srinagar. However, the problem with a ten-year insurgency is that not a lot changes. The Valley is stuck in a cycle of violence that is not necessarily newsworthy. A particularly bloody attack will make the headlines but, even then, it is a short-lived death-toll story. As one seasoned journalist in New Delhi, bored with Kashmir, told me, 'Wake me up when the fighting stops. Then it will be a story.' But as a newcomer I am curious to understand how people live with such violence and the impact it has on them.

I find a few answers at Srinagar's Psychiatric Diseases Hospital, where I'm waved into its calm courtyard by a clawed hand grabbing through a hole in a wall – a cheerless Addams Family 'Thing' trying to escape. A partly open shutter reveals a twitching eye that tracks me as I pass by. The kicking and screaming of a woman behind a padlocked metal door smashes the quiet.

'Don't let that worry you!' grins a man who looks like Luciano Pavarotti dressed in a white lab coat. 'In our society schizophrenics are also taken as saints.'

As Dr Abdul Wahid Khan shakes my hand, it seems his face can't decide between angst and amusement. His more decisive-looking colleague, Dr Mohammed Aslam, wears a criss-cross patterned woollen vest so daggy it is almost cool. Together, they are the keepers of Kashmir's insane. They usher me through to a madman's slumber party.

'Welcome to Ward Three!' Dr Khan smiles with a dramatic flourish, presenting around fifty men squatting on metal beds. Up to four are squeezed onto each one, head to toe, staring blankly from beneath crimson blankets. A kneeling, naked man is locked in a perpetual handshake with his bed-friend. Some have been here for twenty years. The staring silence is broken only by a man greeting me as I slide by.

'*As'salaam aleikum,*' he whispers. Peace be upon you. In the midst of madness and militancy, peace is planted.

The camera is rolling, absorbing what my mind can't grasp. Instinct is the only instruction I have, and I am grateful to take refuge behind the lens. The conditions are appalling, though I know there are worse in India. It is not uncommon for psychiatric patients to be chained to their beds. These are Kashmir's most severe cases – some never had it together, while others have been tipped over the edge by the fighting.

One patient stands out – a dashed good-looking young guy who speaks the well-educated English of a prosperous Kashmiri upbringing. Tariq Ahmad has been here for seven years. Now twenty-nine, he was a promising young man. Until he fell madly in love and the militancy inter-rupted.

As the fighting climbed to its furious peak in the early 1990s, Tariq was studying engineering at Kashmir University. The militancy made for high emotions on campus but Tariq's passions were not political. He fell for a beautiful Hindu girl – a member of Kashmir's small but significant *pandit* community. The way Tariq tells the story, she loved him too and they both believed in marriages of love, not convenience. Marriage between Muslims and Hindus is not unheard of, even in conservative Kashmiri society, but while Tariq wanted to make love not war, his militant mates had other ideas. Kashmir's once thriving Hindu minority, having lived harmoniously with Muslim neighbours for centuries in Srinagar, became the targets of brutal attacks.

'All the *pandits* were scared of the militancy,' Tariq remembers. 'They thought "they will kill us".'

Her family fled their ancestral home, joining the vast *pandit* diaspora, and a devastated Tariq took refuge the same way lovelorn young men do the world over – he smoked a lot of hash, stopped shaving and let his studies slide. Tariq's sprouting beard, however, was grabbing the attention of both Indian authorities and militants – each side reading it as a sign of pious support for the insurgency. His dad feared Tariq was ripe for recruiting by the militants, who often exploit the vulnerable, or that he could be rounded up by Indian security forces on suspicion of militancy, never to be seen again. But Tariq could not tell him the real problem.

'He is a serious guy,' he shrugs. 'I couldn't find the guts to tell him I want to marry this girl.'

Out of ignorance or desperation, he bundled his son off to the psychiatric hospital. Seven years later, 'I am still here,' Tariq smiles. Love in the time of militancy has been costly. 'The fighting hits every corner of your heart,' he sighs through a haze of antidepressants and sedatives, his emotional cocktail for much of his young adult life. Like much of Kashmir, Tariq, it appears, has popped his way to peace, and, as I'm about to discover, he is not alone.

Across the courtyard, a mob is gathering in a doorway. The hall beyond is crammed, the waiting room packed. In one room, jars of brightly coloured pills sparkle like lollies in a milkbar. A man pours spoonfuls of the tablets into makeshift paper parcels as greedy hands grab through the metal window grill. This frenzied scene could be the food distribution point at a desperate refugee camp; but it's the hospital outpatient department. Before the militancy, these doctors would see ten, at most twenty outpatients a day.

Now, two or three psychiatrists assess up to two hundred cases a day – just a minute or two per patient. The only option is to dole out drugs to calm them down. It won't solve their problems, only mask their eventual eruption.

'We are sitting on a volcano of drug abuse,' Dr Khan laments.

Kashmiris' minds have been divided into two clear and irreconcilable spheres: before the militancy and after. The only stopgap for a traumatised population is the epidemic handing out of pills. In my circles, pills are for fun and to escape middle-class boredom; here they're a life staple. As for the doctors, overworked and aware of their flawed care, it's a tormenting job.

'So you can just yourself make out how stressed we must be,' adds Dr Khan, with his mixed look of anxiety and amusement. I leave the stressed doctors and heartbroken Tariq with a mix of personal despair and journalistic satisfaction.

It's not what you'd call a 'good news' story, but I am happy with it. I have fumbled my way through the filming and need only do my piece to camera – the 'PTC' or 'stand up' – that part of the story where the reporter tries to sound intelligent or analytical for a few sentences. They rarely last more than fifteen seconds but hours can be devoted to getting them right. Often it's just a way for the reporter to get their face on the TV or to prove that they're 'in location'. Whatever the reason, if you are filming your PTC without a cameraman, there is little room for vanity. We scour Srinagar for a paramilitary post to use as a backdrop. Not that they're in short supply – it's just that the Indian troops are famously paranoid and sweep us away at the sight of the camera. Finally, we find a spot but know I'll need to be quick. Tripping over the tripod, tangled in the microphone cord, I set up the shot. Adding to the urgency, rain is falling again. 'The story is GRRREAT, brudder,'

Mukhtar beams. I am fast discovering that brother Mukhtar has the unshakeable habit of announcing 'GRRRREAT!' at the first sign of success. It's loud, triumphant and often infectious. I've got my lines in my head and I'm revved up . . .

The words come out fine, the soldiers have not seen us and I only have to do my signoff: '. . . Jonathan Harley, ABC News . . .'

'GRRRREAT!' shouts Mukhtar, off camera but booming down my microphone and ruining the take.

'. . . Srinagar.'

'Mukhtar!!!' I growl. 'What the – !?!'

'Sorry, brudder.'

But it's too late. The soldiers are alerted by Mukhtar's duck-call and move us along before I can do another take. We plod the streets of Srinagar through the now pouring rain looking for another location. By the time we find one, I am soaked to the bone. I film my piece looking like a wet rat with a crowd of halfwits staring over my shoulder. One is scratching his nuts; another is picking his nose. Maybe Kashmir will send me over the edge as well.

The rain is falling softly now and we have retired to the houseboat, where Ramazan has dispensed tea, towels and a plate of cardboard-tasting Kashmiri biscuits. Mukhtar gets a message that the Indian military bureaucracy has approved our visit to the Line of Control. It's great news and I want to leave at dawn but he urges patience.

'Brudder,' Mukhtar says between slurps of steaming milky *chai* laced with cinnamon, 'we must wait till they sweep the roads.'

I'm flabbergasted by the suggestion we wait for clean

streets before leaving but Mukhtar patiently explains they're sweeping for landmines, not litter. At least it's a good excuse to sleep in, so, dry and full of *chai*, we agree to meet in the morning for a houseboat breakfast before leaving.

There will be no sleep in. I am woken before dawn by Fajr – the first of the day's five Muslim calls to prayer. At once song and scowl, laced with yearning and certitude, it grinds across the lake from the neighbouring Hazratbal Mosque – an impressive white marble dome squatting on Dal Lake's edge and boasting what is supposed to be a single strand from the Prophet's beard. The Moe-e Muqaddas, or 'Sacred Lock', is regarded as having come to Hazratbal from Medina via Cochin around the seventeenth century. Whether it's the real deal is immaterial: what matters is that Kashmiris believe it to be so and here, perhaps more than anywhere in the region, truth is infuriatingly elastic. Even by India's incredibly flexible standards, Kashmiri 'fact' is entangled in faith and fancy, customary tales and conspiracy theories. Over countless cups of *chai* I would come to hear equally countless 'truths' about soldiers dressed as militants massacring civilians; about militants dressed as soldiers massacring civilians; of Hindu soldiers killing and eating cows, and militant Muslims feasting on pork. The *shikariwallah* hawking for honeymooners to paddle around Dal Lake, the sandbagged Indian officer on a Srinagar street corner and the Kashmiri trader abandoning his beloved valley for New Delhi squalor will each have their own distinct view through the prism that is Kashmir. My job is to distil all their truths into two minutes of radio or television.

As the first brushstrokes of day sweep across the lake, I quietly consider the irony of India's part in what has become a deadlocked autonomy struggle: a nation defined by its triumph over British Colonial rule has foiled Kashmir's own independence ambitions. Meanwhile Pakistan has

stoked the insurgency with training, funds and arms for militants care of its notorious spy agency, the Inter-Services
Intelligence (ISI), and cannon-fodder in the form of young
men schooled in its hardcore Islamic *madrassas*, or
boarding schools. Through the 1990s, the insurgency played
well to Pakistan's home crowd and periodically pushed
Kashmir onto the international radar. But Islamabad's insis-
tence of innocence – that it provided only moral and diplomatic support to the rebels – wore thin, while Washington
grew steadily sympathetic to New Delhi's forceful message
that Pakistan was a state sponsor of terrorism. The Lahore
Declaration has offered the hope – however slim – of rap-
prochement over Kashmir, and the measure of that will
come through the summer months. Free of the crippling
winter snows, summer is the traditional fighting season
along the Line of Control. With the scorching winds of
nuclear tests still blowing across the region, tempered only
so slightly by Lahore's limp whiff of peace, the world's
newest nuclear powers are facing a key test of strength and
restraint.

'Okay, brudder,' Mukhtar mumbles through a last
mouthful of omelet and toast. As if interpreting an oracle,
he waves his hand to indicate the roads are clear and safe –
or that he has finally finished his gigantic Butt's breakfast.
Fed and ready to go, we shake off Srinagar in our bumbling
Ambassador taxi and plunge into a valley of haunting
beauty. Pines and poplars stretch for the sky as trout-rich
rivers wiggle through soaring mountains. Terraced crops
hug the steep slopes, punctuated by idyllic villages. This
would be stunning anywhere in the world but compared to
India's manic, sun-bleached plains it is a sublime, techni-
colour dream. As our Ambassador battles its way up to
Rustom post, each bend reveals a breathtaking vista and
Mukhtar ascends into ecstasy, radiating excitement and
tranquillity. This powerful, even religious bond to the land

is key to the Kashmiri identity and seeing Mukhtar in his bliss makes me terribly homesick. I miss that feeling of belonging in a patch of bush, on a strip of beach or down a dusty dirt road – born of years of habit and childhood smells. No matter how beautiful another land, it never resonates as richly as your own home.

Any sense of tranquillity is smashed at the summit, where Rustom post sits as a blunt reminder that this is one of the world's most heavily militarised zones. Bunkers and trenches are carved across the 2511 metre-high mountaintop, softened only by sandbags and the sweet smell of spring. Our guide through this battlefield in the clouds is (Lt) Colonel Vijay Pal, Battalion Commander of the 6 Raj Rifles and Indian army officer from Central Casting. Brandishing sunglasses fit for *Hogan's Heroes*, a manicured moustache and crisply ironed cravat, Colonel Pal is all smiles and smooth talking. He is the kind of man who leaves the room to fart, even if it means stepping out of the bunker into the line of enemy fire. Vijay strides around his post like a proud gardener showing off this season's flowers. Here are the trenches. There is the enemy. Here is hot, spicy tea for you and me. I trail with the camera, trying to keep up with his magical military tour.

'Now we can move in the open,' he declares, leaping out of a trench, 'but moment fighting starts, we can't take chance. We have to go in that way,' the Colonel beams, pointing his lovingly polished cane towards a bunker.

'And being out in the open won't draw their fire?' I ask, nervously glancing over my shoulder to the Pakistani positions a thousand metres across the valley as the shell flies.

'They do fire. Now, they're going to start.'

The Colonel stops and glares across to his opponents, as if daring them to start shelling. I stare at the Colonel, as if daring him to get us the hell out of here.

'Take your picture here,' he commands, scratching out

some tripod marks on open ground. 'That hill there is good.' Surveying the image on my camera's fold-out screen, Vijay directs the shoot.

'Up. A little to the left. Up. HALT! Move it right, slowly, slowly, HALT!' It's my first realisation that Indians are experts at everything and, from battle zones to shopping centres, there will be at least one Indian telling me how to shoot my story.

Colonel Pal may be an aspiring Steven Spielberg but he is first and foremost a military man and, like all prudent soldiers, is a pessimist. The fanfare and excitement of Prime Minister Vajpayee's ride to Lahore carries little weight with the men of Rustom post and last summer's intense shelling still rings in their ears.

'I prepare for the worst,' he warns cheerily. 'In case it starts, this year will be much worse than last year.' It's a nod to the fact these men bore more than their share of the post-nuclear testing shelling.

'Not much has changed at the ground level,' he laments. His bluntness underscores the dangerous gap between political gesture and military reality: it's as deep and wide as any valley before us.

The stern assessment is echoed by his junior officers over a prim and proper lunch of *palak panir* – a gluggy curry of spinach and white cheese – accompanied by crispy *chapattis* and, to my shock, ice cold beer. A lunchtime lager in the Officers' Mess was not what I expected in India's only Muslim majority state but the soldiers seem more concerned with pleasing their guest than offending their Kashmiri neighbours' disdain for alcohol. As soldiers in crisp white waistcoats wait on my every whim, I want to compare notes with these young men, explore their thoughts on war, long-distance love lives with their wives, and ask how I, too, could grow a standard-issue Indian army moustache big enough to make even George Negus blush. Instead, my tentative probes fall into a void; whether by order or awkwardness I am met with blank stares and deathly silences. There is a sense of déjà vu as I realise I am trapped in a tragic rerun of my pathetic 'coffee and cake' efforts back at the office. Among these men I am the oddity, the centre of interest and the one expected to entertain. Defeated, I take a top up of beer, settle into my plastic chair and wait for the inevitable.

'Mr Jonathan, tell me, have you met Shane Warne. . .?'

CHAPTER 5

INTO THIN AIR

The Colonel's warnings were prophetic. Back in Srinagar, news is filtering in of heavy shelling around Kargil, a truck-stop town high on the road to Leh, which is famous for its Buddhist monasteries. The fighting seems serious but not earth-shattering until, after three weeks of intense artillery duels between Indian and Pakistani forces, Indian aircraft begin bombing guerrilla positions along the Line of Control around Kargil. It is the first time air-power has been used since the insurgency began in earnest in 1989, and when Pakistan shoots down two Indian MiG fighter jets it says entered its airspace, there is a dark sense that war is falling fast.

The scent of war has brought an oddly quiet air to Srinagar. The streets are absent of the usual phalanxes of military vehicles and troops. They've been redeployed two hundred kilometres away to the effort around Kargil. As the story warms up and my filing demands rise, I reluctantly abandon Butt's houseboat in search of a hotel with a reliable phone in the room. Mukhtar checks me into one of the Maharajah's old palaces, which an optimistic entrepreneur has just converted into a ritzy hotel. While any hopes that tourists would start dribbling back to Kashmir this year have now been smashed, the place is swarming with journalists who have suddenly revived their interest in Kashmir. With fresh military passes, Mukhtar and I leave for Kargil at three in the morning. This time, he's waived his landmine worries and we're soon approaching the mighty Srinagar–Leh Highway.

'Highway' is far too grand a term; this rocky, single-lane track threatens to crumble into plunging valleys at so much as the rumble of a bicycle. In happier, hippier days, this would have been flush with backpackers, smelling of pot and patchouli. Now, only shards of army truck headlights arc through the darkness – and our taxi is dwarfed by them grinding up this glorified donkey trail. As the cool valley air turns icy, streams cutting across the road are frozen and slippery, which is a problem for our doddering Ambassador taxi with barely four working wheels, let alone four-wheel drive. Suddenly, our crawl slows to a stop, our stop slips to a slide and our slide is heading straight for the cliff edge. Next stop valley floor, a hundred metres below, somewhere in the blackness. 'Shhhhiiiiiiiitt!!!!' I scream, reaching for the door, ready to jump out.

But in the time it takes my muscles to catch up with my mind, the wheels grab on the ice and lurch from the abyss with a reluctant groan.

'Does this driver know what the hell he's doing?' I hiss at Mukhtar.

'*Insh'allah*, brudder.' God willing. Kashmir is very *insh'allah*.

But Allah is not willing away Mukhtar's worries.

'My wife told me not to come but I say I must go with my brudder,' he announces as the driver stops for a piss, steam rising in the car lights as his stream hits the snow by the road. 'It is my duty. But she is very worried.'

I'd assumed those living in the midst of conflict become cavalier about it – anaesthetised, fatalistic, reassured that God's will is at work. Truth be known, I'd not thought about it, and as we climb higher into the Himalayas, I realise I had not even asked Mukhtar if he wanted to come along. In my breathless rush, I was oblivious to him and, for that matter, the risks. Mukhtar's cherub face is now a quiet frown; he seems to know something I don't and, for the first time, I realise I am heading into a war zone. I am clueless about what lies at the top of this mountain or how to wear the flak jacket bouncing around the boot; I don't know a tank from a troop truck, an RPG from an APC. In peaceful Australia, the details of war seemed to me a waste of time, if not a wank – lads I knew who were fascinated by combat seemed to have watched too many Rambo films. Now, I am taking the business of battle much more seriously.

Perhaps sensing I'm spooked by his wife's warnings, Mukhtar tries to break the tension with talk of treasure.

'Brudder, can you bring me a vest?'

Like much of the world, India's journalistic fraternity has made the beige fishing vest the essential media fashion accessory, full of pockets for pads, pens and packets of *paan*. As the media caravan gathers pace, a convoy of such vests will crawl up this mountain in the coming days. 'I'll think about it, Mukhtah,' I reply absentmindedly. Providing medicines for an ailing father is one thing, aiding fashion crimes is another altogether.

Soaring peaks emerge against a dark blue dawn. The taxi slips through low banks of snow ploughed to the side of the road. Trucks huddle in an alcove, as men dart into a small hut crowned with red banners which houses a simple shrine to the Hindu god Krishna – a symbol of struggle against doubt and human weakness. Soldiers and commercial truck drivers pressed into duty lay a hand on the shrine for luck before folding back into this giant khaki caterpillar crawling towards the heavens. Finally, the road flattens and straightens, presenting a sun-drenched plateau of craggy, barren fields framed by jagged granite peaks.

It's all about the peaks. Dug into them are around seven hundred *jihadis* who have come to do battle with infidel 'Hindu' India. Many are not Kashmiris but originate from the distant Pakistani provinces of Punjab, Baluchistan or Sindh. Some are Pakistani-trained mercenaries from Afghanistan and, most disturbingly, as many as two thirds are regular Pakistani troops parading as insurgents. They are members of the 3rd and 4th Northern Light Infantry, expert in mountain warfare. These ice-shaved ridges may be uninhabitable but they're not unimportant: from their commanding heights of up to five thousand metres the intruders can cut the Indian army supply route from Srinagar to Leh in the north. Overnight, the eastern approaches to the Kashmir Valley and supply routes to India's armed forces on the Chinese border near Ladakh have been critically compromised.

Having clawed up the jagged, icy slopes in the frozen dead of winter, these intruders now hold bunkers up to seven kilometres inside Indian territory. Conditions are so harsh, Indian troops vacate the bunkers through the winter, and sophisticated logistical support would have been needed to get the intruders into these commanding positions – support that could only have come from the Pakistani army. These fighters are not armed with Kashmiri insurgents' signature cache of Chinese and Russian automatic rifles, grenades and homemade bombs. They have machine guns and rocket-propelled grenades, top of the range cold weather gear and even new snowmobiles.

The driver has slowed the taxi to a crawl and squints down the straight ribbon of road. When he eyeballs me in his rear vision mirror, I don't need to speak Kashmiri to read the universal phrase burning in his eyes:

'What the fuck!?!' he blinks at me.

The next few kilometres to the town of Drass is the most exposed and treacherous stretch – lying in full view of the militants' positions. They are invisible to us but we are sitting ducks. Indian military convoys crawl along here with lights off under cover of darkness, an indication that one of the world's largest armies has humiliatingly had a key supply route crippled by this small enemy force. Comforted by hopes that the military are the target, not the media, we run the gauntlet through abandoned fields never to be planted with this summer's crops, dotted with cattle left to graze on what they can find.

A doctor friend once told me that medicine makes him feel stupid because there is so much to learn. That's how I feel right now. I know nothing about the deafening hardware in front of me. I want to call everything that is loud and terrifying 'bombing'. I can see that the big bullets go in the big guns and make a big bang and presumably kill big groups of people. But that won't give my reports any authority. Saving me from public humiliation, Mukhtar graciously provides a crash course: the big guns are artillery, the big bullets are shells. As for the big groups of people on the receiving end, well, probably best not to think about them.

The roar of shelling rolls across the plateau and bounces off bald cliffs. But it's nothing to really worry about – this is the friendly echo of outgoing fire from Indian artillery nests, huddled close to the cliffs out of enemy range. Scores of giant guns, their barrels angled steeply to deliver their deadly cargo over the mountains, spread out before us. Thousands of troops scamper between artillery and ammunition piles to a chorus of shouted orders. And in absurd contrast, there are pockets of lush beauty, where a picturesque stream weaves through banks of spring grass – more suited to languid picnics than high-altitude war. Such absurdities are of no concern to the Indian troops or, for that matter, their fiercely proud nation. India's idiosyncrasies may be intoxicating, its inefficiencies infuriating and its high dramas hilarious but its nationalism must never be underestimated. And so, this cumbersome creature is setting about reclaiming its dignity. We can move remarkably freely through these ranks, and I walk from gun to gun recording the sound of them firing. I shudder from the force of each blast.

'India is an elephant! A MIGHTY ELEPHANT!' an artilleryman yells at me above the pounding shells while waiting for new coordinates from forward positions. 'An elephant takes much time to move but when it does, the stampede is unstoppable!' To punctuate the point, his 155 mm Bofors howitzer chunders smoke, dust and noise as it sends another shell across the Line of Control. My spine is still rattling twenty seconds later. However, India needs more than its sheer size, strength and shells to purge the enemy from their snug positions. Air strikes are ineffective among the steep and narrow terrain, and already Pakistan has shown it will shoot down anything it says has entered its airspace. If India wants to reclaim its crude bunkers in the clouds, it must do so by dogged and bloody close-quarter combat – and before October's winter snows cement what would effectively become a new border.

Small squads of soldiers, trained in high-altitude fighting inch up the sharp ridges, with special climbing gear and bayonet rifles fixed at the hip. With the enemy shooting directly down on them, progress is agonisingly slow, the effort insane. Each combat soldier needs two or three men close behind him with supplies and weapons support – all this on an oxygen-thin battlefield where a short stroll can be a huge effort. India is ill-prepared and its men are poorly acclimatised to the altitude. From our relatively low vantage point, the ridges look disarmingly calm in the morning sun until another artillery gun blasts my eardrum. Deafened, we press on into town.

Drass bizarrely prides itself as the second coldest inhabited place on the planet – boasting lows of minus sixty
degrees Celsius. Yet in summer, this rustic town built of
stones and timber, with its steep roofs and Himalayan
outlook might seem quaint – except that Drass has been hit
hard. With punctured roofs and walls, many of the buildings look like failed soufflés and it's fast becoming a ghost
town. The children and most of the women left weeks ago,
and now the last of the loiterers are leaving in a battered
bus with shattered windows. On both sides of the divide,
more than fifty thousand Kashmiris have fled their villages
and the raining shells. Blunted and bleary-eyed, with only
the essentials of saucepans and schoolbooks, they are moving to makeshift refugee camps. Soon Drass will consist
only of soldiers and stray dogs.

At the nearby military base, soldiers are furiously typing
up documents in triplicate, sandwiched with tattered sheets
of carbon paper. India remains bureaucratic to the core,
even in war. The commander agrees to see us and offers tea
but not his name – matters are far too sensitive for anyone
to risk being quoted by a foreign journalist, especially when
there is no good news to tell. Masters in New Delhi are
watching closely.

'You should be careful,' the commander frowns, 'we had
incoming here just ten minutes ago.' He glances over at what
seems a fairly flimsy bunker crowned with sandbags and corrugated iron, his expression edged with grim assurance. It
suddenly occurs to me I've spent this whole time not wearing
my flak jacket. I guess I wasn't sure where the war started –
perhaps I was half expecting a signpost to announce:
'Welcome to the battlefield. Click clack flak jacket. Please
don't litter.' I scamper back to the car, and after five minutes
of flapping around with metal plates and velcro tabs, I am
transformed into a weighed-down Michelin Man. Not sure
whether to feel rugged or ridiculous, I turn to Mukhtar for

reassurance, but he looks vulnerable wearing only his woolly jumper and sombre face. His dejection makes me feel like a selfish dickhead. There is only one option.

'Try this, mate!'

I am trying to sound cheery as I unwrap from this blue metal brace.

'Pop this on. It's not a fishing vest but it might be more use.'

Sarah would *kill* me if she knew I was doing this, but Mukhtar has kids and, besides, I am more likely to die of guilt from Mukhtar's sad expression than a shell lobbing in my lap.

'Oh, brudder! No! I couldn't!'

He can, and does, with very little persuading, and in an instant he is beaming. But the driver now casts an expectant look: 'And where is *my* flak jacket?' Sorry. Drivers are the drummers of journalist rock 'n' roll. They always get the bum deal.

With a mix of army men and artillery, refugees and ruins, I have a good radio story and am ahead of most of the media pack. The problem is how to get it to Australia. Indian phones are notoriously dodgy even in the big cities but in these remote heights, they barely work at all. I want to get the story straight to air and on a line clear enough for the audience to understand. Kargil – still another couple of hours' drive away – will be telephone tragedy. More than a few journalists in India have endured unspeakable hardships for a great story, only to be sunk by scratchy phone lines. I am also mindful that at home, this battle is only a mid-ranking story with a limited shelf life. It would take very little – a Prime Ministerial goof, a shift in home interest rates – to bump the story down, if not off, the news agenda. It's best to go back to Srinagar to file, so I farewell the last handful of stayers, who seem determined not to be budged by the battle.

A tattered-faced old woman, Khatija, sits by the road with solemn defiance. In her seventy or so years, Khatija has seen Kashmir carved up and quarrelled over, but never with this ferocity.

'I've seen all the wars and all the troubles here,' she drones into my microphone, 'but there's never been anything like this.' Still, as if to not want to miss the historic show, she stays.

Thanks for your time.

Have a nice war.

Six hours back down the mountain.

To my surprise, Mukhtar suddenly wants to stick around.

'Brudder, please take a photo.'

Flanked by shells roaring over soaring peaks, amid the stench of gunpowder mixed with the sweet smell of Kashmir, Mukhtar grins for the camera, proudly showing off 'his' flak jacket. His childlike enthusiasm is back, like a boy who has just been given a brand new toy. In his heart, this day has sealed our fate as brothers.

'That was war, brudder,' he glows as we rumble down the mountain. 'And we were there.'

It was war, in everything but formal declaration, and we were there but it felt somehow like a letdown. It felt more like catching a taxi to the front line for a day.

'Brudder, do you think the ABC will buy me a flak jacket?'

'Mukhtar, let's work on a fishing vest first.'

If you drive down to central Srinagar and into Mukhtar's street, step over the deep, stinky gutter with the odd dead rat floating face up, enter his front garden with its tall stalks of corn swinging in the summer sun, slip off your shoes at the front door and turn left into his small, simple office, you will see a photo of a man beaming, arms outstretched beyond the blue bulk of a flak jacket, against a backdrop of artillery and sandbags – enlarged, laminated and mounted on the wall. It may just be Mukhtar's proudest professional moment.

So my first taste of war lasts less than a day, stops short of the town at the centre of the battle, involves more time driving than reporting, a driver who silently wants to sacrifice me to the *jihadis* in the hills, a fixer-cum-brother who wants to immortalise the whole fleeting experience, and a reporter who is left with an overall sense of anticlimax. Still, this time I didn't lose any key interviews and my stories got to air ahead of a host of other media outlets. It's certainly an advance on the disaster of Orissa. No tears this time. Not from me, that is.

Sarah is sobbing on the end of the phone. It's been a week since we last spoke and the first she learned of my going to the Line of Control was thanks to my radio report, full of blasting artillery and dire talk of war. I had been purposefully vague about my plans – partly because they were rubbery, but mostly so she would not worry. I was nervous about her reaction and, perhaps like most blokes, decided to deal with it later.

Later has now arrived. She has the staccato stammer of someone caught between weeping and breathing.

'Yooo-huh, yooo-huh, yooo-huh said yooo-huh would not go near-huh the fighting and then I-huh turn on the radio and there is all this bombing and-huh . . .'

'It's not bombing, it's shelling,' I interject, desperate to say something, anything, as she grabs at a breath.

'Whatever. There are all these guns and you-huh . . .'

'It's called artillery . . .' Good, Jonathan, very sensitive. Very helpful.

'I don't care what it's called!' Sarah's stammer evaporates and she lets rip like a machine gun. 'The point is, you didn't tell me you were going, I had to find out on the radio, there's a war between two nuclear powers, you're in the middle of it and I don't want my boyfriend bombed or shelled or whatever you want to call it!'

Thank God she doesn't know about the flak jacket.

The distance, you might say, is starting to strain. Six months since I left, we are living ridiculously different lives, joined by crackling phone lines and each other's broadcasts. Sarah catches me on the news and I try to get up at five in the morning to hear the last hour of her show streamed on the web. Sarah is hopping from work to yoga, then dinner with friends. I am darting from missionary murder to high-altitude battle zone, then wrestling with Mary over where my desk sits when I'm in New Delhi reporting on the coming national elections or astrologists' warning that the world will end this coming weekend. Home feels very far away. I can remember Sarah's world but she must imagine mine and for that, she needs me to tell her. But how much 'compassionate editing' is deception? Secrecy may be relationship poison but so is fear and I feel trapped in a game of truth or dare: whether to tell everything now or dare to wait till all this is over. Besides, I am fast realising that none of this is under my control at all. The region's social and political tectonic plates seem set to shudder into each other with volcanic results.

'Well, the distance will certainly test your love,' I was warmly warned before leaving home and, in a strange, noble manner, such a test seemed attractive in a 'what doesn't kill us makes us strong' sort of way. But any roman-ticising of the lack of romance has taken all of six months to die. Love doesn't need testing, it needs nurturing.

We talk. Sarah feels better for purging her fear, frustra-tion and loneliness. I feel like shit.

India is not feeling much better. As the elephant gathers momentum, it must come to grips with this war. The newspapers are full of analysis and blame – along with stories and photos of brave *jawans* (soldiers) who gave their lives for Mother India. Meanwhile, India's mushrooming satellite television sector is having its Vietnam: for the first time, wall-to-wall war coverage is beaming into the nation's homes. From Mumbai's middle-class drawing rooms to the shared screens of Orissa's villages, the war is live and gory on private networks. For a nation bored to tears by decades of state-run TV, the satellite revolution has been a revelation and a billion pairs of eyeballs are embracing it with evangelical zeal. From game shows to talk shows, endless music videos to twenty-four hour news channels, India became a TV nation over-night. And this televised war is uniting the country.

At times, India seems about to implode in its own diversity – as though its complexities and contradictions will one day prove too much for one nation to sustain. But now it is faced with a common enemy, and Kargil is surpassing India's countless other crises. It's a blessing of sorts for Prime Minister Vajpayee, whose unwieldy coalition government collapsed after losing a confidence motion a few weeks before battle began. With elections in September, the now caretaker government is hoping to capitalise. As the *jawans* claw their way skywards, India is slowly winning the war. It already has the diplomatic upper hand: from Brussels to Washington, the world has turned its back on Pakistan's appeals for international envoys to be sent to ease tensions with India. Prime Minister Nawaz Sharif's ambitions to internationalise the Kashmiri issue have failed. Pakistan's only applause has come from Afghanistan's ruling Taliban.

The first anniversary of India and Pakistan's nuclear tests takes place under the dark clouds of conflict. Pakistan seems psyched up by its new nuclear weapons. At an Islamabad rally to celebrate the first birthday of the world's first 'Islamic bomb', Nawaz Sharif explains why he ordered the tests. 'I wanted to please Allah and not the world. Pakistan is now invincible,' he tells his guests. Meanwhile, speaking to troops at Kargil, India's Prime Minister is steadfast: 'We can go to any extent. We want peace but we are prepared for war. We are determined to get back our territory.'

The Lahore peace process is in tatters and predictions that the balance of nuclear terror would bring peace are shattered. As Nawaz Sharif hosted his Indian counterpart in full Moghul splendour, infiltrators were heading for Indian territory. It's inconceivable that the Pakistani Prime Minister did not give it all a quiet nod, and impossible that his army chief and one-time commando, General Pervez Musharraf, was not intimately involved in the operation. India had not only been caught napping, it had been stabbed in the back.

But the elephant, it seems, is mighty. Despite the intruders' advantages of surprise, height and the latest equipment, their supply lines have become increasingly vulnerable. By July, Nawaz Sharif is on his way to Washington in a desperate effort to win support. Instead, President Bill Clinton spends his Fourth of July holiday reading Mr Sharif the riot act – already the US administration is livid over Pakistan's arming of the Taliban, its failure to help arrest Osama bin Laden, as well as its baulking at the Comprehensive Test Ban Treaty to ban future nuclear explosions. Cowed by Clinton and reliant on international aid to keep his comatose economy on life support, Nawaz Sharif has no option but to order the withdrawal of Pakistani forces. In a desperate attempt to save face, the Prime Minister hails the brave *jihadis* for returning Kashmir to the world stage, but the misadventure has been a humiliating defeat.

The media often like a 'personal' angle on these geopolitical dramas, so I drive across Srinagar in search of understanding – to a place keeping a score on the struggle. The

Garden of Kashmiri Martyrs is not the glorious-looking place you'd expect from such a grand name but I am learning that in Kashmir, grand claims are rarely realised. In such a verdant valley, this is an oddly dry and dusty place. Faded plastic flowers offer the only sign of life; they clap softly against each other in the humid midday breeze. Rows of tombstones pay homage to the young men who have died in the name of Allah and Kashmir. Fresh mounds are draped with shrouds, decorated with garish tinsel. Some seem anonymous; others bear epitaphs in graceful swirls of Urdu. On fabric and chiselled into white marble tombstones, the inscriptions are as much a call to arms as recipe for resting in peace.

The tombstone of a legendary militant reads:

'Do not shun the gun, younger ones. The war of freedom is yet to be won.'

Another urges:

'Lest we forget we have given our todays for tomorrows of yours.'

For many in Kashmir, salvation and insurrection have become as one. To die fighting the Indians is to die for Allah and therefore to find paradise, complete with seventy-two virgins waiting to be of service. What was a nationalist struggle is becoming increasingly pious. As Mukhtar and I walk through the lines of wasted young lives, a group of teenage boys play cricket on the adjoining field; their cheers and laughter provide a welcome distraction from this marble orchard that is steadily swallowing up their playground. Some of these pubescent lads will soon be swapping cricket bat for guerrilla combat. One of them waves and shouts at me cheerfully, as if barracking for his team, 'AZADI! AZADI KASHMIR!'

Azadi is the Kashmiri catch cry. It is a word from Persian, the Latin of Kashmir, that originally meant 'freedom' or 'leisure' but later morphed into 'independence'.

Of course, in Kashmir, it can mean everything and anything to anybody. But its flexibility does not dilute its authority, evoking liberty, justice and, increasingly, religious fervour. For most, it means going it alone, free of India and Pakistan. Many would like to see their homeland become a kind of Switzerland of Asia, although there are still those who hold on to the dream of uniting with Pakistan.

Mohammed Yassin Bhat is carving out one of the last remaining sites in this field of about four hundred plots. Soon, there will be no more room and Srinagar's martyrs will be laid to rest in one of the five hundred other cemeteries springing up like daisies in villages and towns across the Valley. Mohammed has the callused hands of hard work but he talks tenderly of those he buries.

'This is heaven to me and I feel proud to work here,' he grins. 'They were fighting for their right to freedom.'

'And where does freedom lie for you?' I ask.

Mohammed points his scaly finger beyond the cemetery, past the cricket game and over Srinagar's jagged roof line.

'Have you been to Pakistan?' he asks me.

'No, not really,' I reply, thinking that the hermetically sealed Lahore summit, during which I was either at the hotel or official functions, hardly qualifies as any real sort of visit.

'You must go,' he instructs with a serious smile, resting his muddy hand on my shoulder. 'That is the land of *azad*. There lies freedom. Pakistan is the land of the pure.'

CHAPTER 6

SEX AND DRUGS AND THE LAND OF THE PURE

The pre-flight prayer is almost reassuring.

'*Allaaaah-o-Akbaaaar* . . .' wafts through the cabin speakers, elegant and distorted. I act as if it's the most natural thing in the world to catch a flight where its safe arrival – *insh'allah* – is beseeched as stewards hand out steaming refreshment towels.

Cynics quip that PIA stands for Pray It Arrives but my first Pakistan International Airways flight is on time and, compared to some of the Air India fleet, it seems very modern. I'm not even whingeing about it being a dry flight.

But the captain is about to stomp on my budding goodwill.

'Welcome aboard, ladies and gentlemen. Our flight time to Lahore is forty minutes, we'll be travelling at about thirty thousand feet . . .'

So far, so good.

'The weather is clear, so it should be a fairly smooth flight . . .'

Always a good sign.

'So please sit back, relax and please do try to enjoy the flight . . .'

I'd be pleased to.

'. . . despite our many shortcomings.'

Oh.

I don't know whether to laugh or reach for the emergency exit. Fortunately, the hop to Lahore is too short for PIA's shortcomings to become too unbecoming. Besides, the stale cheese and devon sandwiches have a nostalgic school lunch feel about them. The rubbery black olive mounted on a toothpick is almost quaint and the flat Sprite seems homely – it takes me back to being sick as a kid.

Pakistan's prohibitions begin on the flight and intensify when you step into the airport arrivals lounge. The bottle of scotch I had grabbed on the way out at New Delhi duty free is picked up by Detaining Officer Mirza Iqbal, who gently relieves me of my sinful contraband, and neatly completes a DETENTION MEMO, in which 'One Bottle Whisky Ballentines 50c/c' is listed as the 'detained article', with the 'Reason of detention' being that it is 'Not allowed'. (For anyone in Lahore, please feel free to collect it. Quote reference S.No. 9047.) I was hoping the whisky would help lubricate some fast friendships with some local journalists, but unburdened of it, I step out into Pakistan's most indulgent and powerful city.

If New Delhi airport on the night of my arrival was a wall of humanity, cold air and roaring colours, then Lahore is a softer landing to blue and grey – the colours of *salwar kameez*: the long cotton shirts and baggy trousers look as though someone took all the striking saris of India and bleached them to within an inch of their life. Still, there is nothing neutral about Pakistani taxi drivers and soon I am careering into town.

Oppressive monsoon clouds hang over the highway as swarms of black and yellow taxis – much smaller than India's cumbersome Ambassadors – dart around like slot cars. Boys stripped down to their underwear dive into the coffee-coloured waterway hugging Canal Road, their bodies glistening with the oily balm of industrial waste and human effluent. They may be dripping with toxic sludge but they seem the only cool ones in this entire city. A replica of a ballistic missile, lovingly painted in camouflage colours and boasting a big red knob, sits atop a crumbling apartment block – an absurd monument to perverse priorities in one of the poorest parts of the world. The papier-mâché missile is pointing where else but back across the border towards India.

Pakistan may be sliding into economic and political chaos but this city hums with raw, grinding energy. Like a lusty old tart, Lahore refuses to accept that her glory days are fading fast, instead deciding to age disgracefully. Once grand colonial buildings crumble at the corners, rusting buses are packed to the rafters; this city's entire infrastructure seems set to collapse any second. But its dog-eared veneer masks Lahore's importance. The seat of Pakistan's military, political and economic power, it's here that deals are made and betrayed. Lahore is also the hometown of Prime Minister Nawaz Sharif – though if he goes downtown today he's in for a big surprise.

Around fifty thousand men and boys are jamming into Lahore's central streets to curse their country's leader. It's said in Pakistan that any rally less than two hundred thousand is a 'no-show', but it's certainly the most impressive gathering of angry young men I've ever seen. This is a blokes-only affair – they sit in neatly organised rows, stroking their beards, some holding hands, others fiddling with worry beads. The most conscientious or ambitious compete to lead the endless rounds of chanting and ranting:

'*PAKISTAN ZINDABAD*! LONG LIVE PAKISTAN!'

'SHARIF HAS SOLD OUT THE PEOPLE OF KASHMIR!'

Jonathan Harley

'*KASHMIR ZINDABAD!*'

For a fleeting moment it is reminiscent of an Australian afternoon at the football: guys hanging out, bonding, dads spending time with their sons. My comparison is smashed by the sight of a small boy, no older than seven, aloft on his father's shoulders, dressed in full fatigues, waving a toy Kalashnikov and raising his fist in copybook defiance. I think about my young nephews, whose only cause to raise their fist is in protest against no second serves of ice-cream.

This rally is the biggest show of force yet by Pakistan's Islamic hardliners and they're angry about Prime Minister Sharif's humiliating withdrawal from Kargil. Pakistan's oldest and largest Muslim party, Jamaat-e-Islami (literally 'Islamic Party'), is shouting down any talk of peace in Kashmir and vowing the *jihad* there will continue. It's all impressively intimidating.

Jamaat-e-Islami's leader is a short, grey-bearded man with a big message. 'This is shameful for Pakistan!' shouts Qazi Hussain Ahmed. Parts of the crowd bristle with anger, while others pay no attention. 'The only nuclear power in the Islamic world has bowed to Washington and India!'

When Pakistan conducted nuclear tests, many here hailed that they had developed the world's first Muslim bomb – a source of pride and protection from 'Hindu' India. Now some are asking what the point of such an arsenal is if 'conventional' combat ends in humiliating retreat. Still, the faithful seem undeterred: many men are crowned with bandanas signifying they are *jihadis*, returned from fighting in Indian-administered Kashmir. The bandanas have the unfortunate effect of making many of them look like John McEnroe with an unkempt beard but these young men are not to be ridiculed – they are deadly serious about their business. One of them, a nineteen-year-old who refuses to give his name, claims to have returned from Indian-administered Kashmir just two days ago. When this rally is over, he will return to the job of *jihad*.

Pakistan's fundamentalist parties, like Jamaat-e-Islami, are generating a lot of heat but not a lot of votes. They don't pose a direct and immediate threat to the two giants of Pakistani politics – the Muslim League, led by Nawaz Sharif, and Benazir Bhutto's Pakistan People's Party – but their influence has spread cleverly through Pakistan's key institutions, including sections of the army. And they have a direct hand in the upbringing of many of the country's young men through the *madrassa* system. So, after grabbing some great angry material to make my story spicy, I head from the men of words to their friends of letters.

Jamaat-e-Islami's headquarters squat on the outskirts of Lahore. It feels like an Islamic theme park, boasting a medical centre, accommodation, teaching facilities, administrative offices and, of course, the mosque. I am shown around by a party tour guide, who saves his highlight for the finale. The mosque is a functional, no-frills building with a floor space the size of a tennis court; across it are spread gaggles of teenage boys in groups of about a dozen, with a teacher at the head of each. The mood is studious.

Eighteen-year-old Abdul is more studious than most. With his wispy beard and caterpillar eyebrows, he is messy and mildly brooding, but nothing that could not be marketed as the 'thoughtful' member of a teen boy band. However, Abdul's thoughts are not of stardom but martyrdom. He wants to be a *shaheed*, or martyr. *Jihad* is calling Abdul to the border.

'*Insh'allah*, I think *jihad* is the shortest way to paradise so I want to go there,' he says somewhat matter-of-factly.

His only dilemma is which *jihad* to join. Pakistan's *madrassas* made their name by funnelling ideologically moulded young men into Afghanistan to fight the Soviets. After Mikhail Gorbachev withdrew his troops in 1989 and the *mujahideen* factions turned their guns on each other, Pakistan's *madrassas* helped spawn the Taliban and buttressed the militia's ranks. (The word *talib* means religious student, thereby inspiring the name for the young Islamic army.) But there has also been steady demand on *madrassas* to send the boldest and brightest students to Kashmir, and Abdul is hearing the call.

'I prefer to go to Kashmir to find *jihad*. *Insh'allah*, after concluding this course or during this course. *Insh'allah*, I will try.'

'So sacrificing your life for Kashmir, that is something you *want* to do?'

'Yeah, because in every Muslim, a young child wishes that he grow like Salahuddin Ayubi, and Mohammed bin Qasim,' he names some of his Islamic heroes as though they were pin-up stars, 'and I also wish that I will fulfil a role like this. So I think every Muslim and I also wish that I will have a role like this and I pray for God that I will do that.'

'Does it scare you?'

'No. No, I am not afraid.'

'I am.'

Everyone laughs at my expense before Abdul returns to his message.

'Because I am Muslim. I am not afraid because I know that every man's life can end at any second. But Muslim believes if he is *shaheed*, if he is martyr, he will never die.'

Abdul could be talking about his dream to become a pilot, warming to his subject with the excited glint of a teenager dreaming of high hopes and grand plans. There is even something admirable, almost enviable about his sense of purpose, his conviction. My world seems caught in an endless wrestle between ambition and ambivalence but there is no ambiguity afflicting Abdul. His world seems rock-solid, clean-cut, black and white. But it's a clarity born of necessity: if I have option overload, he has its opposite. For

Abdul, death looks like the best option. In a country racked by corruption and crippled by a collapsing economy, Abdul has made a rational decision born of ambition and wrapped in the justification of *jihad*. For a young man wanting to succeed, to do good, Abdul has decided the best way for him to make a mark is to die fighting. It will be his fifteen minutes of fame. Shame he won't be around to enjoy it.

The other dozen young men watch as Abdul and I talk.

'How many of the rest of you want to go to Kashmir?'

My question is met by nervous smiles and deafening silence. Not one hand is raised; I had expected there to be a forest of defiant fists punching high in solidarity with Abdul. Finally, after the awkward quiet, one of the young men parrots the official Pakistani line.

'We can support them morally and diplomatically, that is enough.'

This won't make a very good story, so I persevere. 'So there are not many people here like Abdul?'

More nervous laughs but, no, Abdul's ambitions are not shared by everyone. In fact, they don't seem to be shared by anyone. Perhaps the Kargil drubbing has made prospective *jihadis* think again about the benefits of such a calling, despite the hairy-chested rhetoric of their leaders. Or Abdul may have realised something the others are yet to grasp: in the teenage search for identity, they face two stark cultural choices. They can turn to the west for meaning with its offerings of denim, Channel V and Nike – but know they will receive only a bastardised, leftover product to which they are only half welcome. Or they can embrace militant Islam that offers strength and honour, power and moral superiority, and very much desires them. Suddenly, I understand why militancy looks relatively attractive. With a few more years of ideological training, the rest of these wispy-chinned men may too sign up for sacrifice. The *madrassas* teach obedience and surrender – not individual thought.

After all, the root of the word 'Islam' means 'complete sur-render'. There is only one textbook – the Koran – which is learnt by rote, along with the *hadiths* or narrations of the deeds and sayings of the Holy Prophet.

Pakistan's *madrassa* network flourished through the 1980s under the nurturing gaze of military dictator General Zia ul-Haq, drip-fed by foreign funding and with the CIA seal of approval. Through the Afghan war against the Soviets, they provided Cold War cannon fodder and formed an essential part of the US-backed campaign there. But their role is more complex than that. They offer free education in a country with a failed state education system, and for poor peasant families, the *madrassas* hold out the only chance of literacy for their sons (girls need not apply). Through the 1980s, desperate Afghan refugees sent their boys to the *madrassas*, which also meant one less mouth to feed at home. The good son might then find work in the cities or big towns or even, God willing, in one of the Gulf States, from which they could send money home. The *madrassa* is a valued social service in a country with effectively no func-tioning state. Even many of Pakistan's middle-class sons attend the *madrassas* – and many in this one in Lahore have the telltale broken English of a quasi-bourgeois upbringing. Yet while some boys may come from 'polite' society, the *madrassas* are unabashed recruiting grounds for *jihadis*.

Through the 1990s, Pakistani intelligence officers would provide students with formal training in weapons-handling and bomb-making. Talented *talibs* would be sent for more sophisticated training to camps in Afghanistan, funded by Osama bin Laden. During Taliban offensives against the opposition Northern Alliance, entire *madrassas* would be shut down and the students bussed off to fight. Since 1994, more than eighty thousand Pakistani Islamic militants have trained and fought with the Taliban. They had no choice: the culture of faithful obedience puts the students at the whim of the prayer leader, the *imam*. He who disobeys the *imam* disobeys Allah.

Abdul says he has all the training he needs, though it has not necessarily come through this *madrassa*.

'I get but not very seriously like a full army man. I have learned martial arts but I can work Kalashnikov and these weapons. Every home has a Kalashnikov; we know how to use a gun.'

Pakistan is awash with millions of weapons – the combined legacy of a macho culture, the Afghan wars and a prolific replica industry that painstakingly reproduces the Cold War's most popular weapons at bargain basement prices. When I tell Abdul I have never held a gun in my life, he throws his head back and laughs with teenage abandon.

'No, but that is because you are not American! In America they have a gun in every home. The child can go and get a gun!'

I leave these children of the revolution and go in search of their revered leader, Qazi Hussain Ahmed, who greets me with an astute smile and self-assured handshake. Qazi-*sahib* is also surprisingly softly spoken; a stark contrast to his fierce battle cries at the rally. When I suggest that *madrassas* like his are breeding extremists, he is scornful but measured.

'We are not extremists! We are not militant! We are not intolerant! We are not exclusivist! We are not isolationist! We want to live in this world and with the people and we want dialogue with all the humans. We consider this as a global village and a human family. We are members of this global family.'

It's all said with the poker face of a politician.

'Actually, *jihad* is not war, this is not militancy. This is *jihad* struggle, striving in the way of Allah and this is against oppression. This is the duty of every human being. This is a just struggle.'

Jihad can certainly take many forms in the effort to become a good Muslim, and Pakistan desperately needs a few non-militant struggles to sort itself out.

As my taxi takes me back to town, I flick through some of the sobering statistics that condemn Pakistan to a state of crisis. Two-thirds of Pakistanis are illiterate. Its population of one hundred and forty million is set to double in twenty-five years. The lion's share of government spending goes to the military and debt refinancing, while more than forty per cent of Pakistanis don't have access to safe water or health care. And, increasingly crippled by an exploding regional heroin trade, Pakistan boasts more heroin addicts than tax-payers.

All of which seems surprising in a self-described chosen land.

'Pakistan' is actually an acronym. It stands for Punjab, Afghania, Kashmir and Indus-Sind, with the suffix '-stan', which means 'land'. (Unfortunately for the people of the restless south-western province of Baluchinstan, 'B' did not make it into the mix – which may go some way to explaining the Baluchis' keenness to secede.) To Pakistanis, their nation's name means 'Land of the Pure' – a glorious confection of exclusivity. For all Qazi Hussain Ahmed's talk of a global village, Pakistan is at its core an exclusory experiment; a 'faith-based' state but with borders blurred by cultural and ethnic ties beyond it. And faced with the failure of essential state institutions that should bind a nation, many Pakistanis have only their faith in common.

That is, except for the grinding, threadbare life they share – and nowhere is it more so than here in Lahore. Having met the righteous of this city, I want to explore its seamier side. And for this, I will need a guide.

Mr Parsha's pores seep success like an oily paste. He strides the city streets as a man who owns them – especially those in the old part of town, for it is in these narrow lanes, tight with men on foot and bikes, that Mr Parsha makes his business. At eleven in the evening, it's a scene of studied indulgence: the men of Lahore eat, talk and stare blankly into the middle distance. Down a side alley, a group of withering frames squat around a small pile of aluminium foil strips. Each fingers a foil with a thin river of Afghan heroin running down its centre – ready to heat with a lonely lighter flame for inhaling. They briefly scamper for a plastic bag of rotting bananas a shopkeeper throws them, only to quickly lose interest in their contest and return to their slow death by addiction. And sandwiched between the bored tea houses and busy barber shops are narrow rooms shining with the unforgiving light of fluorescent tubes. They give the street a cruel, blue hue – broken only by the bright pinks, saffrons and reds of *salwar kameez* worn by weary-looking women.

Here, Pakistan is not a Land of the Pure. This quarter of Lahore is the city's sexual underbelly – a zone of confusion and decay. But it's as though I'm the only one who can see it. There is a thin veil of disguise draped over these scenes, euphemistically referred to as the 'entertainment industry'. I film a strange ritual of professional foreplay in which women sing and dance to the tap-tap-tap of tablas and the groan of a harmonium for clients on shabby sofas. It is an undignified scene for everyone: the women's dances are more awkward than alluring. The men stare, impassive, imagining the main performance awaiting them upstairs. Their desire seems pathetic and perverse. Everyone – clients, prostitutes and pimps – are lying to themselves; and Mr Parsha, an 'entertainment agent', is a magnificent cliché. An associate calls him Lahore's President Pimp but after hours of showing an intimate tour of his trade, he parrots the lie.

'There is just dancing and singing going on. I'm an agent for the entertainment industry. There is no prostitution in Pakistan – it is not allowed under Islam. I've never seen such activities and I certainly don't know any call girls.'

His denials seem breathtaking but Mr Parsha is not being totally untruthful. The sex industry is hand-in-glove with Lahore's film industry – a very poor cousin of Bollywood, dubbed Lollywood. The more successful among its murky cast of characters can be found living in Lahore's leafy suburbs, where the inconveniences of Pakistan are kept out by towering brick walls and frosty airconditioning. Mr Parsha knows his coy comments won't make the cut, so he drives me to a large house in a quiet street, to show me the more salubrious aspects of the trade. We're greeted by a middle-aged woman, Sumira, who promptly introduces her daughter, Sumbal, an almost beautiful twenty-year-old. The house is decorated simply – television, sofa, a few photos, a few rooms with nothing more than a bed in them. The place smells of semen and sweat. Sumira is running a neat mother-and-daughter business.

'My husband does not like us doing this work,' Sumira concedes, 'but it helps pay the bills and what can he do?'

In what is supposed to be the more respectable side of Lahore, this has all the class of stale cola. Sumira is matter-of-fact and boasts that she works in one of the few growth industries in Pakistan.

'There's prostitution everywhere,' she drawls indignantly. 'Where isn't there prostitution? If someone has five hundred rupees they think about sex first and bread later.'

Sumira is getting to the end of her marketability but her daughter is very much in demand. And they are always searching for new talent. It won't be long before their domestic helper, a pretty twelve-year-old village girl, is 'promoted' into the family business.

Perhaps you can't judge a country by its sex industry –

except that it is one of the few new growth sectors and no-one acknowledges it exists. Despite its runaway success, Pakistan's fleshy underbelly is shrouded in extraordinary secrecy. AIDS activists cannot openly mention sex in their awareness campaigns. While national leaders puff up over nuclear weapons, Kashmir and the evils of India, there is next to no mention of child sexual abuse which is rife or the soaring trade in sex slaves. (It's estimated that up to four hundred Bangladeshi women are trafficked to Pakistan every month, promised good work only to be enslaved into prostitution.)

It's five in the morning and I snap my camera shut. After a long night, I have two minutes of television. I thank Sumira and Sambal for their hospitality and their honesty, thank Mr Parsha for his seedy tour and dishonesty and head down to Lahore's bus stop. I buy a ticket for an Islamabad bus leaving in an hour's time, race back to the hotel to pick up my bags and climb aboard a journey along one of the world's great white elephants.

The Islamabad–Lahore Motorway is an astounding stretch of concrete that slides through the fecund Punjab plains. Lush fields of wheat and rice flank the route, making for a wholesome scene at a hundred kilometres an hour. But there is nothing else to look at. The motorway has no traffic because no-one can afford to pay the toll of two hundred rupees (five Australian dollars). This brainchild of Nawaz Sharif was supposed to be a bustling link between his home town of Lahore and the capital. It is an empty strip of concrete, a monument to public policy folly.

My coach ends its airconditioned journey in the garrison city of Rawalpindi, which is only a twenty-minute drive from Islamabad. I step down to a bus station that is the same as those the Third World over: an intoxicating brew of commerce and confusion, heavy with the excitement and exhaustion of travel. Conductors hang out of buses painted in a garish splatter of colours, while on the ground men yell that a bus is leaving – '*JALDEE! JALDEE!*' QUICKLY! QUICKLY! – even though the driver is nowhere to be seen. Boys hawk snacks and magazines, keen students in the lessons of commerce. Some boys are not so keen. They stand slightly to the side of the mayhem, hunched, blank-faced, each holding a wire basket containing small bottles of massage oils. A middle-aged man approaches one, chats briefly, nods and they walk off together for one of the hotels circling the bus station. With their trademark oil bottles acting as advertisements, these boys offer the cheapest sex money can buy. It costs as little as a dollar. Child prostitution – especially among young boys – is a highly organised and prospering industry. I unpack my camera and film these broken boys from afar. With this new, distressing side to my story, I climb into a taxi for Islamabad to see if one of Pakistan's few campaigners against child sex abuse is making any progress.

'It's a poor man's pleasure,' Anusha Hussein says from her light and airy Islamabad office, which is dotted with toys and teddy bears. Anusha runs 'Sahil', a non-government organisation, through which she is almost single-handedly trying to take on Pakistan's proclivity for child sex. 'Pakistani men don't even think of sex with boys as sex. They just think of it as fun.' Anusha achieves isolated successes, getting a boy here or there off the streets, but there are many more lads replacing the few who get help. Powerful social, sexual and economic forces conspire to keep Pakistan's child sex trade thriving, and Anusha knows her efforts have marginal impact.

I'm depressed when I leave her office and hail a taxi. We drive through the Pakistani capital, which is, like the nation's name, synthetic. With its wide boulevards and ordered avenues, Islamabad oozes artificiality, diplomacy and bureaucracy. It is as far removed from the exuberance and exhaustion of the rest of South Asia as you could imagine and, with its strange abundance of eucalyptus trees, it seems oddly like Canberra, albeit with mosques and without pubs.

'*Sahib*, Islamabad only twenty minutes' drive from Pakistan!'

My taxi driver squeals with laughter at his joke, even though he has probably told it nearly as many times as he's had cups of tea. Recalling the twenty-minute drive from Rawalpindi, the capital's sister city and home to the military's headquarters, I snigger at the proximity: any general staging a coup need only rumble the tanks a few kilometres down to Parliament House. As we dribble down Islamabad's main boulevard, my driver keeps us both entertained.

'Pakistan named second most corrupt country in the world! Nigeria come first! Verrrry big problem! Why nobody bribe judges so to be number one?!' He shakes so much with laughter that we almost veer into a truck. His self-effacing humour makes me want Pakistan to succeed. I want it to be more than a small, confused cousin of India but I can't see past a fundamental problem. Defining a nation by religion establishes a futile line between 'us and them', which in turn can only present itself as arrogance or paranoia. Or both. Either way, it's a shaky basis for building trust – that essential ingredient which must underwrite any social contract. Pakistan is a monumental study in how not to build a state and society. Its failure to talk honestly with itself – about sex or Kashmir to name just two – blinkers it from reconsidering the failed course charted by a corrupt political elite.

Not that Pakistan hasn't had help in failing.

From 1951, Washington decided Pakistan's military was the best guardian of its Cold War interests in the region. It provided military training, the sale of arms and economic assistance, as well as open support for its leaders, including the brutal regime of General Zia ul-Haq (1977–1988). During the 1980s, the CIA turned a blind eye to the heroin trade that *mujahideen* warlords used to help fund their military campaigns against the Soviets. It kick-started a heroin industry that is choking Pakistan. With the end of the Cold War, Pakistan became an orphan. Its army is still getting used to having been abandoned by Washington, though its people have become all too used to being abandoned by their leaders.

But Pakistan can't be all gloom and doom. Maybe I've just got off on the wrong foot and need a fresh look. I also need a fixer who can help me penetrate Islamabad's cloistered and corrupt bureaucracy, so I contact a man recommended by a colleague. We agree to meet for afternoon tea and, in the meantime, I will try to keep an open mind about his troubled country.

CHAPTER 7

LITTLE OSAMA

Islamabad's Marriott Hotel foyer, a bastion of brass and marble, zips with the ditzy rings of mobile phones as beautiful young women in elegant *salwar kameez* sip tea in the café. This is *the* place to be in Islamabad. Actually, it is the *only* place in Islamabad – another five-star hotel is slowly on the way, but for decades the Marriott has held tight its monopoly over foreign visitors and Islamabad's wealthy.

Irshad Rao is almost tall and almost stylish. In his crisp, black Nehru-suit, he strides across the foyer, half lost, half purposeful, scoping for the young white guy on his own. When he sees me, his pointy moustache curls up with an excited smile revealing teeth stained red from chewing *paan*.

'Welcome to Pakistan!' he grins while weaving between tables, threatening to trip on a chair leg at every turn.

After the small talk is dispensed with, he tells me his story and the history of his country.

As an angry and ambitious young journalist, Irshad became an outspoken opponent of military rule. It cost him four years in prison without charge or trial at the hands of General Zia ul-Haq and he bears the scars to this day – including the glasses that compensate for the near-blindness beaten into him. But Irshad is a survivor. Following the mysterious plane crash that killed General Zia in 1988, and Pakistan's exuberant embrace of Benazir Bhutto, the newly elected Prime Minister appointed Irshad her information adviser. He remained in the job until her first fall from power in 1992.

'Ahhh, it was exciting! Democracy had a real chance. The people loved Benazir. THEY LOVED HER!' He's so excited he almost spits at me. 'But she wasted their affection,' Irshad sighs, listing a legacy of corruption and policy folly.

Irshad was an admirer and friend of Benazir's father, Zulfikar Ali Bhutto, Prime Minister from 1972 until General Zia ousted him in 1977 and arrested him on trumped-up charges of conspiring to murder an opposition political leader. Bhutto was hanged.

'Ahhh, we cried that day. And we cry today because Pakistan has lost its way. But Pakistan will survive, provided the *mullahs* do not take over.'

Ironically, it was Irshad's hero who flirted with the country's Islamic clerics. As well as encouraging a strong public sector role in the economy and approving radical land reforms, Zulfikar Ali Bhutto prohibited alcohol in a bid to woo the *mullahs*. But it was General Zia who set 'Islamicisation' racing across Pakistani social and political life. Among his 'reforms', the US-backed ruler introduced discriminatory 'Black Laws', which included giving the word of one man more weight than that of two women in legal proceedings. When Benazir Bhutto became the first female head of a predominantly Muslim state, one of her first moves was to release all women prisoners charged with crimes other than murder. Many had been convicted under the 'Black Laws'.

After several cups of tea, Irshad's rambling history of Pakistan is descending into a complex coil of unpronounce-able names, machiavellian moves and countless conspiracies, but I like his passion for journalism and irrepressible enthusiasm. When he invites me home for dinner with the family, I'm nervous it will become another historical blur but I'm keen to meet Pakistanis other than *jihadis*, junkies or 'entertainers', so I gratefully accept.

Islamabad is a grid of nameless streets, each marked with a letter and numbers, intended to allow anyone to find their way around once they understand the system. Problem is, the system is so logical and methodical, that nobody here seems to understand it. Everyone seems permanently lost, which may be a metaphor for the whole country. As my driver searches for Irshad's home, I get an unintended tour of some of Islamabad's monuments. Most impressive is Faisal Mosque – a soaring, angular structure with four piercing minarets threatening to puncture the clouds. Much less impressive is the endless array of tanks, fighter planes or ballistic missiles set in the middle of roundabouts. And least impressive of all, but my personal favourite for its sheer absurdity: the replica of the Baluchistan mountain under which Pakistan's first nuclear device was detonated. It looks like a papier-mâché school project writ large.

Finally, as much by luck as logic, we find Irshad's home – a two-storey box set amid a street of McMansions. In a country of crowds and chaos, Islamabad's suburban sterility presents the height of tranquillity. His home is speckled with intricate rugs, a swallowing sofa and a few prized photos of Irshad the young journalist laughing and shaking hands with Zulfikar Ali Bhutto. I am feted with embarrassing warmth and Irshad has even gone to the great trouble and risk of buying me beer from the local Christian bootlegger. It's warm but the first drink I've had in a while, so it's welcome.

Irshad's family is a picture of charm, generosity and secularism. This is the Pakistan that doesn't make the headlines because it's too nice to be newsworthy. But as I get to know them, I begin to think they represent one of the most important stories facing the country: they're leaving home.

Twenty-two-year-old Talha is tall, good-looking and intelligent. The oldest of four, he has just returned from completing his Bachelor in Computer Science and Masters in Business Administration at Canada's University of Regina with outstanding results. He's even been offered a top job in Canada but would prefer to live in Pakistan, if only he could.

'The family factor in our country and our culture is very important,' he tells me, nursing a Pepsi and twiddling his mobile phone. 'The main thing was that when I was away I was missing my family and my home and I was there for one and a half years so I had to come back. I do want to settle here. I'm in love with this country somehow.'

Sadly, investors do not share Talha's affections and, unlike India with its booming software sector, the 'new economy' has all but passed Pakistan by. As for the 'old economy', its decline has steepened since stiff international sanctions were imposed in the wake of Pakistan's nuclear tests. There are a handful of opportunities but, after three months of searching, Talha is finding that being good doesn't guarantee a good job. It's hopeless without contacts.

'I would say so, yes, yes. Not looking at the credentials of the person, just asking them their family background and hiring them, you know, they don't go for the human resource competency. They just go for the, you know, the family competencies.'

Not that his father is badly connected; far from it. It's just that Talha wants to make it on his own and would rather leave than fake it. Actually, he would love to work in India's IT sector but knows he'd never get a visa. For Talha,

India is a land of commercial opportunity, and his little brother, Annas, wants to work there too – though for revenge, not revenue.

'I would probably work in India and then work against it, gather the information for myself and then work for Pakistan again,' he tells me as we sit down to bottomless bowls of spicy chicken and crusty *naan* bread.

'Why work against it?' I ask.

'Because it's against Pakistan.'

I laugh but the deadpan face from this cheeky thirteen-year-old who adores cricket and computers suggests he's quite serious. And both sons are serious about saving their country, if anyone can. But the youngest of two girls, sixteen-year-old Malihar, is less forgiving. Slight and fiery, lounging on the sofa in jeans and t-shirt, Malihar is learning that Pakistan is very much a man's world.

'I'll be a woman soon and there isn't much of a future for women in Pakistan. Actually, everyone here says that Pakistan is progressing and all that, but I'm growing up and I'm realising a lot of things and conservative thinking of the people here. Like there's such a lot of hypocrisy. Everyone would just point at you if you were going around wearing jeans or any western dressing.'

'What do they say? What do they do?'

'They don't say anything, but the look in their eyes like they point you out. They stare at you as though you're some alien in their community.'

'You're sure you're going to leave?'

'Yes, I hope so.'

I look to my host. Irshad seems sad but resigned to losing his children to other lands. This patriot loves his country for what it could be, maybe even what it was, but not what it is becoming. He has been watching the warning signs for years: the long queues snaking outside Islamabad's American, British and Canadian embassies every morning as

Pakistanis patiently apply for work and study visas. The country is losing its most capable and conscientious, and as we chat over hot food, warm beer and cold cola, I'm reminded of the ridiculous ease with which I have been able to pursue my dreams. Education, travel, encouragement have all been in embarrassing abundance and, for the first time, I realise this journey as a correspondent is not of necessity but choice, perhaps even indulgence. It will not go on forever, I have a way out and, unlike these young people, I have no reason to ever despair. One day, I will go home.

There is nothing homely about my hotel, despite the best efforts of its grim-faced doorman, the over-zealous bed-turner and the complimentary stale chocolate left on my pillow every evening. Of greatest concern, however, is that there are no good stories in Islamabad at the moment. I have made some contacts but produced no material, so I abandon Islamabad's artificiality for a city wrapped in history and legend: the frontier city of Peshawar.

It takes only two hours to drive from South Asia to the eastern edge of Central Asia. The Grand Trunk Road sweeps over the stunning confluence of the Kabul and Indus Rivers, cradle to one of history's earliest civilisations. This ancient trading road, stretching from Kabul to Calcutta, was once flush with spices, silks and precious stones, as well as bringing conquering hordes to the subcontinent.

Today, it's anything but grand.

The bitumen heaves with the lead-laced fumes of stinking buses, their brilliant colours glistening in the sun, bursting human cargo flapping like rags, musical horns singing their way through the high-speed maze. Rickety rickshaws and bullying trucks twinkle with sultry depictions of Lollywood starlets swinging on mudflaps, smiling from side panels. They are a welcome distraction from the insanity flashing past my window. Like any road in the region, traffic is governed by a brutal battle of the biggest. To the stuffy sensibilities of western, law-abiding drivers, it seems mad, bad and downright dangerous. But there is a quirky justice at work: the drivers of these clumsy trucks are hardworking men with little money and even less power. (In January 1998, a transport worker who had not been paid in two years doused himself in petrol and set himself ablaze outside the Press Club. He left behind a letter that included: 'My family is starving and I am fed up with quarrels. I don't have a right to live. I am sure the flames of my body will reach the houses of the rich one day.') Behind the wheel, these powerless men are kings of the concrete, bosses of the bitumen. Their rule of the road is the sole revenge of the little man.

Peshawar is the ultimate frontier town, a hub for trading in everything from carpets to Kalashnikovs, Arab horses to Afghan heroin. Its smuggling markets or *baras* are awash with duty-free Japanese stereos, televisions, washing machines and airconditioners, which have comprehensively crushed Pakistani manufacturing, adding to the country's economic woes. Like most border towns, it is a furious casserole of commerce and culture – and for those wanting to get a taste of Afghanistan, it is as close as you can get in reasonable safety. From here on, the tea will no longer be strong and milky but green and watery, the men will be crowned with untidy turbans, and the women will be shrouded from top to toe in ghostly *burqas*. For its more than a million Afghan refugees, Peshawar is a window to a wider world – free of Taliban austerity, flush with trade and, by Afghan standards, good facilities. The cinemas are crowded with excited teenagers and the streets screech with blaring, distorted music.

I go straight to the office of Peshawar's legendary journalist, Rahimullah Yusufzai. He is famous for many things but most recently as one of the last reporters to have interviewed Osama bin Laden. With his unrivalled ties to the Taliban, Rahimullah walks one of the most difficult lines in journalism: to be trusted by the Taliban but respected as impartial. As Peshawar's BBC correspondent, he is nothing short of a star in Afghanistan, where his Pashto-language radio reports are a lifeline for a people otherwise cut off from the outside world. He's a celebrity here too, so I must wait for hours for him outside his office – and I am not the only one. Fatima, a young woman from Kabul, is also killing time in the queue and she's bored enough to chat to a sloppy-looking stranger.

'I am a journalist,' she tells me, and explains in excellent English: 'Well, *was* a journalist. Until the Taliban came to Kabul and it was too much for me. I could stay during the civil war – then I could still work as a journalist with foreign reporters. But when the end of the war meant the Taliban, it was time to leave. I cannot live life inside of my home, like a rat in a cage. So I am here in Peshawar looking for work or to travel to another country. Can you help me go to Australia?'

'No, I'm sorry, I can't. I don't think there is anything I can do for you,' I reply in my best broadcast voice – trying to sound friendly, forceful and final.

'Do you not have a friend at the Australian Embassy? I have some money I can pay them,' she persists.

To Fatima, bribing an immigration officer is a necessary formality, not an impossible risk. I tell her it's not done like that in Australia. Fatima gives a look of total incomprehension. I'm not sure what she finds more incredible: that I can't help, or that bribing won't, or that I have given her a straight answer.

'Please do not lie to me,' she pleads. 'Too many people say they will help and then do nothing.'

'That's why I'm telling you now that I can't help. I'm

sorry but I don't want to lead you down the garden path.'

'What is garden path?'

Fatima is looking increasingly perplexed and I can see this getting very messy. Thankfully, Rahimullah arrives.

I expected a rough, tough guy in the mould of a rugged frontier legend, but Rahimullah is impeccably polite and a little shaky on his feet. His greying beard indicates he's seen Peshawar in all its hues over the last few decades – as the Afghan *mujahideen* factions set up their bases against the Soviets, as the refugees flooded in only to stay and, more recently, the growing idolisation of Osama bin Laden.

'Osama is becoming a hero here,' Rahimullah tells me as we step onto the street for this afternoon's planned rally. Climbing into his tiny car, we review the last twelve months of the rise and rise of bin Laden. When Washington retaliated to the August 1998 bombing of US embassies in Kenya and Tanzania, Osama bin Laden was implicated and targeted. It's nearly a year since around seventy US cruise missiles struck six camps around the eastern Afghan town of Khost. Few will commemorate the anniversary in Australia but the people of Peshawar remember it well. They saw the wounded who were brought here, and many had relatives who had gone to the camps for training. Certainly the retaliation greatly fuelled bin Laden's already simmering popularity and he is now taking on cult status.

As Rahimullah takes me downtown, air-brushed portraits of bin Laden stare from posters in shop windows, from auto-rickshaw mudflaps and taxi dashboards. We pass 'Osama bin Laden bazaar' – just one of many businesses in and around Peshawar named after the Saudi billionaire turned Islamic billboard star. Some of the posters depict him looking like Rambo, complete with Koranic-verse-inscribed-bandana, swathed in bullet belts and wielding an enormous automatic rifle.

'It is a little surprising,' Rahimullah smiles, 'because he is a very shy person and now he is a celebrity. You know, he was an unknown man a few years ago. He came here in the eighties, he took part physically in the Afghan *jihad* and he also gave huge donations to the Afghan *mujahideen* and he helped the Afghan widows and orphans but he was not very well known. But he became known when he was attacked by the Americans and he has become a rallying point for the Muslims.'

En route to the protest, Rahimullah promised to take me to see Osama, right here in Peshawar. We find him in a well-kept, prosperous living room, giggling and happy with all the attention. He rolls around the lush Afghan carpet, beneath the glass coffee table, gurgling at his own cleverness for having clapped hands, rolled over and stood up in one seamless motion. Turning one next week, little Osama is the bouncing son of an insurance salesman, Ahmer Mohammed, who wanted to give his son the name of a great Muslim. Ahmer leans toward me to gently press his point.

'I admire Osama bin Laden and I want my son to have the same qualities when he grows up. Osama has shown he's a brave man because he's fighting for Islam, so I gave my son the same name.'

While my friends in Sydney are naming their boys Tom, Ben and Jack, Peshawar's proud parents are calling their sons Osama. Some are even renaming their children. Ahmer does not strike me as a militant Muslim – his polite manner, business suit and comfortable home suggest middle-class Peshawar rather than the gun-wielding cliché of hardline Islam. But he resents America's role in the region, its relationship with Israel and, especially, Washington's track-record of buying and trading Pakistani cooperation. Humiliated, Ahmer sees a biblical-sized battle looming and he's already conscripted his son.

'My son will fight, if need be, in a *jihad* against America in the future. It will come. I tell you, it will come.'

Blessed are the insurance salesmen. If mild-mannered

Ahmer is bracing for a showdown, then I'd hate to see what the angriest hardliners have in mind. We leave Ahmer tickling Osama's toes and as we drive to the rally, I feel uneasy about this region's future.

We park the car and walk the final few blocks towards the roar of rhetoric, and meet a re-run of the Lahore rally; only here, the focus is Afghanistan, not Kashmir. My timing is perfect: it's the first of a series of rallies in support of Osama bin Laden and in condemnation of America. I film a human river of sweat, spit and spite. It looks like Pakistan's answer to running with the bulls – minus the beasts and booze but with all the bravado. The mob tumbles through gorges of narrow streets in the old part of Peshawar, fists punching the air in defiance, beards dripping with sweat and saliva – scenes my camera will love.

'LONG LIVE OSAMA BIN LADEN! LONG LIVE AFGHANISTAN! DEATH TO BILL CLINTON AND DEATH TO AMERICA!' Their screams bounce off the crumbling buildings, shutters drawn in case the rally turns ugly.

'IF IT STRIKES AFGHANISTAN, AMERICA WILL MEET ITS END!'

The niceties of dinner at Irshad's or afternoon tea at Ahmer's playing with little Osama are swept away by the screams of the street. It makes me think back to Abdul, the ambitious *jihadi* in Lahore, and whether his young life has months or years left to run. And I wonder if all of this street theatre is really to be taken that seriously, or whether these men – young and old – are just letting off steam. Perhaps this is just their equivalent of the mosh pit.

'Nawaz Sharif is American puppet!' a young man screams down my lens as he hurtles past. 'And the puppet must go!'

The puppet does go – and more quickly than anyone could imagine. Two months later, Nawaz Sharif is ousted in a bloodless coup when he tries to sack his Chief of Army Staff, General Pervez Musharraf. With the rest of New Delhi's media pack, I race to Islamabad, expecting tanks and soldiers on the streets but, arriving after midnight, the streets are silent and unarmed. In daylight, also, the army does not flex its renewed power. It does not need to. The Pakistani people, cynical and exhausted, neither weep for Sharif nor their latest loss of democracy. Pervez Musharraf names himself 'Chief Executive', speaks with surprising frankness about his country's chronic problems and promises to rebuild Pakistan's failed democracy and economy. For the fourth time in half a century, the generals are back in power and Pakistan swings between military autocracy and failed civilian democracy. It also plunges into deeper international isolation – banned by the Commonwealth and scorned by Washington. But two years from now, General Musharraf and his country will come in from the cold. They will be saved by events beyond anyone's wildest imaginings. Overnight, Pakistan will be transformed from international pariah to vital partner in Washington's war on terrorism. And Afghanistan will see yet another war. But on this autumn day at the end of the millennium, no-one can see what the new century holds. Besides, just across the border, men are busy recreating the seventh century.

If I can't see the future, I may as well get a glimpse of the past.

It's time I met the Taliban.

CHAPTER 8

FROM CHAIRMAN TO CHAMAN

The man who calls himself the Chairman wants two thousand dollars. US, of course. The three thousand dollars I have brought with me has stretched the ABC's coffers but it clearly won't go very far. His rectangular jaw follows a shallow smile and makes a little laugh. Between us sits a nervous Irshad.

'Irshad, please tell the Chairman that the ABC is a poor media organisation and I don't have a lot of money. If we were rich there would be more than just me. See: no cameraman, no producer, just a one-man band. Very poor ABC.' The Chairman's English is actually not bad but we both feel less threatened by using Irshad as the intermediary, who might soften the edges of cultural sensitivity. Irshad translates, increasingly uncomfortable with what is becoming a very prickly cultural and commercial exchange. I have come to Quetta, the provincial capital of Baluchistan and Pakistan's other great smuggling gateway, on the assurance that I could get a Taliban visa. And to be fair, the Chairman has delivered on his promise: a thick, wet visa stamp is in my passport, but now, and only now, is there any mention of a fee.

The Chairman's business card reads:

Chairman and Company
Government Contractor and General Order Supplies
Proprietor:
Abdul Ali (CHAIRMAN)

He dresses simply in traditional flowing trousers and shirt, more grey than white and stained with fatty splashes from lunch. The Chairman should be in silk: he has made millions building roads and other public works across Baluchistan, managing the lucrative system of kickbacks. For a bit of pocket money, the Chairman cashes in on his local contacts when the occasional journalist blows in looking for a visa. I am totally out of my depth, haggling with a seasoned schemer in one of the most remote and ruthless parts of the world.

'Two thousand, my friend,' the Chairman repeats, thumbing his worry beads. Not that he need worry; he knows I still need him. I may have the visa but it is useless without an escort through the tribal badlands to the border. My piece of paper, on its own, is worthless. At least I have been making some progress. His opening fee was two thousand dollars per visa, which, with Irshad's, would put me, or the ABC, severely into hock. I am more scared of what my bosses will say about such a bill than I am of the Chairman's next move. He and Irshad walk out of my hotel room, leaving my imagination to run wild. But twenty minutes later they're back, Irshad intact and with a new offer.

'One thousand, my friend. But only because you my friend.'

Some friend. I should take it but I can't.

'Mr Chairman, I am sorry, sir, but I can only afford five hundred dollars for both visas. I just don't have the money.'

It really is all I can afford, and I'm feeling bad for paying anything at all, but in Afghanistan and Pakistan, no doors open without money. In fact, the Taliban have battened down the hatches over the last six months, effectively banning foreign journalists, so the visa in my passport is journalistic gold.

The Chairman laughs a little more, which makes me all the more nervous. Behind the smiles, I fear he's fuming at this plucky young white guy trying to haggle him down to an eighth of his asking price. He is a member of the Pashtun tribe, legendary for their ferocious courage and the ease with which they can be rubbed up the wrong way. The Taliban are also predominantly Pashtun. Struggling for some sort of social nicety, I order tea to the room, which only has the effect of dragging out the whole episode. Finally, he breaks the silence.

'I want to come to Austraaalia.'

Oh, shit, here we go.

'Yes, Mr Chairman, you should, it's very beautiful.'

I can see where this is heading, and I am dreading it.

'You help me get viiiiisa.'

'Well,' I begin, preparing to roll out the same Australia-is-not-corrupt spiel I gave Fatima in Peshawar. But who am I kidding? 'Yeeees, of course, Mr Chairman, my friends at the Australian Embassy are very helpful.'

When in Rome . . . What does it matter that I bend the truth for this guy? I may live to regret it but right now I don't care: I need any bargaining chip I can get my hands on and I really want to get going.

'I love come to Austraaalia for holiday.'

'Holiday?'

'Yes, Great Barrier Reef, Seeedaneee Harbour and big rock.'

'You want a tourist visa?'

'Yes, yes. Quetta my home. Me tourist.'

How hard can that be? Well, probably quite hard, but maybe I don't have to lie that much after all.

'Chairman, I would be honoured to help in any way I can.'

I can't see this bulky bloke lying around Bondi Beach but, then, I can barely picture myself on Bondi any more.

'Okay. Five hundred dollar. No problem.' The Chairman laughs his hollow laugh, stands up for what I assume will be a manly handshake but instead grips me with a spine-crushing hug, which I think is meant affectionately but might just as likely be a gentle threat. After two hours of draining negotiations, I pay the cash and we arrange for him to drive us to the border in the morning.

I hop into a spluttering auto-rickshaw and head for Jinnah Road to get some Afghanis – Afghanistan's near-worthless currency. Quetta's money-changing street is dotted with men huddled in shawls against the early evening chill. Their rates are all the same, so I pick one at random. The man opens his shawl to reveal brick-size wads of notes; I hand him five hundred dollars, he hands me several bricks. I check it, Irshad checks it, we hop back into our rickshaw and head for the hotel.

'Irshad, are you sure this is right?'

As I recount the wads on the way, they don't seem to add up to five hundred dollars.

'Yeesss, I am sure,' Irshad replies confidently.

I am not so confident. Back at the hotel I check again and confirm we've been ripped off. The guy short-changed me a hundred bucks worth of bricks.

The Chairman arrives with his sparkling new Toyota four-wheel drive and a crate of freshly picked peaches.

'This for journey,' he declares with a benevolent wave. 'You go Afghanistan, you need food for journey.'

I think I'm touched by the gesture but have given up trying to read him. I'm wondering if our little dance yesterday was nothing more than a little light amusement for the chairman. No longer caring, I throw my gear in the back and we head for the border.

'It's a very good road,' I offer as we pick up speed out of town.

'Yes, my friend, my road! I build!'

The Chairman seems in high spirits, the road really is good and the bare Baluchistan landscape slides by: harsh, haunting hills rise out of faded plains. There is not a sign of water, crops or stock. Incredibly, villages dot the route, in defiance of the damning environment. Many are made up of Afghan refugees who came twenty years ago when the Soviets invaded. Certainly, anyone living here has nowhere else to go. Stalls offer baskets of rotting fruit while bloody, fly-blown sheep carcasses swing and stink in the morning sun. We stop at a check-post to collect two lads in black *salwar kameez*, baseball-style caps stamped with official provincial badges and each cradling semi-automatic rifles. These tribal area guards will escort us to the border, through lawless lands far from the reach of Islamabad. For all intents and purposes, we are moving through the Republic of Baluchistan (except for the Chairman's road, which comes under Pakistani federal law), and if the Baluchis had their way, theirs would be a completely independent land. As it is, these parts are governed by the tribal code of *pasthunwali*, which permits the free carrying of any sort of arms, not to mention abduction and the odd honour killing.

'This your insurance!' Mr Chairman laughs, waving at the guards.

'And what is your insurance?'

'This!' He laughs loudly, this time genuinely amused by himself as he pulls his turban from the glove box. As he nestles it onto his head, I feel more secure about the protection offered by his long coil of material indicating his

Pashtun tribal status than by the boys in baseball caps wielding weapons. They are as young as I was the last time I played cowboys and Indians with plastic pistols. One of them falls asleep, his gun resting between his knees, pointing directly towards my head.

The Chairman is driving me to Chaman. It's Pakistan's final town before the Durand Line – the artificial border scratched out by the British in the late nineteenth century but which no Afghan regime has ever recognised. It served its imperial purpose by creating a buffer between the Russian and British Empires but more than a century later, it is a resented colonial legacy: it also divided the vast Pasthun tribe between Afghanistan and what eventually became Pakistan. As we cross the Khozak Pass, an enormous desert plain presents itself. Cut into the western flank of the mountain pass above it, concrete Pakistani army pillboxes keep watch on a country it can't decide is friend or foe. For now, these neighbours have a marriage of convenience. The last few miles of Pakistan's railway line shine in the sun, a silver slither marking out one welcome British legacy. This is the end of the line.

The word 'Chaman' is Persian and means a prosperous, poetic garden, or orchid. It's a cruel joke: whirls of dust dance around the town which is completely treeless and soulless. However, it is an oasis of sorts: Chaman is buzzing with activity, almost all of it illegal. The Chairman drops us outside an office, unpacks the gear and peaches, shakes my hand, and heads straight back to Quetta. This time there is no smile; his performance is over. He leaves us with a young guy called Ahmed, who takes us upstairs into a sparsely furnished room where a large plastic sheet is spread on the floor, followed by huge plates of rice, kebabs and *naan*. We shovel fistfuls of food in silence, mostly because it is the custom and also because none of my hosts speak any English. I don't know who they are, what this decrepit office represents and what will happen next. In fact, in my mental map, I could not say where Chaman is, except somewhere along the border in Pakistan's south-western corner. I would ask Irshad for some guidance but, frankly, he looks even more confused. As far as I can tell, I am one of a few, if not the only, foreign journalist to be entering Afghanistan at this time. After the Taliban's repeated refusals to hand over Osama bin Laden for his alleged masterminding of last year's US embassy bombings in Africa, UN Security Council sanctions on trade, air services and any financial dealings with the militia, come into force today. The imposition of the sanctions will plunge the country into even greater isolation, and it's not a bad news hook for taking a look inside this hermit kingdom. But I cannot imagine what lies ahead and, most critically, if I will be able to film anything in a country that has banned television and filming.

Yet, strangely, I feel right at home. I am sitting on the floor, eating lunch with my hands, in an anonymous office, in a frontier smuggling town, with total strangers but for a fixer I think I like but barely know, heading to a country racked by years of war and ruled by a medieval, Islamic regime. I feel so removed from my former life, I'm mystified as to what else you would do on a Sunday.

Downstairs, the tea houses are humming with drivers, customs officials and tribal men chatting happily. They've got a lot to smile about. Huge consignments of smuggled goods flow through here in a parade of illegal trade. Chaman is a glorified truck stop and because it is a much smaller town than Peshawar, the illicit business is so much more explicit. As many as three hundred trucks pass through every day: many of them are stolen, carry false number plates and the goods have no invoices. The drivers, sporting several false licences and perhaps passports, may cross six international frontiers, stretching from Karachi on the Arabian Sea to the Central Asia republics. The cargo is everything you need and a lot you don't: electronic goods, petrol and, of course, heroin. This is the twentieth century Silk Route, and the descendants of those ancient trading tribesmen and nomads make up the transport and drug mafias of today, with their dons based in Quetta and Peshawar. Instead of enormous camel caravans, they use Mercedes and Bedford semitrailers in a highly organised and extensive system worth billions of dollars, while bankrupt Pakistan loses enormous sums in customs revenue.

We climb into Ahmed's pick-up, head for the border post and, without warning, we are in Afghanistan, pulling into Spin Baldak. This is a town as furiously busy as Chaman, but instead of a bitumen street and proper shops, there is a dirt road and rows of cargo containers. Taliban skulk up and down the 'main street', their black turbans wrapped like gigantic lengths of liquorice around their heads. The container doors open onto the main drag, displaying their wares – tyres, car stereos, spare parts, fridges and food. The only vaguely permanent structure is the brick passport office, though it looks like it won't last as long as the containers. The Taliban passport officer is heading out for prayers, but he grudgingly delays it to stamp our passports. Ahmed picks up a cheap car cassette deck from one of the cargo containers, quickly weaves together the wires with the car speakers and roars off in a storm of dust and blaring Bollywood soundtracks, bound for Kandahar.

The road is a jumble of gravel and rubble, the boundary between it and the desert impossible to define. Drivers regard this as an advantage and swing far beyond the verge – if it exists at all – to overtake each other. Some drivers are laughing and tooting, others are hunched over the wheel with stressed expressions. Ahmed likes to chat about business.

'That is my family's truck!' He points to a huge semitrailer bulging with a load of tyres. 'We have been waiting for it to come all day.'

Irshad translates the remark, which I don't really give much thought, until a few minutes later when my twenty-three-year-old rally driver points out another semi stacked with brand new fridges, still in their boxes.

'That truck, too. Good. That is coming.'

Crunching through cavernous potholes and plunging corrugations, he singles out yet another truck. It seems this is not just some kid the Chairman arranged to drive us to Kandahar but the eldest son of one of Baluchistan's biggest smuggling mafia bosses. Perhaps it is Pashtun honour that dictates I be looked after, or perhaps the Chairman just wanted to be sure that he got us well out of his hair. For Ahmed, it's a fun Sunday drive and a chance to see some family business contacts in Kandahar. The heir to a smuggling empire is being groomed by his father, himself taught by his dad. The family has been trading for decades, and now boasts a conglomerate which stretches the region and, according to Ahmed, includes offices in Sudan, New York and Zurich. I can't tell how much Ahmed is gilding the lily but I am impressed by his chunky, diamond-encrusted gold watch. Whoever is running Afghanistan's smuggling show, business has boomed.

'Before the Taliban we could not drive along this road without being pulled over by the warlords,' Ahmed tells me above the music. 'Now you can travel anywhere with a bag full of gold.'

Through the first half of the 1990s, this road was hatched with the roadblocks of warlords, extorting traders and travellers, controlling who passed, what they paid and, ultimately, who would live and die. The Taliban challenged their power and rackets. (A key early triumph for the Taliban militia was the freeing of a thirty-truck Pakistani convoy waylaid by warlords near Kandahar in November 1994. It took four days of fighting and fifty dead, but the convoy was freed and the Taliban took control of

Kandahar.) In a lucrative deal, the Taliban enjoyed early backing from the Quetta mafia, who helped fund the militia's military conquests, which, in turn, opened up safe routes to Iran and Turkmenistan with significantly cheaper levies than what they had been previously paying warlords. With the support of Pakistan funnelling fuel, cash and arms, the Taliban seemed unstoppable. This force of young, desert illiterates was forging a nexus with transport and drug mafia, corrupt Pakistani customs officials and a Pakistani establishment scrambling for a winner in its civil war-torn neighbourhood.

The road might be free of warlords today but it still looks threatening to me. At times, the dust is so thick we can barely see our own bonnet, let alone the car in front or any oncoming vehicles. Where there once were bridges now lie folded concrete and metal; the vehicles drive around the debris and through dried-up creekbeds. A group of road workers is boiling bitumen to revive one stretch of road, but it is a pointless gesture. Further along, boys shovel dirt into a pothole as we approach, but it is a hopeless form of begging. Ahmed doesn't stop, and I can't imagine many do.

As we near Kandahar, Ahmed takes out his Bollywood tape, shoves it beneath his shirt and tunes into the proselytising and propaganda of Taliban mouthpiece Radio Shariat. Between prayers, the announcer reminds listeners of the decrees relating to women:

'If women are going outside with fashionable, ornamental, tight and charming clothes to show themselves, they will be cursed by the Islamic Sharia and should never expect to go to heaven.'

Irshad translates the crackling voice but I am soon lost in thoughts about Sarah. I miss her laugh and 'charming clothes', though she'd find nothing funny in these decrees. The distance is really starting to wear and we need more than a fleeting holiday together. I will call her in Kandahar, despite the knowledge that a short, distorted chat on the satellite phone won't close the gap.

The approach to the Taliban's spiritual capital is announced by the leftovers of war and smuggling. Old Soviet tank tracks are unrolled across the road to serve as speed humps. A blown-apart cargo container is a mind-bending reminder of the practice of capturing an enemy, throwing a hand grenade in behind and locking the door. A lamppost is draped with audio and video cassette gizzards, a testimony to the Taliban ban on music and television, edicts enforced by the much-feared religious police – agents of the wonderfully Orwellian-titled Department of the Promotion of Virtue and Prevention of Vice. With my camera and bag full of tape stock in the boot, the lamppost decorations make me feel less than welcome. Adding to the intimidation, a stream of Toyota pick-up trucks rolls by, each with five or six young men trying to look menacing as they sit on bench seats in the back. They are Afghanistan's equivalent of the lads sussin' the strip at Bondi in souped-up Toranas – minus the booming stereo, of course. A few of them appear to be Arab – foreign fighters whose loyalty lies not with the Taliban but with Osama bin Laden and his al-Qaeda network. The pick-up is the Taliban vehicle of choice and each man wields his weapon of preference – either the hardy AK-47 rifle or bulbous-nosed rocket-propelled grenades. These student warriors rule with the Koran in one hand and Kalashnikov in the other.

I feel like I have been tossed into a perverse time machine, chundering me both backwards and forwards. It's at once a violent jolt to the seventh century and a tumultuous thrust into a dark, dysfunctional post-apocalyptic future. First came the Dark Ages. Then came Mad Max. And somewhere between, suspended in time, space and sanity, in a whirlwind of dust and devastation, came the Taliban. I've landed in an Islamic utopia with Cold War weaponry.

CHAPTER 9

THE SOUND OF MUSIC

Kandahar is a silent city. Once comfortable suburbs are now honeycomb rows of hollowed homes; the only sound the tentative taps of landmine-clearing teams picking their way through the debris. In a cleared area marked 'OK' in sloppy whitewash, two brothers recently returned from years in Pakistan, are rebuilding their family home, hopeful the Taliban will make good their promise to maintain stability and safety. The Taliban's seat of power is showing signs of recovery. Most obvious are the construction projects funded by a grateful Osama bin Laden, including road works and a sprawling compound residence for Mullah Mohammed Omar. But it's not only bin Laden largesse which is kick-starting Kandahar. Public confidence is up too: encouraged by several years of Taliban-governed stability, an entrepreneur is building a three-storey apartment block, while street stalls offer sumptuous carpets or pots glistening in the afternoon light. Still, amid this activity, there is an absence difficult to isolate. It takes me a while to realise what is missing but it's so obvious.

Music.

The screeching speakers of India and Pakistan are nowhere to be heard, and I miss the distorted delivery of

Bollywood soundtracks or America's discarded hits of the 1980s. The Taliban's ban on music – along with TV and just about everything else that's fun – leaves a gaping hole in a region characterised by its wall of noise. Welcome to Nofunistan. Although, entertainment of sorts is on offer this afternoon. Dust-crusted from the journey, we edge through a stream of people flowing towards the sport stadium, which happens to be just a few hundred metres from the United Nations' guesthouse, where Irshad and I are staying. We pull up outside the high, blue UN gates, unpack my gear and farewell Ahmed as we're greeted by the guard.

'Who is playing?' I ask, pointing to the crowd.

'It's not a game,' he giggles, looking at me as though my pants are on back-to-front.

Alongside other international public relations coups such as their effective house arrest of women, the Taliban have earned a notorious reputation for melding play and piety. With their retaliatory brand of Sharia justice, a body of Islamic law based on the Koran, the Taliban have made capital punishment a central, public plank of their power, transforming soccer stadiums into execution arenas. By claiming to enforce the laws of Allah, as channelled by Mohammed, the regime stamps its authority as sole interpreter of God and his prophet's intentions. Whoever challenges the Taliban challenges divine authority. For this afternoon's circus event, a murderer, convicted by Sharia court, will be shot by a relative of the victim. With a mix of journalistic thrill and personal revulsion at the whole prospect, I dump my bags in the guesthouse, and head for the stadium with Irshad. The stadium outskirts are sprinkled with religious police wielding rubber straps for herding the crowd. I approach one of them, a guy who looks like a young Rudolph Giuliani with an oily beard, tattered black turban, and a bad taste in his mouth.

'Can I go in?' I ask through Irshad.

'You are welcome. But you need guard.'

'How do I get a guard?'

'There are none now.'

'When will there be one?'

'*Insh'allah*, it will be soon.'

'How soon?'

'*Insh'allah*, when the almighty Prophet, peace be upon Him, is ready, guard will be ready.'

'When does the execution happen?'

'*Insh'allah*, Sharia justice will happen soon.'

'Sooner than a guard is available?'

'*Insh'allah*, it will happen.'

'The guard or the execution?'

'*Insh'allah*, everything will happen.'

Ask a simple question, get a righteous answer. I'm learning that throughout this region, Muslims, Hindus and everyone in between can't seem to manage a straight 'no' between them. I had never realised the priceless value of a direct refusal or denial, and it's times like these I pine for Australians' blunt ways. Several lads from the religious police posse seem to be doing nothing but staring slack-jawed at our little chat and one of them could presumably be my guard, but it's clear I won't be going inside the stadium.

'*Manena*.' Thank you. Not.

'*Jor Osi*.' You're welcome. Not.

Rudy the Righteous Ruminator makes easy a dilemma I was avoiding: truth is, I am not sure if I want to go in. For all his evasiveness, I am more troubled by my moral fibre – or lack of it. I face a kaleidoscope of emotions: curiosity, disgust, fear. I had always assumed I opposed capital punishment but am suddenly drawn to the visceral drama of a public execution. Revenge suddenly has a nice primal appeal.

As I linger, a crowd gathers around and with it an air of resentment: the United Nations' economic sanctions, designed to force the Taliban to hand over bin Laden, are already driving up the price of wheat and other staples. Disappointed and intimidated, but relieved, I walk back to the guesthouse, comforted by a cosy November sun.

At least the UN gate guard is pleased to see me.

'Very dangerous for you. Maybe you Australian, but crowd think you American. Come, come,' he gestures while locking the gates behind us, 'take tea.'

If in doubt in Afghanistan, take tea. Lost your moral map? Take tea. Caught between publicly executing a man and delivering mercy? Take tea. Torn between doing your job as a journalist and being human? Take tea. So, I do, warm, green and sweet, in the compound courtyard, with its floppy roses and elderly pomegranate trees, the fruit of which, sunburnt and bursting, lies scattered on the ground. Irshad heads off through the deserted streets to request an interview for me with the Foreign Minister, while I sit and listen to the buzz of anticipation coming from the stadium as Kandahar awaits the afternoon attraction. They hush and the guard translates as the public address system announces that Taliban Supreme Leader Mullah Mohammed Omar is appealing to the victim's family to show eleventh-hour forgiveness. But his supremacy does not inspire clemency and, through the still afternoon air, five shots of Sharia justice sing over Kandahar. They hang like a choir's last note.

As if to compensate for my moral stagnation, my imagination fires. I hear the rapid, short breaths of the convicted, sense a thick knot of fear in his stomach as he kneels below the soccer posts, the palms of his tied hands thick and sticky with sweat. Perhaps his family has come to the stadium, to watch his last, undignified breaths. I imagine the short gasp among the crowd, almost imperceptible with the first bullet, as blood starts to seep into the hard, baked ground. I wonder if the women feel a freedom behind their *burqas*, hidden to react as they wish: to grimace or grin at the messy trigger work. I wonder if my imagination is more disturbing than the reality of being in the stadium.

The quiet of Kandahar and the noise in my mind are interrupted by the siren of the ambulance that is removing the body. As the sound pours over the compound walls, I wonder why they need the siren at all. There is no traffic and certainly no hurry. There is never a need to rush to the morgue.

Their state-sponsored entertainment over for another week, the crowd heads home. Irshad returns with news that the Foreign Minister will see me straight away at the Radio Shariat offices. Never have I had such immediate access to a foreign minister, let alone in a country where journalism is effectively illegal; but as the regime slides into near total international isolation, moderate elements want to send conciliatory signals. The shrivelled shell of the radio station is dimpled with bullet and mortar holes; inside the halls have no lights, the doors were kicked down long ago. A minder shows us upstairs to the interview room, where I gingerly unpack my camera, wondering at what point the minders will remind me that filming is forbidden in the Islamic Emirate of Afghanistan. They don't, I set up hurriedly and wait.

An hour and copious cups of tea later, the Foreign Minister arrives. Mullah Wakil Ahmed Mutawakil is not your typical Taliban minister: for a start, he's in one piece. The Taliban are the most disabled leadership in the world, their wounds telling of a country crippled by two decades of fighting, in which more than one and a half million people have been killed. Taliban Supreme Leader Mullah Mohammed Omar is minus his right eye, many of his most senior ministers have lost at least one limb. Another unusual thing about the Foreign Minister is that he works after lunch. The government, as it is, functions for just a few hours in the morning, if at all. In the official capital, Kabul, some ministers spend their afternoons at the front line to the north, commanding the effort against the opposition Northern Alliance who still control ten per cent of the country. Many ministers never go to the office at all.

Mullah Wakil Ahmed Mutawakil is not only comparatively conscientious, he is also the relatively moderate voice of the Taliban. With his soft but not especially long beard, and moustache trimmed as a sign of piety, he is the public face of the regime. I assume he is much older but he is only my age – another young achiever in this student army desperate for international legitimacy. Yet another unusual thing about Mullah Mutawakil is his preparedness to be filmed, which should make him a willing participant in heresy – since the Taliban believe that the portrayal of any living thing attracts the curse of Mohammed. But he shows no signs of discomfort before my camera, as he insists the Taliban are merely misunderstood – girls can go to school (if there were the money), a Taliban television network is planned (if there were the money) and women can work (sort of).

'We have a culture where we don't give strong work to women. We wouldn't like our women to be a pilot or a fighter because it's not the tradition, but for other things, like we have a gaol for women here, so the person who is controlling this would be a woman.'

While the Taliban has won no plaudits for its women's policy, that's not why the west has become so wary of the regime. Their problem is, Osama bin Laden: The Foreign Minister is defiant, and in the face of new sanctions, threatening.

'We are an Islamic country and Allah is the true judge. America will receive something from our God, they will face strong storms and they will face a lot of problems.'

'Is Osama bin Laden in Afghanistan?'

He pauses, as if tossing the question around in his mind before offering his answer.

'*Balay*.' Yes.

And with a nod to his minder, the interview is over. However, the most important chat of all is yet to be had.

'Your Excellency, I respectfully request that I could seek your permission to film a few buildings and other inanimate objects in Kandahar to demonstrate the reconstruction effort led by the Taliban and the need for international assistance.'

Pride has no place for a journalist in need and I have slid to grovelling in a blink. As my words are translated, he sits motionless, utterly unreadable, which I take as a cue to keep going.

'Your Excellency, it is clear from the little I have seen of Kandahar that this city is returning to its former glory. Clearly, the Taliban are misunderstood by the outside world, and your efforts at education and other measures are great and wonderful developments by your government. I humbly suggest it would be worthwhile to show some of these efforts to the outside world.'

I can't believe the crap coming out of my mouth and I am certain the Foreign Minister is going to look straight through me, but he nods solemnly and, perhaps to save us both our dignity, scrawls his answer onto a piece of paper, hands it to a flunky standing by and slides out of the room with a shake of my hand and a slim smile. So authorised and fitted with a Taliban minder, we head out to film the non-living of Kandahar. As we drive back through town, I snatch only the odd shaky shot from the back seat of the car through the dust-covered windows. I can't focus, can't change the exposure, can't even put my eye to the view-finder. Mr Minder is nervous about the religious police, who are unlikely to recognise the authority of the Foreign

Minister in this matter; filming – or, rather, preventing it – is their gig.

He takes me to Kandahar's once majestic high court, that now looks like an abandoned industrial site halfway to demolition. Gaping rocket holes pierce the walls, not a single window is intact. Inside, once authoritative offices and court rooms have been claimed by Kuchi families – Afghanistan's legendary and resilient nomads. Their goats munch and stare while chickens scurry away. But here, behind these battered walls, I am in relative heaven – free to film, even to take the time to do a piece to camera. Still, the setting sun is robbing me of light, and as it seems like an eon has passed since I left Quetta this morning, I am happy to call it a day. It's clear I will need my energy and patience over the coming days: making television under the Taliban is like swimming through molasses.

My week is an endless stream of talk, tea and trying to steal shots. At a rate of ten secret attempts for one successful shot, and prohibited from speaking to women or visiting people's homes, this feels like Afghanistan Lite. But for all the limitations, I am still glancing into life under one of the most bizarre regimes in history and it's intoxicating. Some foreign correspondents I've met along this trail are so worldly they seem bored with everything, as though life has become one long anticlimax. I never want to become that person. Even after a year, I feel my eyes have been hardening, but Afghanistan is jamming them wide open. Perhaps it is the high blue skies, or the timeless deserts, but my head feels like it can breathe and for the first time all year I feel I am getting the hang of the job.

I have milked Kandahar for material and it has milked

most of my money but I am hungry for more. Kabul calls. Not surprisingly in a bankrupt country with no formal banking system left, nobody will give me a cash advance on my credit card, but I am assured that it will be no problem at the capital's Hotel InterContinental. Sounds like a plausible plan; the only question is how to get there. The idea of fifteen hours' carving a track through the lunar landscape from Kandahar to Kabul does not thrill me but nor does the prospect of catching an antique aircraft care of Ariana Afghan Airlines. In the end, curiosity and impatience get the better of me and I cough up forty dollars for two plane tickets and Irshad and I head for Kandahar airport.

This 1950s gift from an America trying to cultivate a little Cold War closeness is a grand construction of steep concrete arches, which might look funky in Phoenix, Arizona, but in Kandahar, Afghanistan, look absurd. It is retro, war ravaged and vacant. I want to buy a crappy magazine, drink a cruddy cup of coffee, but there is not a single shop or stall. Instead, I'm swamped by young boys wanting to scab, not serve.

'You have magazine, mister?'

'No, sorry, nothing.'

'*Newsweek*? *Time* magazine? *Playboy*? *Penthouse*?'

At least the Taliban can't change some things.

After two hours of waiting, the passengers are gathered, and the luggage is weighed, but there is no plane, no baggage check and no guarantee the flight will happen today. Finally, a sullen Taliban lad skulks out and asks to check baggage. If ever there was electronic security equipment it was long ago shot or stolen, so the search is sock by sock, shirt by shirt. Mum always told me to wear clean undies but she didn't warn me that one day my dirty ones would be airport exhibits. I was expecting my camera gear to cause the greatest grief but instead my personal belongings become a source of fascination and distraction: the pattern on my boxer shorts, photos of Sarah and, most of all, my toilet bag.

'What is this?' the inspector asks. Irshad translates.

'Shaving cream,' I reply.

The inspector holds the can as though it were a steaming shit, his contempt for infidels and their shaving ways all too visible.

'Here, I will show you!' Irshad interrupts, taking the can and squeezing a huge glob of cream in the palm of the inspector's hand. Now, if not before, he really does look like he's holding steaming faeces. Irshad beams a wide grin, unable to contain the pleasure of his prank. The inspector violently shakes away the cream before snatching a clean t-shirt from my bag to wipe his hand. The inspection is over.

As our twin-propeller plane taxis towards us, I wonder how many thousands of flights this Russian-built Antonov has made and whether one more trip is too much to ask. The new UN sanctions ban the Ariana fleet from flying internationally and therefore from getting its only proper mechanical service. Now, the planes are sustained only by Afghan ingenuity and faith.

'*Insh'allah*, you will make it to Kabul,' offers one of the ground staff. 'He keeps Afghan planes flying. And sanctions new, so planes okay. Six months from now, big problem.'

I'll remember not to fly Ariana next year.

Once on board, concerns about the plane's condition give way to fear of deep vein thrombosis. The seats are packed so tightly, I cannot fit in my legs and, having wedged myself in, I lose all sensation below the knees. I try to clip on my seat belt but it's broken. My safety sensitivities don't seem to be shared by anyone else: children play on parents' laps, there is no safety demonstration and passengers stand in the aisle chatting, even as we accelerate down the runway. It's more like catching a bus across town than a flight across the country.

The only consolation is the emergency window next to me with a large red lever, and clear instructions: USE ONLY IN EMERGENCY. There are several around the cabin but at least I could make a swift exit if need be. However, as we lift off, the corpses of aircraft littering the tarmac edge suggest this big red lever won't be any help. Still, I am learning to surrender to the forces of fate, or perhaps the will of Allah. So, with lower legs paralysed, I sit back in this sardine-tin seat and wait for the bearded stewards to present the in-flight snack of a biscuit, banana and Coca-Cola – yes, even in a country at ideological war with Washington, the great symbol of American culture pervades.

Below, the scene seems strangely familiar, almost Australian. Parched desert hills roll across a land apparently void of life. The Kabul–Kandahar road is a thin ribbon, much like the dirt tracks criss-crossing the Australian outback, joining somewhere with nowhere. Afghanistan's isolation and the richness of its ancient heritage resonate in familiar ways, though it is in so many ways Australia's opposite. One is landlocked, the other an island continent. One is a democracy, the other a theocracy. One is racked by war, the other prides itself on its peaceful distance from the world's troubles. And, apart from the greatly overstated Great Dividing Range, Australia is deadpan flat, while Afghanistan is crowned by the awesome Hindu Kush. As it comes into view a thrill zips through me, like a kid who has never seen snow before. An icy white blanket draped across its peaks, shining in the morning sun, the Hindu Kush holds court over the entire country.

However, the drama of the vista is overtaken by some unwelcome in-flight entertainment: a few seats in front, a young man decides that the temptation of an EMERGENCY EXIT lever is too big and red and enticing to ignore. He tugs the handle and in one deft effort pulls in the whole window frame. Air sucks out of the cabin, though it's not clear if it's from loss of pressure or the chorus of passengers' gasps. Some scream. Some pray. Some appear not to notice anything unusual. The rest of us laugh – especially when three elderly men pick the window up off the floor and try to fix it back in place by casually leaning against it. I would add my weight to the effort but my legs won't move. Amazingly, there is no serious loss of pressure because the plane is flying so low anyway. So, with a chilly breeze flowing through the cabin, we hobble into Kabul.

In Australia, the offending lad might have been met by men in white coats, waiting to slip him into a straitjacket. Instead, he is ignored and it is me the authorities show most interest in. I walk directly into the arms of some Taliban minders and I haven't felt safer all day. They tell me I must go straight to the Foreign Ministry to register my arrival in the capital, but I head straight to the Hotel InterContinental because I know that without cash I won't be staying long. Surprise, surprise, they don't take credit cards or cheques, and with only a few hundred dollars to my name there is no way we can stay.

Midday. If the taxi driver is good, I am told, we can be at the border by five, when the gates to Pakistan will shut for the night. Disappointed, I have no choice. I try to reconcile myself to the fact that I have just risked life and limb by flying to Kabul, only to hop in a taxi to head straight for the border. Not wanting to leave completely empty handed, we drive a few laps of town and I sneak some shots from the taxi. Kabul is a pumped-up version of Kandahar: bigger and busier. Which, in a country shut off from the world and bled of its productive population, means there is still just a splutter of activity. Kabul also seems much more bomb-battered, thanks to the vengeful rocket attacks of rival warlords. It is as arresting as it is depressing, but this crumbling capital forms just a fleeting image before we head east for Jalalabad and then the Torkham border post.

Around hair-raising hairpin turns and along the muddy Kabul River, our young driver races for the border but he's no match for the road's potholes and yawning crevices. We arrive a shade after six o'clock to gates closed long ago. The Taliban guards let us out but the Pakistanis won't let us in. Stuck in no-man's-land, we face the prospect of sleeping, and freezing, under the stars. After hours of haggling and the subtle offering of bribes, the Pakistani authorities reluctantly agree to open the gate but take no money. I want to press on to Peshawar but they refuse us permission to travel through the lawless North West Frontier Province tribal areas, even with the compulsory armed escort. Instead, they show us to a guest room in the guards' house and bring big plates of steaming spicy chicken and warm *naan* – strictly free of charge. I've not eaten since the morning's sugary in-flight snack so I devour the food. As for my appetite for Afghanistan, that has been whetted and is far from satisfied. So, I crash on the high, hard bed, tired but content, and, in the moonlit shadow of the Khyber Pass, vow to return.

However, for now, I must return to India.

CHAPTER 10

IMRAN'S ARMY

Long-distance love sucks and, after a year apart, Sarah is throwing in her job at Triple J, bidding farewell to friends, family and her ocean view and heading for New Delhi. The ABC apartment offers no vista, almost no furniture and absolutely no charm, so it's a scramble to make it comfortable, maybe even a bit romantic. I have been so preoccupied with work that my new home has been the lowest priority. So I get busy, paying too much for a limp little rug from a Kashmiri carpet-*wallah*, securing a few bottles of black-market champagne from the local bootlegger, and trying to rustle up fifty roses from the roadside flower-*wallah*. The bunches are droopy and diesel-stained but his big piles of loose rose petals present possibilities; I grab a bag-full to scatter around the bedroom before heading to the airport. The traffic is terrible and, despite Abraham's best efforts, Sarah has already been waiting for ten minutes by the time I arrive. That's long enough to be harassed by twenty taxi drivers, a pilot trying to pick up and a beggar unimpressed by her offering of an Australian twenty-cent piece.

'You're late!'

Shit. 'Sorry.'

Sarah tries to look angry but by the time we're out of the car park, we're smiling our way through the thick New Delhi night smog. She looks even better than when I left home a year ago: tanned, slim in tight jeans, and her face bright with the abandon of someone embracing uncertainty. We are buzzing to see each other but there is also an unspoken nervousness: we have spent more time apart than together and Sarah makes no secret of her disdain for India. After a disastrous backpacking trip ten years earlier, she swore never, ever to return. And that was before New Delhi had mutated from sleepy political town of a few million to a monster of twelve times that size. As if it knew she was coming, the city has greeted her with its first pea-soup fog for the winter – just as it welcomed me a year earlier.

'How does anyone breathe in this city?'

'What do you mean?'

'This pollution is unbelievable. I mean, it's disgusting.'

'Oh, yeah. That.'

Sarah shows the same wide-eyed shock I did a year ago. However, now I don't see the pollution or, for that matter, the traffic we're trapped in or the beggars tapping on the car window. It happens slowly, imperceptibly, so that you don't notice yourself changing. Then, as if by in-built survival mechanism, India has taught you to ignore its sensory overload. It takes a newcomer, with a fresh set of eyes, ears, nose and throat, to remind you how corroded your organs of observation have become. We crawl through the traffic, climb upstairs to the apartment, open a bottle of champagne and make plans in the most plan-hostile country on the planet.

Our first goal is simply to spend the festive season together, but five Islamic militants have other plans. On Christmas Eve, they hijack Indian Airlines flight 814 from Kathmandu, eventually settling at Kandahar airport after harrowing touchdowns in the Indian city of Amritsar, the Pakistani city of Lahore and the United Arab Emirates. Christmas Day becomes a blur of filing stories, as does every day for the following week – largely because an Australian banker is among the one hundred and eighty-nine passengers, which gives Australia a direct stake in the story. India is in meltdown as the government considers whether to give into the hijackers' demands to release Pakistani Muslim cleric Maulana Masood Azhar, who was arrested in Indian-administered Kashmir in 1994 but has never been tried. His group, the Harakat ul-Mujahideen is considered more ruthless than most and is on Washington's terrorist black-list. It's a good running story but I can't do it on my own. The digicam won't do; this time I'll need a crew with a proper Beta camera to avoid delays in editing and dubbing. That way, my update reports can be fed more quickly via satellite as the story is breaking. For once, I can hire a crew, but all the good ones are snapped up by the big networks.

Peter eventually finds a small media Moghul army: cameraman Imran and his assistant, along with the sound recordist and his assistant, the tripod carrier and his assistant. And, of course, the driver. At a squeeze, there is room for me in their van, so we head down to the Prime Minister's residence, where a growing crowd is demanding the government bow to the hijackers' demands. On the way, I establish the terms of our contract.

'Imran, what is your fee?'

'As you like, sir.'

'As *I* like?'

'Yes, sir.'

I have had this conversation with countless taxi-*wallahs*

and hawkers but I had expected the supposedly professional world of the media to be a little less tedious.

'Well, what do you normally charge?'

'Up to you, sir.'

'Yes, but what do you *normally* charge?'

'As you like, sir.'

'Okay, how about a hundred dollars for the day?'

'OH-HO-NO, sir! Pleeeassse!'

'You said as I like.'

'Yes, but, sir, it is too little.'

'So what you mean is as *I* like as long as you like it also?'

'OH-HO-NO, sir! Pleeeassse!'

'Okay, Imran, four hundred dollars a day. That's the going rate.'

'Yes, sir.'

'Okay.'

'And petrol, sir.'

'And petrol?'

'Yes, sir. And food for the boys.'

'Anything else?'

'Tea, sir.'

'That's it?'

'Yes, sir.'

We shake on it.

The crowd outside the Prime Minister's official residence is angry and afraid. Most are relatives of the hostages, unsure whether they will ever see their loved ones again. Imran's army tumbles out of the van and they take an eternity to get their gear together, just as the crowd really revs up. Imran is quick on his feet but his assistant trips over the tripod, the soundman gets tangled in his cords. We scramble over to the mob as Imran opens up his camera.

'Sir, tape, please.'

'Tape?'

'Yes, sir. Tape for camera.'

'What do you mean, "Tape for camera"?'

'You bring tape, sir.'

'*I* bring tape?'

'Yes, sir.'

'*I* bring tape?'

'Yes, sir.'

'What the fuck do you mean *I* bring tape? You're the camera crew!'

'Sir?'

'You haggle over petrol, food and tea . . . and you forget to mention *tapes*?!?'

I'm not sure who is more outraged at this moment: the protestors or me. Fortunately, a friendly cameraman from an Indian network overhears and offers a spare tape. Once he gets going, Imran is purposeful. He gets among the crowd, is not intimidated by the police with their long *lathi* sticks, and takes no crap from the other cameramen competing for the same slice of action. His army of assistants trail, more hindrance than help, and while Imran is keen, his English is borderline, so I have to point at anything I want filmed. Still, it goes well enough, and before heading to his office to cut the material, I want to get a passing shot from the car.

'Imran, as we drive past, film the crowd.'

'Yes, sir.'

A truck gets in the way, ruining the shot.

'Did you get it, Imran?'

'Sir, not so good. Truck is problem. Again, please, sir.'

'Okay, let's do it again.'

The driver turns around and we pass again but Imran just rests his camera in his lap.

'Imran?'

'Yes, sir?'

'Are you going to film the crowd?'

'Sir?'

'The crowd. Are you going to film it again?'

'Have shot, sir.'

'I thought the shot was no good. The truck was in the way. You wanted to go again.'

'Sir?'

'First time. The truck. TRRUCCCK! Shot no good.'

'No, sir. No good.'

'Film again? Make good shot?'

'Yes, sir.'

We do. And then we go.

Imran's studio is a forty-minute drive across town. Because the ABC has no TV gear, I can't edit at my office, so we crawl through the afternoon rush, only to discover the edit suite is busy with another client, despite assurances it would be free. After two hours' waiting, I am in the suite with an editor who speaks such little English he makes Imran seem fluent.

'Play tape.'

'No problem, sir.'

'Stop tape.'

'No problem, sir.'

'Go back to the top of that shot.'

'Sir?'

'Rewind.'

'No problem, sir.'

The tape spins back.

'Stop.'

The tape keeps whirling.

'STOP!'

Still it whirls.

'STOP! STOP! STOP!'

I scramble for my taxi-Hindi.

'BUUUUUSSSSS!' Enough!

He stops the tape, three minutes from where I want it. And so it goes through the course of the edit, a farcical blend of sign language, screaming and shonky Hindi. I'm angry because he doesn't speak my language, even though I'm the one living in his country. What should be a routine one-hour cut takes three to complete and I am punch drunk by the end of the process. Abraham picks me up and as we drive home, I wonder whether hiring a crew is such help after all.

As I walk through the door, Sarah pours me a vodka.

'You look terrible.'

'Thanks.'

'What happened?'

'India happened.'

I have some dinner before heading upstairs to file radio material for the morning bulletins, certain this is the worst festive season I've ever had. Sarah returns to the TV to fuel her blossoming love affair with Bollywood – and resigns herself to my working weird hours and putting the job before everything.

Just as the newsroom starts to tire of my incremental updates, New Year's Eve brings a breakthrough. In a deal brokered by the Taliban, India bows to the hijackers and agrees to hand over three imprisoned militants, including Maulana Masood Azhar. Another of the three is the lesser known Omar Sheikh, who has been jailed in India since 1994 on charges of organising the kidnapping of four westeners. It is not the last the world will hear of Omar Sheikh. For now, however, Foreign Minister Jaswant Singh will fly to Kandahar to hand over the three freed prisoners and return with the hostages. The hijackers are allowed to run free, given ten hours by the Taliban to leave Afghanistan. New Delhi politicians often declare with all their pomposity that 'India is not a soft state!' and insist it will never bow to the demands of militants, especially in relation to Kashmir. However, after a seven-day standoff, popular pressure has proved too great – though the concessions are less than the release of thirty-five militants and payment of two hundred million dollars (US) demanded at one stage.

The hostages are expected back in New Delhi at ten o'clock tonight. Imran and the boys travel in their van, Abraham drives me, and Sarah comes for the ride. She and I know the wait may drag well beyond midnight and we are determined to see in the new year and millennium together – even if it is with a few thousand of our closest Indian strangers at the world's most impersonal airport. New Delhi is already excited with pre-2000 celebrations and news of the hostages' return is zapping the city like a bolt of electricity. It might be the only power the capital enjoys for the next few days if the dreaded computer millennium bug brings trains, planes and telecommunications to a standstill. Considering the usual unreliability of Indian infrastructure, though, I'm not sure anyone would notice if the bug works its worst.

The airport is heaving – even by New Delhi standards. The departure area is swirling with relatives, well-wishers and media, a mass of hysteria as the first of the freed hostages appear. After a week stuck in their seats on the Kandahar tarmac, often blindfolded, only occasionally fed and always fearing what fate awaited them, they look drained and dishevelled. Still, they're heroes and the crowd swarms them as if they were rock stars. The police are too excited to offer any protection and the passengers are helpless against the garlands of marigolds, the showers of flowers and the shaking of hands. A few appear calm, as if their flight had been routinely delayed, but many collapse in a heap of tears and relief. There is no sign of the Australian, Peter Ward: diplomats whisk him out a secret side exit. All but one passenger is grateful for India's concession: a *sadhu*, or Hindu holy man, draped in saffron, his white beard showing most of his years are already spent, chides his Hindu–Nationalist government for putting the interests of individuals above those of the nation. For most, however, this is a night of victory and the crowd chants till throats are hoarse.

'*INDIA ZINDABAD! INDIA ZINDABAD!* LONG LIVE INDIA!'

Imran's army is thrilled to the verge of hyperventilating but the cameraman seems to be catching the action. This time I brought a tape and Imran had the forethought to bring a stepladder, which now gets him above the crowd. However, they forget headphones, so it's impossible to check my piece to camera over the din – just another hurdle to overcome, alongside the man shoving two grinning sons under my arms and the stunned-mullet mob staring from behind me as I say my piece. India is drunk on a brew of relief and nationalism and it all seems perfectly normal. In Australia, I would watch such TV scenes with a mix of awe and bemusement, disbelieving the unbridled excitement and endless mass of humanity. Now, it seems as natural and believable as the pollution that hangs over this city like an old wet rag. While Sydney is celebrating the start of 2000 with fireworks and friends, there is nowhere I would rather be than here, amid this chaos and these overexcited strangers. As the hostages return home, I am starting to feel that this may also be a home of sorts for me.

That feeling is helped hugely by Sarah's arrival. Suddenly I have someone with whom to share the mayhem, to laugh and swear and wonder out loud about the impossibility that is India. And as if a sign of things to come, we share the strangest start to a new century we could imagine. With the filming complete, I thank Imran, grab the tape and head back to quickly file for radio. I send the stories, lock up the office and race onto the roof, where a bottle of champagne and smog-filled sky will bring in the millennium. The fireworks are a fizzer, the champagne is flat and the fog is freezing but we are together.

Unity does not bring invincibility and the next morning Sarah wakes with a terrible flu, which worsens into pneumonia, which worsens into double pneumonia, complete with terrifying hallucinations. In New Delhi's poisonous pollution, that can be deadly. So against her protests, we follow doctor's advice and check in to New Delhi's largest, newest private hospital. She is X-rayed, jabbed and fitted with an oxygen mask. The room resembles that of a five-star hotel but such luxury is cold comfort: it is Sarah's first time in hospital and India is not where she'd like to be making this debut.

I ring her parents, who take the news well, in the circumstances. If they suspected I was reckless for wandering off to India, they'll be convinced of it now. Boy meets girl. Boy abandons her for India. Girl throws in great career to follow him. Girl gets life-threatening pneumonia. Boy looks and feels like one-hundred-percent first-class arsehole.

Sarah looks gaunt and weak but is in surprisingly good spirits. The antibiotics are working and, despite the medics' obsession with her coughing up large amounts of gooey phlegm, the care seems good. After a week, Sarah is discharged, provided she sucks on a strange steam contraption that looks like a giant bong but is supposed to help clear her lungs.

At the apartment, Sarah rests and slowly regains her strength. Thankfully, work is slow so I take a moment to catch my breath. Sarah's illness has shaken both of us and quickly stripped away my New Year revelation about feeling at home in India. It has proven to be a thin veneer. New Delhi is a big city with big facilities for those, like us, who can afford them, but in times of trouble there is no substitute for friends and family. After a year here, I must admit I have few friends and feel I know nothing of this place. The more I learn, the more I realise I don't know. I may be a little older but not much the wiser. From the intricacies of managing the ABC office to the absurdities of Afghanistan, absolute truths are few and far between. Stories are a crude clash of time, space and what (I think) matters: the Big Bang on a daily basis. I have learned to love the job but often it leaves the taste of frustration in my mouth. Compressing the complexity of South Asia into a few minutes of radio or television seems an exercise in superficiality.

There's no sense of inner revolution. Boy into man. The sudden appearance of a hairy chest. If anything, I feel quieter. More shy. Perhaps even more stupid. Amid the noise of Delhi, more important things are going on. For a city of fifteen million people, a correspondent at his computer is none of their business.

And of little interest to them.

CHAPTER 11

POOR MAN'S AMERICA

My new humility hurts, and realising all I don't know is just making work more difficult. I can't muster the gumption to write stories like I used to. After a year, the stereotypes of India are wearing thin. I need to find a path through India's contradictions that makes sense to me, that goes beyond the clichés.

For India stares down its clichés, sticks out its tongue and holds up a finger to the stereotypes. It is the richest, poorest, most charming, infuriating, beautiful and hideous land in the history of time. And it can be as efficient as it can be chaotic. I am learning a universal and merciful law of the land: everything you say about India is right and so is its opposite. And strange, bizarre things begin to make sense. At a dinner at the Press Club I barely snicker when Indian journalists discuss the benefits of drinking one's own urine. Yet when they then proceed to tell me just how Australia should begin its path to becoming a 'true democratic republic', I feel my self-confidence return. Indians are quick to give authoritative advice on anything and everything, so why shouldn't I? I have nothing to lose by posing my own pet thesis for understanding this impossible land.

So here goes.

India is a poor man's America.

It may seem absurd that the world's richest and most powerful country could be cultural cousin to one of the poorest and historically marginalised. However, the more I see India, the more I see the United States. Both great nations share an unshakeable sense of historical destiny; they each take immense pride in their democracy, social diversity and incredible cultural creativity. Their nation's imaginations are captivated by their prolific and usually trashy film industries. Both peoples take themselves far too seriously and take refuge in jingoism. Each nation seems to need an enemy: for Washington it was the Soviet Union, then Saddam Hussein and Osama bin Laden; for New Delhi it has always been Pakistan. They each boast massive armies and nuclear arms. And in both societies, those with power and money are respected and fawned upon in a way that rubs against Australian anti-authoritarianism. In short, both countries believe they're the centre of the universe.

Perhaps the strongest thread they share is that spun by the furious turbine of enterprise. Despite their reputation as a nation of laggards and incompetents, I increasingly see Indians as extraordinarily hardworking. To be sure, its bumbling bureaucracy is a story of late starts and long lunches, lack of accountability and chronic corruption, but the country works despite its public service, not because of it. Indians hold dear the dream of climbing from rags to riches – a dream drawn all the larger since India began to deregulate and open up its economy in 1992, inviting in a world of consumer possibilities. Our local shopping centre is crowded with sickly cows munching on rotting garbage and urchins tugging to clean my shoes, but behind sparkling glass windows, the latest Nike and Benetton fashions compete for space with Japanese white goods, while teenagers queue for McDonald's and Pizza Hut. At times, India feels like 1950s America, a society fascinated with the new, naïvely excited by cheesy ads broadcast via the exploding range of cable television channels.

India is also finding its place in the new world economic order. Its burgeoning information technology sector, having made its name doing the grind of decoding the world's millennium bugs, now provides a third of the world's software workers. So, with the region taking a break from coups and catastrophes, I set out to find India's least clichéd, most efficient enterprise. I track it down, not in India's pristine, new Silicon Valleys in the southern cities of Bangalore or Hyderabad, but amid the rubbish and bustle of Bombay. It's a story for ABC's *Foreign Correspondent* and for me – does the Poor Man's America thesis hold up to closer scrutiny?

As my plane sinks down through the muggy Bombay smog, Asia's largest slum spreads around the city in a quilt of corrugated iron, cardboard and plastic. It is stitched by muddy tracks and paths, along which people scramble like worker ants. Morning fires make breakfast. Children are bathed in buckets.

Bombay is awake, if it ever slept.

Most of these families are not from here. They have been drawn to the city by the lure of riches, however small. Indians go to New Delhi for power. They go to Calcutta for charm. And they go to Bombay for money: you can smell it when you step off the plane. The air in this west coast megatropolis is thick and sticky with the stench of wealth – the desperate pursuit of it, the fearful clutching to it, the squalid absence of it. Bombay is also called Mumbai, recently recast in its original Maharati name by the city's Hindu–Nationalist leaders, though Bombay is a tag too rich in romance to completely shake from usage.

'Taxxeeeeee!? Taxxeeeeee!?'

'Sir! Sir! *Sahib*!'

'Cheap taxxeeeeee!'

My Bombay welcome is the furious dance of the taxi drivers. The long line snakes off into the distance – too far to see the end. As I run the gauntlet, each man lunges forward with the same flash of insistent optimism.

'Taxi, *sahib*?'

'*No.*'

'*Taxi, sahib*?'

'*NO.*'

'*TAXXXIIIEEE, SAHIIIIIB?*'

'*NOOOOOOOOOOOOOOO!*'

All the way along the line.

Every driver is oblivious to my previous refusals; and it is this in-your-face hustling that is the heart of Indian enter-prise and optimism – albeit in stark contrast to its soporific service.

I pick a driver randomly – a lottery for the both of us.

'Lucky day, *sahib*,' he grins widely. 'My very lucky day.'

Mahesh launches into his life-story as he lurches into the morning traffic. He has four children. He wants school for them, to provide opportunities denied to him. His family lives in a slummy part of town. He does not see them often, sleeping most of the time in his taxi – always ready for the off-chance of work. Beneath his eyes, the deep, dark rings of ingrained exhaustion.

'You must be happy for what you have, *sahib*,' he wheezes, nudging his taxi through gridlock. 'Ganesh will provide everything you need. You want a lot but you need only a little.'

Ganesh is the beloved Hindu elephant-god who keeps watch over Bombay. With the head of an elephant on the roly-poly body of a man, he is the city's favourite son and his cheeky nature seems to touch everyone. Ganesh is the embodiment of wisdom, the lord of beginnings and the clearer of hurdles, so I figure he's a good deity to adopt as my own mascot on the road. Mahesh rubs the round tummy of his mini Ganesh on the dashboard as he drives, talks and eats. Last night he went home and his wife packed a *tiffin* full of hot, spicy homemade food. As we grind to a standstill, defeated by the congestion, Mahesh tucks into a steaming steel container of mustardy *dhal* (stewed lentils) scooped up with *chapatti*, a piece of flat bread.

The *tiffin* is the mighty Indian lunchbox – and much more impressive than the plastic number your mum packed with stale sandwiches and burnt cupcakes. It is a neat culinary column of small tins that fit into each other: the smallest may be just one container, the largest may have several and can tower a foot high. The British originally coined the term *tiffin* to describe a light lunch. This Anglo–Indian word lingered long after Independence, and has come to describe on institution greater than the Raj. *Dabba* – literally meaning 'box' – is also widely used.

Whether you call it a *tiffin* or *dabba*, it sits at the centre of one of the world's most efficient enterprises. Attracted by a tale that does not involve tyranny or territorial disputes, I have come to film a story involving home-cooked food, clockwork timing, supreme coordination, a lot of men and very hard work. I am especially excited because I am treated to a producer – Tony, an expat Aussie living in Bombay. I have also managed to poach a great cameraman from the Japanese broadcaster NHK for the day. Rakesh is skilled, speaks perfect English, and is not slowed down by a small army of hopeless helpers. He even brings tapes and head-phones. I am playing TV grown-ups.

The next morning the team and I watch as Mrs Lalla-poria puts the notion of a cut lunch to shame. From her spotlessly clean kitchen, the smell of onions frying wafts through her third-floor apartment. It's not yet eight o'clock but lunch is well on the way. Today she is cooking curry and rice with a cheeky chutney, a simple salad and *chapatti*.

In her orange and yellow floral-print dress, and with care-fully kept silver hair, Mrs Lallaporia looks like a budgie who won't stop singing. She laughs uncontrollably at my hopeless Hindi while tenderly dishing lunch into the separate *dabba* compartments. It's a routine she's kept for nearly half a century, first for her husband and then her darling son, Manosh.

'I don't like my son to eat outside,' she smilingly sneers. 'Outside food is no good. The food is not so healthy.'

I always thought only wimpy westerners worried about the hygiene of India's restaurants and dodgy roadside diners, and I frown at foreigners who limit themselves to boring hotel food. My best meals have been in the dirtiest of *dhabas* but it seems Bombay's middle class can be just as picky as the tourists. Maybe this family knows something I don't. The Lallaporias are members of Bombay's unique Parsi community – followers of the ancient Persian Prophet Zarathustra, who handed down a strong code of conduct. Parsis are obsessive about cleanliness and purification, so it's only the best for Mrs Lallaporia's son and that means home-cooked lunch.

However, Manosh is no schoolboy in shorts and long socks. He is a forty-three-year-old insurance worker. What's more, he's married. But his working wife, Roxanne, won't make Manosh lunch and there is no way he is going to do it himself. Now, I am not the most reconstructed guy in the world, but I can do a few kitchen things. Mum's motto 'Just because you're male, doesn't mean you have to be useless', still rings like a brainwash. Such radical ideas cut no mustard with Mrs Lallaporia. She believes men were born to be useless. The only problem is how to get her steaming chicken curry to her son.

Enter the mighty *tiffin* or *dabba*. However, a *dabba* is not much use without a *wallah*. Together, they make one of Bombay's most remarkable institutions: the *dabbawallah*.

While Mrs Lallaporia performs her morning ritual for her domestically challenged Manosh, another ritual is taking place in the streets of Bombay. A skinny-legged man in khaki shorts cycles through the pouring rain: at stake is the city-wide delivery system. He knocks on Mrs Lallaporia's door, bang on nine o'clock. Her packed *dabba* is passed to him without a word and so begins Bombay's extraordinary meals on wheels.

We leave Mrs Lallaporia and follow Bhikaji to film him as he works his way through the streets of his patch – darting in and out of apartment blocks to collect containers like a sparrow gathers twigs. He needs no notes or maps and never locks his bike. (An unspoken code ensures a *dabbawallah*'s cycle is never stolen.) Methodically, this fifty-year-old waiter on wheels brings about a dozen *dabbas* to the local station, where he and a gaggle of *wallahs* sort hundreds of lunchboxes into piles by an intricate coding system of colours, numbers and letters. The same ceremony is mirrored at stations across the city.

'Our *tiffins* are sent everywhere in Bombay,' Bhikaji tells me as he lifts a thirty-kilo plank of lunches onto his head as if it were no heavier than a surfboard. 'It is the question of filling one's stomach.'

The system relies on trust and cooperation. Bhikaji will collect Manosh's lunch but he will not deliver it. The codes brightly painted onto the *tiffins* map their journey: the station, street and floor of the office where they're bound and the homes to which they will return. Everything but the name of the lunch muncher – there's no need as most of Bombay's five thousand *dabbawallahs* are illiterate or semiliterate. Yet their efficiency and effectiveness is exceptional. When the respected American business magazine *Forbes* assessed the *tiffin*-men it found a world-class success rate of 99.999999 per cent or better. In other words, one error in six million transactions. It's the sort of run rate to make Don Bradman proud – and certainly matches any high-flying corporate giant.

Even more incredible is that this world-class act performs in one of the most congested, chaotic cities on the planet. If the traffic is not in gridlock and torrential rains have not washed the roads away, a raft of less usual crises would get in the *wallah*'s way. So, the only reliable way to zigzag more than a hundred and fifty thousand lunches across town is by train.

It's ten o'clock and Manosh's lunch is all aboard the train to Churchgate, in the heart of central business Bombay. As Tony, Rakesh and I squeeze into the compartment with the planks of *dabbas* and scores of sweaty, moustached men, I wonder if rush hour ever stops in this city. I should be grateful as this train is relatively roomy. Often, Bombay's passengers must climb onto the roof, or hang onto the sides, making a caterpillar of commuters. However, on this Orient Express, we are all firmly tucked inside – just a handful of the more than thirteen million Indians who hop on a train across the country every day. There is not a woman in sight: the cramped conditions provide the perfect opportunity for blokes to go the grope so women commute by other means.

The *dabbawallahs* themselves seem quiet, polite types. They are a closed community of workers – almost all come from a small area of Maharashtra State a few hours from Bombay. Most dress in traditional long, collarless white shirt, knee-length *dhoti*, which looks a bit like a baggy sarong, and wear the light cotton Gandhi cap, which looks like the upside-down hull of a ship. They are short, strong and straightforward.

After keeping ourselves out of the way of a furious exchange of pallets dropped off and thrown on at stations along the way, we groan into Churchgate. This is *tiffin* central. On the footpath just outside, amid swarming crowds, swirling garbage and a pall of pollution, rows and rows of lunches are methodically arranged. At this daily *dabba* convention, stainless steel and plastic-covered containers conceal their delicious secrets – the most divine home-cooked food. In a city with as many food rules as religions, matching the *dabba* to the desk is about more than just pleasing fussy eaters. Ganesh may be the favourite son, and Hindu–Nationalists may rule this town, but Bombay boasts myriad faiths, including a significant Islamic community. If a Muslim's beef *biryani* got mixed up with a Jain's strictly vegetarian *dhal* and rice, Bombay's notorious religious tensions might reignite. It doesn't take much.

The shots on the station are television magic, but we are struggling to keep up with our *tiffin*. We film a few scenes and realise within moments that *dabbas* are on the move again. The *tiffins* are piled onto huge carts pushed by half a dozen *wallahs*. The early morning downpour is now a distant memory and the streets are steaming, but the mugginess won't slow these men as they clip through the streets, dodge taxis and auto-rickshaws, circle around the odd holy cow and dart between overflowing dustbins. We can barely keep pace. Every time we pause to film them running past, they are out of eyeshot by the time we have gathered up our gear. Then, disaster. In the confusion, we lose sight of our lad's lunch. In the closing moments of the shoot, a missing *tiffin* threatens to unravel the whole day's filming. If we're not there to film Manosh taking delivery of his *dabba* and tucking in, we will have a major hole in our story. We must find his curry in a hurry. Tony and I are sweating profusely and I am starting to panic. Some frantic enquiries, a bit of guess work and a smidgen of luck leads us back to

Manosh's *dabba*. Panting and sweating, we find the last *dabbawallah* in the chain, showing barely a bead of sweat, strolling into the lift at Manosh's office block.

Midday and lunch is delivered to the third floor, without a hitch or hurrah. For just six (Australian) dollars a month, Bombay's meals on wheels are a legend in Manosh's lunchtime. Our camera jumps in front of Manosh as he opens up his lid to smell Mumma's work.

'If it's not there for a day, I find it very difficult,' he smiles, squeezing a quarter of lime over his curry. 'I have to go to a restaurant, wait in a long queue and God knows what I'm eating there.'

Manosh is a creature of habit. In his long sleeves and sensible slacks, and with his neatly parted hair, this is hardly one of life's great adventurers. He works nine to five, files piled neatly, calculator covered in plastic to keep it clean. I just can't get past the fact that here is a forty-three-year-old bloke having his ageing mum make him lunch every day, and question him about the fairness of it all.

'It's one of her hobbies,' he implores pathetically. 'That's how she kills time.'

I have come to admire India's extended family structure and especially the care it provides the elderly. It's a far cry from the western way of throwing the old into nursing homes as soon as they pass their use-by-date, but this familial system has its many burdens – lack of privacy, independence, freedom. It also locks people into rigid role plays. I want to slap this guy around the ears, wake him, shake the smug schoolboy grin from his face. In this macho, moustached paradise, too many men seem trapped half in adolescence. They stroke their dicks like a string of worry beads, goggle at women and giggle at their bouncing breasts and at forty-three, still have their mums make their lunch.

But Manosh knows his mother's cooking can't last forever. A small crisis is brewing in their household because his working wife, Roxanne, refuses to *ever* take over *dabba* duties. As more Indian women take up paid work, they're not hanging around to make meals for hubby. It's a problem not just for Manosh, but also for the *dabbawallahs* whose business is dwindling. However, the demise of the mighty Indian housewife is only part of the story.

The humble *dabbawallahs* – with their world-class efficiency rating – cannot escape global corporate forces. With money to spend, Bombay's expanding middle class is venturing out. The posh head to ritzy restaurants with names like Indigo and Olive. The rest head for a new wave of funky, local eateries – clean, airconditioned, convenient – inspired by the American family diners. But these new Indian eateries are not necessarily competing with McDonald's or Pizza Hut. They're taking on home cooking.

We go to one for a lunch break. Men in brightly coloured uniforms, complete with matching baseball caps, march out of the kitchen and toss our steaming *dosas* onto well-scrubbed tables. To Tony and I the food is good, but Rakesh calls it 'bland'.

Yet, despite the rise of the diner and the demise of the traditional housewife, the *dabbawallahs* are a sacrosanct institution, and they are optimistic about their future. They have a magnificently named union, The Honourable Company of Tiffin Box Carriers, to look after their interests, and we head there after lunch. The office is not as impressive as the name but these are men of few means and needs. The union helps organise the rounds, securing a monthly pay of around two hundred dollars for everyone, settles disputes and stares down attempted coups and takeovers. Union leader Ganga Ram waves away any talk of the *dabbawallahs* disappearing. With a relaxed flick of his wrist and a modest wobble of his head, Ganga Ram gets back to basics.

'This trade is not going to be closed down, because

everybody needs food to live.' As he talks, a soft bead of sweat dribbles from beneath his cap past the red *tikka* on his forehead. 'It doesn't matter if there are ten, five or two people. There will always be someone asking for a *dabba*.'

As his posse nod in agreement, a warm Bombay breeze teases through the window. We all breathe a quiet sigh of relief. The story is over and the *dabbawallahs* will survive. It's reassuring to know the winds of change carrying corporate forces from overseas may have met their match in a bunch of blokes in *dhotis* delivering *dabbas*.

God bless India.

CHAPTER 12

A MASTER OF DESTINY

A heavy groan descends over Delhi. The apartment shakes as if Armageddon is tumbling down from the Himalayas, and Sarah gives me what is becoming an all too familiar look of 'what the fff . . .?'. This is no earthquake; the rumble rolls from the sky and I race onto the roof to see a plane flying so low I can almost scratch its fat metal belly.

Bill Clinton is coming to town.

Air Force One is the biggest thing with wings I've ever seen and this visit seems the biggest thing to happen to India since winning the 1983 cricket World Cup. It's already brought an extraordinary transformation to New Delhi: thousands of workers have been scrubbing the world's dirtiest capital, painting fences with rags, preening dusty shrubs and erecting giant air-brushed portraits of the US President. Sadly, no-one can clean up the air.

But not everyone is trying to tart up the place. A Marxist Party activist scrawls on a wall in big red letters:

'CLINTON GO HOME!'

A wit more interested in getting a green card than waving the red flag adds in even bigger black letters:

'AND TAKE ME WITH YOU!'

In a country that so often takes itself so seriously, it's rare to see nationalism and cheeky realism side by side. It's also strangely comforting. But I'm the only one in this city who has time to enjoy the joke. New Delhi is severely stressed about how best to receive the first American President to visit in twenty-two years. The bureaucrats – or *babus* – are in meltdown about media accreditation. They phone daily to bombard with *babu* babble:

'Mr Harley, unless and until you provide advance intimation of your intention to attend the joint press conference by Prime Minister Vajpayee and President Clinton, we will regrettably be non-permitted to issue you with the relevant media accreditation.'

'Non-permitted?' I tease.

'Sir, you will do one thing. Please be advancing your intimation via facsimile *post-haste* and I will do the needful at an earliest convenience.'

'Well, I . . .?'

'Mr Harley, you must get a wriggle on! The felicitation of Mr Clinton is nigh! Please be dispatching your driver immediately.'

'I will send him straight away . . .'

'You will be needing to giddy-up!'

'Consider me giddied-up.'

'Right you are. Cheerio.'

I send Abraham off with an intimation to attend.

India's bureaucrats are the masters of mangling English with Hindi, Victorian idioms, military metaphors and cricketing imagery. Hinglish is as formal as it is ridiculous and I am also grateful to India's English-language newspapers for providing a daily stream of entertaining examples. It is a world in which criminals are 'miscreants', where they're pursued not by police but 'sleuths', and sex scandals involve 'dalliances' between 'paramours'.

With America's Presidential paramour about to flirt with a billion people, the *Times of India* ponders:

'Will Clinton get the sanity check Americans usually look for when they arrive in a strange country – that crucial can of Coke for their soul – or will he be overwhelmed by the ennui?'

As I laugh over this headline I can't help pondering that India doesn't have much 'ennui' – to the newcomer, the country is as subtle as a sledgehammer. But at times this place is oddly coy. A friend recently told me his grandmother 'was not very well'. She had died. It took another week of my asking if she was feeling any better before he finally told me she'd 'expired' two weeks earlier.

When they're not speaking in polite code, Indians are often waxing forth on anything and everything. This is a nation of experts – most of them self-appointed. Whether it's tensions with Pakistan or when best to eat mangoes, India is a country of a billion boffins. And they're currently engaged in a frenzy of interpreting and explaining the importance of the Presidential visit. Commentators hit the late-night news shows to talk about an 'unparalleled meeting of the minds'. The visit is significant. Lured by burgeoning business and strategic interests, Bill Clinton's whistlestop tour of Delhi will end a Cold War legacy of estrangement. For all their similarities, these two empires have historically had tense ties – during the Cold War Washington backed Pakistan, and New Delhi grew cosy with Moscow. Now, with the Berlin Wall long gone, America is finally realising it has a long-lost cousin – and a potentially profitable one, at that. One billion consumers are crying out for product. Bill Clinton is spending only a few hours in Islamabad but days in India. There's triumph in the air. Enemy Pakistan is out, Mother India is in!

But Kashmir is off the agenda.

While revelling in the world leader's attention, India is keeping its pride. It flatly rejects Bill Clinton's offer to mediate and is showing no sign of talking directly with

Pakistan in the wake of the Kargil debacle. Both sides remain raw and there's new dread over what this summer may bring. The US President recently called Kashmir 'the most dangerous place in the world today', and India responded with a cool sniff and a major hike in defence spending of twenty-eight per cent. Right on cue, Kashmir provides a chilling curtain-raiser to the Clinton caravan: gunmen storm the mainly Sikh village of Chattisinghpora south of Srinagar and murder thirty-five men.

Bill Clinton expresses his sorrow but keeps his mediation skills on hold. It works for him – when he addresses the Indian parliament with a brilliant speech weaving flattery, knowledge, diplomacy and charm, the proud parliamentarians rise as one to applaud. They mob him like he's a Hollywood celebrity, and parties afterwards are full of sari-clad women describing how 'Bill' reached to touch their arm at a meet-and-greet. Indians may not like the fact that America rules the world but they love a celebrity with star-power. Bill Clinton has it. He also seems to have a genuine interest in the region and a concern for its issues and dangers.

South Asians may be more wary of the future President. In November 1999, a year out from the polls, Texas Governor George W. Bush was settling into his Presidential campaign, when he was embarrassingly tripped up by an impromptu foreign policy quiz. Asked to name the leaders of India and Pakistan, he could not.

Bush: 'The new Pakistani General has just been elected. He's not elected; this guy took over office. He appears he's going to bring stability to the country, and I think that's good news for the subcontinent.'

Journalist: 'And can you name him?'

Bush: 'General. I can name the General.'

Journalist: 'And it's?'

Bush: 'General.'

Journalist: 'And the Prime Minister of India?'
Bush: 'The new Prime Minister of India is . . . no.'

I'm no Bill Clinton but I'm managing to feel a little more on top of the nuances of India, as well as the complexities of playing *sahib* with the ABC staff. I feel ready to take a risk: I decide to move the bureau from our flat of crumbling neglect to a slightly less crumbling house. While the looking and negotiating is hell, the move goes surprisingly smoothly and the staff settle in and seem content. Abraham in particular is unusually happy. He smiles as he drives and whistles around the office – even his furrowed brow has gone. This behaviour is so unusual I would be worried if I didn't know why he's so thrilled. After years of push starts and rusting parts, Abraham has a shiny, white (and, thanks to the opening of the Indian economy, Japanese) sedan. It gives him new status on the road and, most importantly, provides us all with airconditioning. It is no small victory: sometimes the intricacies of the ABC bureaucracy can rival India's and organising the money was more complicated than any story.

Inspired by Abraham's new lease on life and my ability to arrange my own, I figure it's time I took a bit of control. I'm even feeling confident enough, or should I say cocky enough, to try driving. When Abe's off duty I've been catching cabs but it's time to show India I know what I'm doing. A friend, Melissa, is about to arrive from Sydney so I figure a quick trip to the airport is a good way to start. The flight comes in late, the traffic should be quiet and there's no need to drag Abraham out of bed.

As I slide into the seat, turn up the stereo and pull onto the ring road to the airport, I realise I've not driven since leaving home eighteen months ago. It's a weird feeling of freedom and a reminder of how little I do for myself in India. I don't drive, wash or iron, I don't even make my morning coffee. And I no longer notice. I have become part of the modern Raj – hopelessly dependent, and resentful when 'staff' make mistakes or don't read your mind. I may be in control of the bureau and its workers but I'm not in control of my life. They run the show; I just pay their wages. And as for my working day, that's at the mercy of events and editors.

As if to highlight how hopeless I've become, I realise I've left my wallet at home and I don't have the fifty rupees needed for the airport car park. Foreign correspondents can usually bluff their way through but the guard won't budge – I don't even have a wallet with a press pass to wave at him. No fifty rupees, no entry.

My only option is the James Bond park – right outside the arrivals gate. It's free and nobody says I can't, so in the long tradition of foreigners acting arrogantly, I zip in as if the space is meant for me. I stride inside to find Melissa's flight is delayed, but I can keep an eye on the car through the windows at the end of the arrivals lounge. Why should I worry anyway? It's time I started acting more like a foreign correspondent: pushing the limits, bending the rules, keeping cool. For too long I've been too meek and mild. I'm a boss, a bureau chief, for God's sake, and I should act like one. Who does it hurt if I do the odd illegal park, don't get an Indian driver's licence or abuse the odd bureaucrat? It comes with the territory. I'm getting a handle on the job, on the place, so why not throw my weight around a bit? I'm a foreign correspondent and master of my destiny.

I look back out the window. The car is being hoisted onto a tow truck.

'FUUUUUUUUUUCCCCCCCKKKKKKKKK!!!!!!' I scream as I bolt through the crowd, a blubbering ball of panic. My brain is pumping with images and all of them are bad. I can see the ABC's sparkling car ripped up for parts, sold off in some dodgy car yard or held hostage by a fat bureaucrat running a racket. I see myself on the phone trying to explain to my boss how I lost the week-old car. And then I think about telling Abraham. Oh God. I stumble in fear.

'STTTTOOOOPPPP!!!' By the time I'm outside, the tow truck is fifty metres down the road and gaining speed. I am screaming, sprinting like the Six Million Dollar Man.

'STTTTOOOOPPPP!!!'

The airport crowd is laughing at me. Even the beggars are giggling. This is not the look of a man who is master of his destiny, it is the look of a desperado. The only mercy is that the truck is old and slow. I catch up.

I bang on the driver's window. 'STOP! STOP! STOP! THAT'S MY CAR!'

He ignores me and accelerates, so I do what any confident boss would. I jump on.

The crowd is bent over in hysterics and I am bent over on the back of a truck gasping for air, with the ABC car bobbing behind me, headed for who knows where.

'STOP!' I bang on the driver's cabin. 'STOP!'

Finally, perhaps fearing the damage I may do to his truck, the driver relents and he pulls over on the outskirts of the airport. He gets out, as does a policeman. Shit. I didn't know *he* was there. Quick, split-second decision: do I seem calm or crazy, clean or corrupt? I take a leaf out of the *babu* babble book of bullshit and go with crazy and corrupt. Barely able to breathe from the run, words come in rapid fire.

'Sir, sir, sir, I'm terribly sorry, I have a friend coming from Sydney and she has never been to India before and I am terribly worried for her and she is my responsibility and it is my duty to give her a warm Indian welcome and India is now my home and it would be a disgrace on my family and the whole country if I am not there to greet her and her

flight has been delayed and I think she is not well so I have
been waiting and my wallet has been stolen so I have no
money for parking and now my friend will be arriving any
moment and she won't know why I am not there and she
may be collected by some unsavoury character and you
know it is unsafe and . . .'

The policeman looks as if he wishes he'd left the car
where it was parked. But I'm not sure he's going to let me
off. He moves to get back in the truck, the driver spits and
turns to follow him. Then, from some deep desire to
survive, my mind clears and throws up an all-important line
– the discreet way to offer a policeman a bribe.

'Sir, can't we settle this with a fine?'

He responds as if I had merely asked for directions: 'Five
hundred rupees.'

Just a lazy five hundred, the equivalent of twenty bucks?
No haggling, no delicate negotiation over my contribution
to his son's education fund? Could it be this simple? I don't
want to tempt complications.

'Sir, of course. I just need to meet my friend and get some
money from her.'

'I will wait here. With your car.' Now *here* is a man in
command of my destiny.

I run back to the arrivals area, past the still-giggling
beggars, to find Melissa emerging from customs.

'Melissa! Hi! Have you got any money?'

'What?'

'Oh, hi. I mean, HI! WELCOME TO INDIA.'

Melissa regards my frazzled face with a look of regret:
Delhi's taxi drivers would have been more welcoming.

'Hi. Thanks . . . I think.' She's beginning to look nervous.

'Money, have you got any money? I'll explain later. I
need money.'

She pulls out a wad of Australian dollars, from which I
grab a hundred to change before ushering Melissa and her

bags into the night. Back at the tow truck, the car is already lowered. Melissa looks at me aghast but the transaction with the policeman is fast and hassle free.

'You need receipt?' he offers, insincerely.

'No, really, thank you.'

'No problem.'

We get in the car, I bleat the whole embarrassing story to Melissa and swear her to secrecy. I don't tell Abraham, Peter or anyone in Sydney. It is the best five hundred rupees I've ever spent, and at home, soothed by a strong vodka, I figure I'm at least getting a feel for doing business in India.

My near-death airport experience has not diminished my driving desires. If anything, it has increased them. So, with no world leaders dropping into town, I decide to drive to Rajasthan for a weekend away with Sarah. In Australia, heading away for a couple of days was the most natural thing in the world, but here it feels indulgent. It's a correspondent's nightmare to be on holidays when a huge story breaks, so we head for a place just two hours away – an easy bolt back to Delhi if need be. I take my satellite phone and laptop just for good measure. Sarah is incredulous.

'You've got to let go of your work sometimes,' she says with frustration.

'I am letting go. I'm *going* away for the weekend.'

'Yeah, with all your work gear.'

'It's not *all* my gear. It's half.'

Sarah replies with the cock of an eyebrow and a look of resignation.

We head off for the Rajasthan border complete with my gear and a bottle of Australian wine we've been saving for a special occasion. As the new car purrs down the Delhi–Jaipur

Highway, I earn a new respect for Abraham and his calm hand. Driving in India is like an endless bungy jump: as exhilarating as it is terrifying and death is high on your mind. At first I play safe – sticking to my lane, using my indicator religiously and obeying the speed limit – but it only leads to a barrage of abuse. The Indian driver's answer to everything is to lean on the horn, and a symphony is blurting around me. When I ignore the speed limit, take up two lanes and cut in and out of the traffic like I'm in a scene from *Starsky & Hutch*, then things calm down. The Indian road is a mighty, rushing river – there's no option but to go with the flow and hope not to hit the rocks. Or the cows.

After two hours of dodging trucks, buses, bicycles and camel carts, we arrive at Rajasthan's Neemrana Fort Palace. This restored fourteenth-century bastion is now a hotel, and as we walk in, I see why it has become an oasis for the well-to-do of New Delhi. Medieval wooden doors with huge metal spikes sticking out of them open onto a garden overflowing with bougainvillea and jasmine; a long ramp leads to courtyards where tea and cakes are served by waiters in pressed crimson jackets. The Raj is not dead – it's just on holiday at Neemrana. The room is a beautiful blend of richly coloured Indian art and Euro-chic simplicity, with a tiny balcony overlooking mustard fields. Directly below is the much less romantic Neemrana village, a crowded place with muddy paths and sickly cows – and it's here that most of the hotel's cleaners, porters and labourers live. The realities of Indian luxury are never far from view.

There is no television or radio here and the silence is bittersweet. Away from the office, the world of news seems of little consequence. Well, it should seem that way. But I can't relax. Always lurking in my mind is a fear I'm missing something. Every few hours I hang the satellite phone out the palace window and ring Sydney's foreign desk to make sure everything is 'quiet'. Only once reassured can I sleep, eat and stroll through mustard fields framed by dusty tracks, watching boys play cricket as we pass by. For once, India seems at peace. At least, my India does.

But even a holiday has a nasty surprise in store.

Any sense of relaxation wears off on the drive back to Delhi. Desperate to make sure I haven't missed anything while in the traffic, I dump my bags on the office floor and rush to check the wire service, the internet and emails. Of course, in a part of the world as large as this, many things have happened, but nothing that will make the Australian news. I breathe a sigh of relief and lean back on my chair to put my feet up, only to be jolted by a stabbing sensation in my hand. I'm used to geckos, crickets and angry ants but the sharp shot of pain tells me this is something much more. On the floor is a small, squashed scorpion that must have hitched a ride on my bag from Rajasthan which I have unknowingly stepped on it after it stung me. I'm reluctant to drive across town to the big hospital, so I go to the private clinic at the local shopping mall. With the squashed remains of the scorpion in an envelope, I walk into a place that appears small but clean and adequate. I'm feeling all right, if a little numb, but when I tell the doctor what happened, he looks at me with wide-eyed panic.

'Do you want to see the scorpion?' I try to pass him the envelope.

'No! No! No!' He pushes back on his chair as though I'd just pulled a knife. Without asking one question, he furiously writes a prescription for tetanus, a pain killer and antihistamine. I'm perplexed and angry, as I explain I'm not in much pain and am already covered for tetanus. Before leaving Sydney, I had taken every jab in the book – from malaria to meningitis, from rubella to rabies. But all those shots combined were nothing compared with what's about to come.

As I fill out the official paperwork, the scorpion-phobic doctor disappears and in his place is a nurse wearing one of those high, white hats I thought nurses stopped wearing in the 1950s. Walking into the room, she is already transferring my antihistamine into a syringe. I didn't see her unwrap the needle so can't be sure it's new.

'Excuse me, is that a clean needle?' I feel like a snob but I have to check. There are too many stories of dodgy needles, AIDS, hepatitis and the like swimming in my head.

'Of course!' She is clearly offended, though not as much as she is about to be.

'Would you mind if I see a fresh needle taken out of its packet?'

With a Bollywood roll of her eyes, the nurse melodramatically opens a new syringe. She then transfers the same antihistamine from original syringe to new one. I try to contain my outrage at this display of sanitary insanity.

'I'm sorry . . .' I try to sound calm '. . . but I would like to see a brand new syringe and a brand new dose of antihistamine, opened in front of me. Can we start all over again?'

The nurse is fuming at my whingeing, western paranoia.

'You will have to pay for it.'

'Not a problem. I will pay for it.'

She doesn't just mean money.

So back to square one we go. Fresh, sealed syringe. New phial of antihistamine. Slowly, deliberately, disdainfully, she transfers medicine to syringe.

Then, revenge.

'Bend over, sir.'

It is clear who is now in control.

'Bend over?'

'Bend over.'

'Not in the arm?'

'No, sir, drop your trousers and bend over.'

Feeling more than a bit vulnerable and in a somewhat

compromising position, I can't see the nurse's technique but I can be sure it involves an energetic run-up and major muscle. She drives the needle deep into my derrière and smiles as I swear. However, credit where it's due – the therapy works perfectly. By the time I return to the office, I can hardly feel the scorpion bite. It's just that I can't sit down for days.

Wanting to find some good in the experience, I write my scorpion sob story for ABC Radio's *Correspondents Report* but this only ads insult to injury. It's the one story that family and friends, strangers and colleagues will ring and write to me about. Even years later, it's the thing about me they will be most likely to remember. I'll meet people at parties who'll look at me blankly if I talk about dangerous assignments in Kashmir or Afghanistan but then click their fingers when I mention India.

'Hey, you're the guy who got stung by a scorpion.'

Amid the tragedy, turmoil and overload of broadcast news, the absurd will stay lodged in memories long after the daring.

For now, however, I wonder if it's worth risking my life for a story that most will forget. For it's time to head back to Kabul. I may be acting more confident and cocky but as I tell Peter to arrange the journey, and say goodbye to Sarah, leaving her alone in New Delhi, I grow increasingly nervous. I'm well aware that when you try to be a master of destiny in South Asia there's usually a sting in the tail.

CHAPTER 13

THURSDAY NIGHT FEVER

Kabul is drowning in dust. The once fertile Shomali Plain is dumping a blanket of dirt on the Afghan capital – a nation's breadbasket is now blowing in the wind. The city seems oblivious to this biblical haze. Only my driver, a fading man with a straight nose and crooked sense of direction, makes mention of Afghanistan's worst drought in thirty years.

'Last night,' he mumbles, 'I dreamt it was raining.'

The only thing raining on Kabul has been rockets. Poets once praised its setting on the Kabul River, ringed by mountains and made prosperous by trade, but today, much of the city is rubble, the river is a trickle and the UN sanctions block commerce with the outside world. The little visible economic activity keeps Kabul barely functioning – a teenage boy fans coals cooking kebabs; a withered figure hauls a garbage cart, each step threatening to be his last.

The moment I hopped off my UN flight from Islamabad, I was greeted by and 'registered' with the Taliban Foreign Ministry, just as I was last November. Then, Kabul's autumn air seemed crisp and clear but now my eyes soak in a fuller scene that's dry and devastated. We drive for hours, past wheat silos once bursting with grain, now hollow and broken. A bus depot looks strange and morbid, stacked high with junked, stripped and crushed vehicles that once took girls to school – now both buses and girls are on the scrap heap. In the worst-hit areas, the jagged remains of bombed homes look like stalagmites. Entire districts are that way, while other areas are relatively unscathed. In its doomed battle with the *mujahideen*, the Soviets sheltered the capital but when they left and the Afghan factions turned their weapons on each other, parts of Kabul were shelled into the Stone Age.

However, I am not here to report Kabul's usual story of devastation and despair. I am not covering the sputtering civil war, with its front line about an hour's drive north of here. I have not come to question the Taliban on its unshakeable stand on women.

I have come to report on sport.

Australia, the world and the ABC newsroom have had enough of the war story and the drought has been going for months. The biggest story in Sydney at the moment is the upcoming Olympics and news editors are keen for an Olympic angle on foreign news. I can give them one: the UN sanctions effectively stop the Taliban from sending athletes to Sydney. I figure this story about the clash of sport and politics will offer a new way of looking at the increasing isolation of the Taliban and might hopefully strike a chord with sports-mad Australians. It's also the only way I can wedge myself into the wall-to-wall Olympics coverage dominating bulletins at home.

Driving past boys kicking a saggy soccer ball around a park with no grass, I wonder how anyone in this malnourished, war-torn land has the energy for any sport at all. On the edge of the park, young men are playing cricket – Afghanistan's latest import from the refugee camps of Pakistan. And I see signs advertising gyms, portraying men with bulging pecs and giant biceps. Under the Taliban, sport has become the new television. It is one pastime allowed by the regime, although some *mullahs* are known to frown on anything that might distract from pious pursuits.

My Taliban minder, Masood, loves to body build. He also likes to sing.

'I'm staaaarAAAAArrrrrting with the maaAAAAAaan in the miiirrror . . .'

With the car windows wound up against the dust storm and religious police, Masood is crooning, illegally and against all laws of good taste – he is ear-splittingly out of tune. I curse the Taliban that prevent me from putting on a tape to drown him out. Masood prefers Michael Jackson's mediocre later nineties releases (despite the fact that no music is meant to have entered the country since the Taliban took over four years ago) to those from the days when the artist's nose and music had credibility.

'If you wanna make the woOOOorld a beeetter place take a look at yourself and then make a chaaaaAAAAAAnnnge . . .'

Masood wants change any way he can get it. Dressed in traditional baggy *salwar kameez* with a dog-eared denim jacket tossed over the top, he's as modern a young man as you'll meet under the Taliban. Good-looking and likeable, despite making me wish I were deaf, Masood is my compulsory Taliban-appointed translator – a none too subtle way for the regime to keep a close eye on journalists. For thirty dollars a day, translators are minders, spies and spoilers. Their skill with English and, most importantly, their trustworthiness are the luck of the draw but on this first real visit to Kabul, luck is with me. This twenty-one-year-old is shrewd, discreet and opposed to the regime. In a land of dangerous strangers Masood is fast becoming this journalist's closest thing to a foreign friend.

'So what do you do for fun?' Masood asks, his eyes mischievous. The wisps of his piss-poor moustache are twitching with delight and he's clearly pleased with his question. I suspect the joke is on me but I'm happy to play along. After all, fun is in short supply here: this is Nofunistan.

'Well, Masood,' I begin, trying to cast my mind back to Sydney, when I had time for fun in my life, 'what I do for fun is not the sort of fun you have around here. Films, which you're not allowed. TV, which is banned. And music – that other no-no. Or I'd go to the beach, which, unless we feel like driving for the next five days across a couple of countries, is not likely.'

The grin under Masood's moustache is spreading to his Dan-the-Diver chin, tickling the lame carpet of hair there. His amusement is contagious.

'Come, come, Jonathan, it's Thursday night. I'll show you a good time.'

For Kabul's young and restless, Thursday night is as close as they get to a Saturday night vibe. Thursday is for letting your beard down because Friday, the Muslim day of prayer, is when the pathetic excuse for a government puts up its feet – officially, at least. For residents of this once cosmopolitan city, Thursday's as boring as any other night. However, Masood and his mates have a club and after cruising Kabul's evening dust bowl, our driver slides into their gangland at the end of an unpaved alley. It's a place that doesn't appear to promise much fun.

A queue of women snakes along the alley, waiting for bread handouts from a bakery next to the stairs that lead down to Masood's club. These women are just some of the twenty-five thousand war widows in Kabul – among the most desperate people in the world. Their husbands were killed in the struggle against the Soviets, or in the civil war, or at the holy hands of the Taliban. With the regime's ban on them working, women without husbands are women without means. In all, four hundred thousand people in

Kabul depend on bakeries like this one run by the World Food Program.

'Walk quickly, do not look at the women,' Masood warns me as we get out of the car.

I assume he is trying to avoid detection by Taliban informers but a forceful grab at my sleeve reveals another danger. Widows are circling, having surrendered their place in the queue to try their luck at begging. As they crowd in, red glaucoma-ridden eyes peer through the blue mesh of their *burqas*. Some have lifted the shrouds over their heads and look like toothless brides left at the altar. Spit sprays across my face as they squawk stories of suffering.

I can't understand but I'm guessing it goes something like this:

'Dead husband . . . six children . . . no work . . . seven children . . . Allah, peace be upon him . . .'

The appeals are heart-wrenching and depressing. Their strategy is simple but effective: smother the subject till he coughs up cash. Masood tries to shoo them away but these women have faced far fiercer foes and he's quickly put in his place with fiery snarls. Boxed in and gripped by guilt, I delve into my pocket for a fistful of Afghanis, but the notes are not out before the women lunge like seagulls, snatching at my meagre offering of a few dollars. As they scrape on the ground, a gap appears in the ruck; Masood grabs my arm and pulls me down the stairs.

With the rabble at our heels, I'm swept inside in a tumbling jumble of gasps and guilt. I catch my breath, the door locks and the widows' frenzy fades away. Slowly, I begin to make out shapes and faces in the room, lit by a dull light in one corner and the flicker of a computer screen in another.

'What is this place, Masood?'

His devious grin returns.

'This,' he declares, pausing for dramatic effect, 'is where we teach English.'

'Teaching English is your idea of a Thursday night on the town?'

'And other things,' he adds.

He shows me over to the computer, where a young man is transfixed in the blue glare of a monitor, the sound loud in his headphones. Masood and his friends run English classes for some extra money, telling the Taliban their computer is for 'teaching purposes'. As I look at the monitor, my brain struggles to translate what he is watching: something familiar but totally foreign. Till suddenly, in a wave of understanding, it hits me like an iceberg.

Titanic.

The Hollywood blockbuster was released three years ago but here it is hot property. Scratchy CD-ROM and video copies are smuggled from house to house and, despite Taliban efforts to plunge life back to before video killed the radio star, Kabul is determined to be entertained. Some have bricked up their TVs behind false walls but those more bold simply stash them behind a couch, ready for regular use. The well-to-do have VCRs and, incredibly, in a country where the average monthly income is just a few dollars, some even have DVDs. Just metres from where widows are fighting for a few pathetic Afghanis, I am staring at a brand new PC, playing *Titanic*.

'Down here,' shouts Masood, arcing his arms wide and leaning over an imaginary bow, 'I AM THE KIIIING OF THE WOOOORLD! I am Leonardo DiCaprio!'

'And where is your Kate Winslet?'

'Well, Jonathan,' the wind goes out of his sails, 'that is a problem.'

I instantly regret my quip. Fantasies are the secret to sanity in this place – lose them and you lose that shining corner of your mind in which anything is possible. Masood doesn't need some stranger from Australia ruining his fun.

'All you know is war, all you know is killing, bloodshed, things of that sort,' Masood tells me in his American-accented English, parroted straight from Voice of America and Hollywood. His words are punctuated by the clunky tones of an enamel teapot, pouring the first of many cups of green tea, like the Magic Pudding, endlessly dispensing comfort and company. 'Especially for this generation,' he continues, 'we are very sorry because we have seen no luxuries and no happiness of life, and now we know nothing about the realities of life.'

It strikes me these guys have seen too many realities of life. Youth may be wasted on the young, but in Afghanistan the youth don't get any time to waste on being young. There is no margin for error, to explore or to pretend you will be a rock star and get really drunk and deaf failing. The Taliban's ban on fun is just the latest blow to young lives of struggle.

This teetotalling nightclub is a long way from friends in Sydney gearing up for the glamour of the 2000 Olympics. Instead of sharing the champagne and cheering, I am in the least glamorous city in the world, on the banks of the Kabul River's drought-stricken trickle, in a landlocked, war-weary country. Strange as it seems, it's just what I want, albeit with the unwanted cost of separation from Sarah, family and friends. Australia is an oddity of peace, prosperity and blissful ignorance and I needed to switch off the TV and see for myself. I may be no master of my destiny but I love where destiny has taken me.

Tonight, what these young men would love most is female company. Hushed sexual tension hangs heavy in the air. It is no accident that *Titanic*'s romantic tragedy has struck a chord: happiness found and lost is the story of Kabul, and yearning is the state of the men in this room. Many of them are parading a long-fringed hairstyle that is supposed to emulate Leonardo DiCaprio's. On most, it looks like a lank bum-part, made all the more ridiculous when offset by the compulsory beard. The trend continues despite a Taliban edict banning barbers from creating 'The Leonardo'. For once, I agree with the Taliban.

'Actually I prefer Indian cinema. Bollywood is my favourite,' Masood glows, rattling off a long list of Bombay pin-ups. 'Amitabh Bachchan, Sushmita Sen, Aishwarya Rai. These are my favourite stars.' His half a dozen friends nod and you can almost hear the screeching Hindi soundtracks imagined in their minds, their eyes glazing as they skip from tree to tree with their sari-clad lovers. 'A lot of Hollywood is pornography to us,' says Masood. 'Bollywood is better because all the family can enjoy it together.'

Here I am in the den of rebellious, young Kabul, only to find that *Titanic* is as racy as it gets. Not only that, if it's not on for the whole family it's not on at all. In my late teens or early twenties, the idea of doing anything with the family, let alone sitting down to a video with them, was the last thing on my mind. Here, what little fun there is, must be shared around.

If consuming 'adult themes' on the small screen is delicate, then talking about them openly is torturous. Thoughts may centre on sex, but words are hard to find.

'Girlfriends, I have never thought about this one because . . .' Abdul, a tall, serious guy, is painfully nervous about where the conversation is heading. As he trails off, I offer a little help.

'Even to talk about having girlfriends is forbidden?'

'I think according to Islam it's forbidden,' he replies.

I have to pinch myself not to laugh. I am, after all, a guest and a grateful one at that. However, I am stunned by the suggestion that Mohammed decreed young men should not talk about young women. The Taliban's thought police are making great progress in the battle for minds over groins.

Not everyone's as shy as Abdul. Sitting next to him is Yama, who is laughing on my behalf. The proud owner of a fat face with crooked teeth to match, Yama is as expressive as the Taliban are suppressive.

'Yeah. Yeah. I have many girlfriends in Afghanistan, especially in Kabul,' he declares, standing up. 'I'm not care about the Taliban. All the time playing with girls.'

'And Yama, what does playing with girls involve?' I can't contain my curiosity.

'Ah, just walking in the street, just talking. If it is possible, I'm going to buy some gifts for them.'

The commercial laws of courtship appear universal.

'Just shirts and some shoes, bracelets, some things,' Yama says as he tops up my tea for the fiftieth time.

'And how many girlfriends do you buy gifts for?'

Yama looks to the crumbling ceiling to list them in his mind. 'Maybe more than ten girlfriends.'

I choke, spraying tea all over him. Everyone roars with laughter as I try to regain my breath and a dash of dignity. My mind races with the possibilities of Yama's love life – the logistical and political problems of juggling ten girlfriends, not to mention avoiding the religious police. But Yama won't bow to the Taliban.

'Yeah, I not care about it,' he laughs with defiance and nervousness.

'But what is the point when you can't even *see* your girlfriends?' I ask.

The lads nod knowingly. The *burqa* has kept half the population out of sight, work and schools. It has come to embody Afghan women's house arrest and it's the source of endless romantic frustration for young lovers in this town. Yama and his mates agree that, of all the forms of rebellion and defiance under the Taliban, seeing the face of a girl – who is not your sister or some other close relative – is the most important and demanding challenge.

'It's very difficult,' Yama concedes, 'but in private, in the corner of somewhere, I see her face.' Then that laugh again. Nervous defiance.

Encouraged, Abdul is starting to come out of his shell and declares he possesses a special gift. 'I can tell how beautiful a woman is by the shoes she wears,' he says. There is not a hint of humour or irony in his declaration and it is met by more knowing nods all round the room. I would hear Afghan men proudly declare this depressing romantic art many times. It gives a whole new meaning to the notion of 'having a perv'.

In this room of Romeos and Leonardos, Masood sits silently. He is not interested in girlfriends, for he knows where love, or at least marriage, will take him. Masood is already engaged to a distant cousin who, it so happens, he likes. Love would be too strong a word: Masood has not seen his fiancé for five years. She has been living in Sweden since her family fled in 1995 – the year before the Taliban rolled into Kabul.

'I got really happy when I heard that my mother is going to arrange that engagement,' he says with a sip of tea and a blink of anticipation. 'Because she's living in Europe and that is going to be another source of support for us.' Marriage, money and exit strategies are inextricably entwined.

As the eldest son, Masood is the sole pillar of support for his widowed mother and younger brother and sister. His father was an academic, a voice of moderation against the hardline Islamists fighting for control of Kabul. When he was killed in a rocket attack in 1992 Masood, at fourteen, became the head of the house, equipped with only his quick mind and sprouting English. In a rare miracle of meritocracy in a land of nepotism, he won work with the Foreign Ministry as a translator, providing a crucial source of income for his family. It also created the opportunity for Masood and me to meet.

He would soon wish that had never happened.

CHAPTER 14

BEND IT LIKE
ALLAH-O-AKBAR

I wake up to metal mouth, as if I've been licking an enamel teapot all night. My veins are pumping rivers of sugar. The big night with the Kabul boys has produced a green tea hangover, nowhere as nauseating as the alcohol equivalent but my jaw is grinding and my head is hazy from too much of the sweet brew. There's no going back to sleep – the Central Asian sun is streaming into the room, delivering a view certainly worth waking for: dawn flares from behind parched mountains, the city below seems at peace and yesterday's dust storm is a distant nightmare. Fruit carts are already taking their place on street corners as songbirds dance between poplars and quiet fires brew breakfast tea. Out of the rubble, Kabul's charms emerge.

Perched majestically on the city's western saddle, the Hotel InterContinental offers Kabul's best vista and a glance into the minds of Afghanistan's modernisers. The two hundred-room icon was supposed to be a bridge between east and west, a 1960s symbol of Islamic liberalism and modernity, but its heyday would be short lived. It is itself a shell-scarred hulk – a gloomy reminder of the battles for the heart and soul of this forsaken country. Only the first two floors are useable and I am the only guest. Sanctions keep away the non-smuggling businessmen and most visiting aid workers make their own arrangements. Journalists are few and far between. Tight Taliban visa restrictions help limit the flow to a trickle and almost all media outlets have simply given up on Afghanistan – it costs too much time and money to send journalists there for stories centred on an insignificant regime. One day, the world will be stunned by its own stupidity for ignoring this place, but for now, I have a hotel and (I hope) a story largely to myself.

If I sit still, I can almost hear the echoes of 1970s abandon seeping out of the plaster – the laughter of diplomats escaping tedious Islamabad, the splash of women in bikinis, the tap of dancing toes from the top floor Pamir Supper Club.

But mostly, I hear the drone of the *muezzin* calling people to prayer.

I walk downstairs (the elevator is out of order), to find the only sign of life in the once-chic Bamiyan Brasserie. Men in tattered black jackets are polishing cutlery with filthy rags, waiting for their only guest to appear for breakfast. They've maintained what standards they can, trying to preserve a modicum of style through Kabul's darkest years – when the power was out, the water did not flow and the only guests were journalists keeping tabs on the bloodshed. Against anarchy or tyranny, routine becomes ritual, a shaky line to sanity. With the sacred study of a monk, each waiter goes through their motions of service: the order of the cutlery drawer, the serviettes and menu have not changed in three decades.

As I order an omelet and tea, four young Taliban slouch in as if they own the place. They behave like rich teenagers let loose with dad's Amex card and display the universal language of condescension – one which denies dignity to all involved. However, these tattered waiters know how to wait: they've seen rulers rise and fall and they, too, will see the Taliban tumble. I love their exhausted, undiminished dignity and their discreet glares of disdain. Theirs is a good-humoured hatred.

Masood bounds through the door, bright-eyed and inspired by our 'night out', heading for my table.

'*As'salaam aleikum*,' he greets every man in his path, warmly shaking each and every hand. While Afghans have a feared reputation for bloodshed and treachery, they are meticulously polite and habitually wish peace upon you. Greetings usually include an exchange at breakneck speed in Pashto:

How are you?
Fine, thank you.
Fine?
Fine.
Are you well?
Very well.
Are you fine?
Fine.
Fit?
Very fit, thank you. Are you fit?
Yes, fit, fit, very fit.
Family well?
Very well. Your family is well?
Yes, fine.
Fine?
Fine.
Fit?
Fit.
Good.
Good.

The exchange is compressed into incomprehensible banter – after all, everyone knows the answers. It's a long way from Australia, where social graces are simple, especially among men. Where the Australian male is 'a man of few words', Afghan guys don't shut up. It is a guy's paradise. The bond is more than football team camaraderie or the comfortable masculinity of having a beer with a mate. Afghan men are bound by myth and a history of repelling aggressors, whether the British Empire in the nineteenth century or the 1980s Soviets. Afghan man is part warrior, part poet. He may skin an enemy alive or relax under the spring sun with his nose buried in a rose. When Afghans shake and embrace – and there is almost always an embrace – there is a shared understanding about the way of men and the world.

It's a world in which I feel a welcome member – if for no other reason than that I have a member. The typical Australian male is no less, and perhaps more, butch but the stories that define us are very different. Lessons of battle are enshrined in both identities but while Australia's sacred stories are tempered with military defeats and suicidal swagmen, Afghan mythology seems to be a stream of straightforward tales of dogged defence and glorious conquests. Scanning this shell-shattered dining room, with its barking Taliban and fraying waiters, the Afghan myth seems way out of date – this failed state is starving, its people are crippled, the rulers are Pakistani-sponsored zealots impregnated with ten thousand foreign al-Qaeda mercenaries. Yet, against the evidence, Afghans are convinced theirs is the greatest country on earth.

Eventually, Masood makes it to my table, where he greets me with a handshake and embrace.

'So, Jonathan, big game today,' he gleefully declares as he helps himself to tea. 'Kabul plays Peshawar.'

There is only one thing bigger in Masood's life than his Thursday night – the Friday soccer match. For most boys and men, the weekly game in Kabul's infamous Ghazi

Stadium is the highlight of the week. For me, the soccer game will be essential for my story. If I can film it.

We have a long lazy breakfast and I check in with the foreign desk on the satellite phone before heading into town. Other than closed government buildings, there's no sign that this is a day of rest. The local *burqa* stall is open – its summer range of shrouds (in blue *and* grey) flap limply in the breeze. Business only stops for Friday prayers and once they're done, the crowd starts to make its way to the stadium. It's been months since the sounds of executions, amputations or floggings have rung out from Ghazi Stadium – proof, say the Taliban, that their iron-fisted tactics of deterrence are working. Today, the only thrashing fans are expecting is that of the visiting soccer team. As the crowd pours into the stalls, we climb collapsing stairs to the man who holds court over this concrete colosseum.

Taliban Sports Minister, Mullah Abdul Shukur Mutmaen, greets me with the hug of a long-lost cousin. He is a bear of a man, a Pashtun giant with a beard as coarse as steel wool tumbling down his chest. He would have no trouble passing the standard Taliban test that a beard fill a fist. His hands are as big as boxing gloves and appear able to crush the skull of an enemy. Yet, like many of the *mullahs* – those men who traditionally lead prayers at local mosques and form the backbone of religious observance – he has a quiet manner that defies his imposing appearance. He sits us down on a tattered vinyl lounge, then resumes his place at the window.

Mullah Abdul Shukur Mutmaen is a picture of success: he has one of the cushiest jobs in the city, with an office overlooking the weekly game. It has the air of a corporate box with tea flowing freely and large bowls overflowing with boiled sweets. The windows are opened wide – the panes of glass were blasted away long ago and in their place, opaque plastic sheets are stretched across the frames.

Satisfaction fills the air among men savouring their position of privilege. The minister's closest gaggle of goons lounge on chairs, laugh at his jokes and nod along to his commentary on the game below.

I, too, am paying homage to the big man. We all want favours from him and I am no different from this pathetic posse.

'You shall film,' he assures me, with that ever present rider, '*insh'allah*.'

I will need all the help Allah can offer. The boys from the Department of the Promotion of Virtue and Prevention of Vice are out in force. Taliban religious rigidity is often mistaken as unity, but beneath their pious veneer, the Taliban are factionalised. In the battle between the ultra orthodox and relatively moderate, Mullah Abdul Shukur Mutmaen is high on pragmatism and low on real power. He may hold court over this stadium but does not really control it. He, like everyone, fears the religious police.

With their kohl-lined eyes and Kalashnikovs over the shoulder, the religious police prowl the stalls like vultures circling a corpse. Hollywood could not design more sinister-looking dudes. They even seem to have the worst teeth in Afghanistan. When they're not playing moral enforcers or issuing ludicrous edicts such as that women do not make a noise when their shoes hit the ground, they're operating as the Taliban's most effective spy agency.

Halftime is prayer time and, when the whistle blows, the religious police swoop into action. They herd the crowd and players onto the field, where they lay down their shawls as makeshift prayer mats. As the crowd-cum-congregation faces Mecca, those seen to be dawdling are whipped and hit. Men cower as these mostly illiterate teenagers turn prayer into punishment. Many of the religious police are from the most impoverished and conservative southern parts of the country or recruited from Pakistan's *madrassas*. Across this field of faith and fury, the setting sun casts a sticky, apricot glow. With the scuffing of the ground, the light bounces off the rising dust creating a glowing curtain of gold – a flash of the divine in the midst of madness. At the harshest times, this stark land provides the most magical moments.

Suddenly, the plastic-covered windows are slammed shut. I have seen too much and there is no way I can watch – let alone film – the prayers themselves. The Taliban have become so precious and paranoid about their interpretation of Islam that they frequently forbid infidels from entering mosques, watching prayers or even discussing Islam. It's a far cry from the open door policy I have been used to among Muslims in Pakistan or India. So, the stadium prays beyond my gaze and I can only entreat the soulless god of television. I ask that I might film something, anything, before the end of the match . . . or the daylight. Whichever comes first.

When the Taliban first came to power in Kabul in September 1996, with the full force of their religious zeal, they banned all sports events. Even the most innocent forms of fun such as kite-flying were not permitted and remain that way, though these bans are only very loosely enforced. Some games like *buzkashi* – the highly skilled if grisly sport involving two teams of horse riders fighting over a headless goat or calf – have never returned. The southern Taliban banned *buzkashi* because it is a northern Afghan pastime. Soccer, on the other hand, made a quick comeback. After all, legend has it that *mujahideen* played football with the heads of vanquished Soviet soldiers. While the Taliban have allowed soccer to flourish, they still try to exercise strict control over crowd behaviour. Clapping is supposed to be banned. Instead, fans should chant '*Allah-o-Akbar*' – God is Great.

Today, there is not a lot for the crowd to applaud. The visiting Peshawar team – easily recognisable by their trimmed beards or mere moustaches – are making short work of their hosts. The *mullah* looks nervous and beads of sweat trickle down his beard. He smells of salt and kebabs. I, too, am starting to sweat as the sun sets. Soon there won't be enough light to film, but Taliban time starts for no man – least of all a clean-shaven infidel from Australia. In a quiet cry for help, I make moves towards my kitbag but my gesture is quashed. I am poured more tea, a clear signal I am going nowhere soon. The trusty, dusty AK-47s of the *mullah*'s men reinforce the message. To them, their weapons are little more than fashion accessories, but to me, they speak of authority. Power perceived is power achieved.

In typical Afghan fashion, the waiting breaks without warning. The minister clears the room of his goons and ushers Masood and me into a small, adjacent office. The only light is the filtered hue of dusk and, like all the windows, opaque plastic sheets are stretched where glass should be. I can't see a thing, and I give this bear of a man a look of desperate disdain.

'This won't work. My camera can see through this plastic no more than you can.'

I don't have time for Afghan niceties. Poor Masood has to translate the substance of my words, without the terse tone. The *mullah* chortles like a magician about to pull a rabbit from his beard, instead producing a penknife. He cuts a small incision through the plastic sheeting – not even three fingers' thickness.

'You have got to be joking. I am supposed to film through this? It's not even wide enough for my lens.'

With another small stroke on the plastic, he concedes barely another inch and strides out of the room barking a blunt instruction: 'Be quick!'

It's the first time I have heard him use a harsh tone. He is as nervous as I am. As he leaves, the *mullah* padlocks the door from the outside, giving us no way out and giving the impression to anyone passing that the room is empty. I am aghast but have no time to whinge. With my own penknife I make the hole in the plastic large enough to poke the lens through and begin filming my way around the stadium. It is now almost too dark, especially beneath the shade of the awning, but I grab what I can.

I'm concentrating so hard on getting some shots, I don't notice the bang on the door.

'What was that?' Masood gasps.

Still, filming furiously, I don't hear a thing. Then I hear a hard, determined bang, more kick than knock, more boot than fist. It's certainly not polite. We can't open the door, even if we wanted to – it's locked from the outside. My brain freezes, suspended between fear of the Taliban and fear of failure. I have only half a minute of shaky footage.

My brain kick starts and I shove my camera into my kitbag, fumbling with the zip.

Three more kicks, the crack of metal on wood, some shouting, a manly groan then – THWACK! The door slams open in a shower of splinters, dust, beards and guns. Religious police pour into the room in a stream of testosterone. In a triumph for absurdity, they cock their weapons. My gear is as good as gone and, more importantly, Masood is in serious trouble. They drag him by the jacket, yelling and bouncing him between the walls of the hall. They're not interested in me; I don't know whether to be relieved, or nervous that they might be keeping me for later.

The *mullah* walks out of his office, trying and failing to look calm. He smiles foolishly. The senior religious cop admonishes the *mullah* as though he were a small boy. You don't need to speak a word of Pashto to follow this show of strength. Here is a Taliban minister being torn to shreds by the real holders of authority. Slowly, the tension dissolves, they stop pushing Masood around and, amazingly, no-one searches my kitbag. They're more interested in my sunglasses.

A very young guy lifts them from my shirt pocket.

'I like your glasses,' he smooches in good English, 'I will have them.'

With my brain frozen again, my response is pure instinct.

'No, you won't.' I'm shocked at the words coming out of my mouth but I'm glad – I don't want to be seen to be intimidated. I figure it's better to take no shit from the start, even if I am shit scared. What follows is a hopelessly blokey eyeballing moment that feels suspended in eternity. This kid has to prove his power – not so much to me as to his mates – but, incredibly, he returns my glasses and, as suddenly as the whole drama began, it ends.

'Come,' Masood mutters, 'we can go.'

His eyes are flaring as we race down the stairs.

'Masood, what happened? What did they say to you?'

He stays silent as we make our way to the car, through the crowd outside the stadium and past the boys selling nuts, dried fruit and melon. We climb into the back of our taxi, the driver weaves through the mob, and the last rays of the day are almost gone. As I wonder how they could still see to play soccer, a roar pours from the stadium; Kabul has scored. Masood turns to me from the front seat, tears welling in his eyes. He looks much younger than his twenty-one years. For the first time, he looks vulnerable.

'They slapped my face. Fuck them. They humiliated me. They slapped me.' He is half weeping, half cursing – half boy, half man. I see clearly that manhood does not come at once; it is a slow and uneven process. One moment we are kings of the world, the next cowering kids.

Driving through dusk streets, there is nothing to say. I may yet have my gear confiscated or get kicked out of the country. It's an occupational hazard of filming under the Taliban and I'd quietly thought it could happen at any time. Yet while my fate is unclear, we know what awaits Masood.

He will lose his job.

The sole breadwinner for a widowed mother and two

younger siblings is sacrificed by a foreign stranger for a few seconds of poorly lit, shaky footage taken through a small incision in a plastic window. In the fickle world of daily news, the pictures may or may not make it onto the television.

As the car grinds up the hill to the hotel, I rack my brain for something to say. I can only think of the predictable and pathetic.

'Sorry, Masood,' I offer sheepishly. 'Sorry.'

He offers no reply.

The following days are tense and frustrating. The Taliban won't confront Masood till I am gone so spies track us around town – as much to keep an eye on him as me. We dart in and out of gyms, where we film buff blokes and karate classes behind closed doors. The soccer footage is so shaky and short, I am desperate for any sporting pictures I can get and something is better than nothing. Slowly, I piece together a story. However, it is getting harder to meet with people. They know the Taliban are watching even more closely than normal and won't have anything to do with me. It's time to go.

As we head to the airport, I give Masood an extra two hundred dollars to appease my guilt. He seems philosophical about the ordeal.

'Don't worry,' he reassures me. 'I would never be able to work for the Taliban long. I think you say in English "it would end in tears"?'

With tears and smiles in our eyes, we say goodbye. As the small UN plane circles over Kabul, I feel guilty for creating a mess for Masood and I feel guilty for leaving. I can see why some foreigners stay in Afghanistan. The place will hold on to a particular type of person and never release its grip. Afghanistan is the perfect country for the compassionate adventurer. One aid worker told me he will leave when his work is done. He's been here fifteen years. A few years ago, I might have stayed and made myself useful in a place where the need is great. But not any more – I am not compassionate, independent or adventurous enough to turn away from home forever.

Home is where I must go. But I will have to take the long way: Kabul to Islamabad, then fly to New Delhi to sign cheques and clear the piles of mail from my desk. Sarah will already be in Sydney and I follow next week. We have a wedding to attend.

Ours.

CHAPTER 15

WELCOME HOME

This glistening city can't possibly be my home – it's too orderly; too *hygienic*. The toilets flush, I can drink the water and the sky does not look like a desert. In fact, Sydney a week before Christmas can't be real at all. Its twinkling beaches and laidback parties are a surreal wonderland. As Sydney airport customs officials comb my bags, I recall the warning I received here two years ago: that I was heading to 'another bloody universe'. That immigration officer was almost right. But we are the weird ones, not them. If anything, ours is the more distant planet, the more bizarre place. By sheer weight of numbers, India and its neighbours are more 'normal' than Australia. More than a billion people cannot be the exception. We, from the Lucky Country, are the odd ones out.

And now I feel odd in my lucky land.

I've missed Australia's informality – wearing shorts to parties, the way people laugh and touch, the first-name basis among strangers. I did not pine for home but I did idealise it. Now, Sydney feels foreign and flat. Well, boring, if truth be known. In contrast to the danger of Delhi's roads, the traffic seems stilted and slow. People actually *obey* stop signs and speed limits. As for sticking to one lane, stop cramping my style! I am back in the land of limits and laws; and, like the traffic, everything seems tedious. Sydney airport is not heaving with hostages returned from a week's ordeal in Kandahar. My family and friends are not as fascinating as Masood and his mates. There is no crisis or coup to race off to. After two years' running to stand still, I have a new best friend. Adrenalin.

In the absence of excitement, I search for nostalgia. I need to hunt out old friends, especially ones who can tell me what's happening. Matt is the coolest guy I know – big, blond and with a BMW bike – and always has his finger on the pulse of the city. We became friends working together at the Hopetoun Hotel – a smoke-filled venue where your feet would stick to the beer-soaked carpet and your ears would bleed from the bad bands. The Hopetoun was an inner-city institution and Matt one of its icons. At the time, we were both students in our early twenties but his size and worldliness made Matt seem much older. Adulthood came to him early and comfortably – he found his manly boots and ran with them, while I was still doing up my teenage sneakers. Through the 1990s we'd run into each other at pubs and parties but like so many friendships I've neglected, I'd lost touch since leaving town. With no stories to distract me, it's time to reconnect.

I head to the Hopetoun, as much to track him down as to check out the old haunt. Like much of this Olympics city, the Hopetoun has had a makeover. The mission brown paint has been stripped back and buffed to create that fake aged look that is the interior designer's answer to pre-faded denim. Where there was once adhesive carpet, now lies shiny floorboards; the fridges twinkle with imported beers and fine wines; the Hopetoun has been gentrified. There's no sign of Matt but I find a mutual friend playing the pokies, so I buy a beer and sit down to chat.

'So, do you keep in touch with Matt?'

A pregnant pause; never encouraging.

'Er,' he mumbles, eyes held tight on the pokies screen, 'I assumed you knew.'

I don't want to know but I have to ask. 'How did he do it?'

His mate looks down.

'Overdose.' His tone is matter of fact. 'Matt knew what he was doing.' It's a nice display of Aussie male understatement – or perhaps, with time, he has got used to news that once shocked him, too.

Junkies would always wander into this pub, trying to sell some car stereo they'd just stolen. Matt was contemptuous of them and with his massive frame would throw them out. 'Fuckin' junkies,' he'd growl. I doubt Matt lived like a junkie, but he died like one.

I can see him, sitting in his groovy living room. Spoon. Flame. Needle. Vein. Just enough of a hit to do the job. Just enough to step off.

I have come from a place where so many with so little struggle to survive – to a place where so many have so much, and where a bright young guy turns out his light willingly.

Welcome home.

News of Matt's suicide hits me hard, dumping a football-sized knot of grief in my gut and a dense Delhi fog across my forehead. This city of Sydney, which yesterday seemed so slow, is suddenly too fast and I am confronted with how much I've come to depend on my adrenalin high. My work is fantastic or infuriating but always challenging. And when things go wrong, there is always another story. You don't need to take responsibility for anything – you can always move on and leave any mess you create behind. Another burst of buzz is just around the corner. There is accountability to the audience and ABC, but rarely to the people whose lives I invade.

However, the most responsible thing I've ever done is about to happen. Marriage. Surrounded by family and friends, dappled in summer afternoon light, Sarah and I vow 'I do'. Long-distance love has survived and thrived despite South Asia's best efforts to make mayhem.

Along with my wedding vows, I make some New Year's resolutions. I am going to stem my adrenalin addiction, keep my cool and take greater time and care with the people I meet. Life is to be savoured.

We have one more year in South Asia and I want it to be memorable. It will be – but not as I, or anyone, could ever imagine.

CHAPTER 16

SHAKEN AND STIRRED

We dive into married life with ten million of our closest friends. Before us on the sandy banks of the Ganges stretches the Hindu party from heaven, a festival of the spiritual and the spectacular at the confluence of three sacred rivers. The Maha Kumbh Mela is a smorgasbord of spiritual celebrities: the *sadhu*, or Hindu holy man, who never cuts his nails; another who sits on a throne of nails. There's the towering temples made of bamboo, lit up like Christmas trees and garlanded with the holy word 'OM' flashing in neon glory. And there are the beggars, who stampede every evening for free meals and bask in the best treatment they've had since the last Kumbh. (Giving to the poor builds up good karma for their benefactors.) It's an intoxicating Hindu high and a heavenly way to return to work. Sarah and I are still gliding on beach honeymoon bliss and this is the perfect way for us to keep hanging out and work – she's working on some stories she's been writing about India, and I've got a story planned for *Foreign Correspondent*.

Sadhus' ganja-packed chillums fill the air with the whiff of weed, though most people seem high simply on the nirvana of the Ganges' purifying powers. Everyone smiles, waits patiently and gives generously to beggars. We are strolling through the biggest human event in history and, despite fears of deadly stampedes, this is the best organised Indian gathering I have ever seen – and it's open to all castes, classes and ethnicities. It's as though someone took all that's grating and unjust about India and flushed it out to sea. Actually, that's exactly what they're doing. The bathing is endless – *sadhus*, soldiers, peasant farmers and politicians come to the freezing winter waters to dunk as one.

Everyone here is ecstatic. They will bathe and be absolved of their sins, thereby breaking free of the cycle of reincarnation and, therefore, from the suffering of this world. On the Kumbh Mela's most auspicious day, an estimated twenty-five million pilgrims are dunked en masse in pursuit of instant karma. I like it here. Maybe I can even incorporate some of India's spiritual offerings of tolerance, humility and patience into my resolution-packed new year.

The bliss is broken by the ring of my mobile phone. It's a colleague from the Canadian Broadcasting Corporation.

'Mate, have you heard about the earthquake?' His voice is pumped with the thrill of a new story. My heart sinks.

'Ummm, I guess not.' This human rumble right here feels like an earthquake in the making, but I know that's not what he's talking about. 'What's the story?'

'Gujarat. It looks bad. Really bad. Don't mind me saying but you're at the wrong story.'

He's right: I'm in the wrong place at the wrong time. It takes a sharply rising earthquake death toll for me to resign myself to the fact that my Mela happiness will be short lived. Again, India's art for anarchy is ruling my life. By four in the morning, with the hum of the Kumbh Mela fading behind me, I'm in a taxi heading for the city of Lucknow – it's a five-hour drive away but offers the earliest flight back to New Delhi. Sarah stays on, cursing India and my job anew for their skill at scuttling fun.

The adrenalin is back like an old friend. As my taxi

rumbles through the dark, the foreign desk feeds me information and a rundown of the agency pictures coming in via satellite. I am more than a thousand kilometres from the story but my coverage will start in the back of a taxi, in the northern state of Uttar Pradesh.

It's a poor alternative to being there but better than no story at all. The global news agencies are my lifeline and, on a mobile phone that drops out between towns, I piece together a picture of the earthquake, tapping a TV script on my laptop as the taxi bounces along the road.

All I need is an email connection.

The deadline is too tight to wait till Lucknow, so we pull up at a phone office along the highway, identical to millions across the country: featuring an attendant, a phone or two and a timer tallying the cost of your call. Not so long ago, correspondents would file their reports straight down a phone line; in the case of television, editors would then cut the voice to the pictures. The voice quality was invariably scratchy and muffled but it certainly sounded of India. However, with hi-technology has come high expectations, and now the norm is to send digitally recorded voice tracks over the web for a clear, crisp product. Sometimes it can sound sterile but it's the way of the future; the atmospheric days of croaky phone lines are fading fast.

First, I need to record my voice-track away from the noise of the traffic so I step into the small, unassuming office that is my link to the outside world. As I unpack my gear, the attendant telepathically anticipates my need for silence. Unprompted, he shows me to the back of his office and opens a door to the basement, which is dark and damp but nice and quiet. By the glow of my laptop screen, sitting on the bottom step leading down to the basement, I record my voice and save the file. Perfect . . . provided I get an internet connection. I climb back up to the office to discover the phone is like one of those old bakelite sets your grand-parents had, so there's no prospect of plugging the phone line straight into my laptop. I rustle around where the line joins the wall. No access there. But the timing device has some wires exposed so I unscrew the cover and, with alli-gator clips and one of the myriad converter plugs in my kit, get a connection. First time. I struggle for quick dial-ups in New Delhi but in the back blocks of the very backward state of Uttar Pradesh, it works perfectly.

One story down, who knows how many to go before the world loses interest in this disaster. I hop to New Delhi, grab my satellite phone and sleeping bag, file a couple of radio news stories and head for Gujarat.

Ahmadabad airport is a foretaste of the chaos to come. Pouring out are mostly women and children who can afford to leave by plane (an estimated million people are on the move, most of them by road). Pouring in are those whose job it is to follow disasters – international aid and rescue workers greet media friends warmly, giving the appearance of a club moving from crisis to crisis. Rwanda. Sarajevo. Gujarat.

As I walk out of the airport, the *Washington Post*'s Pamela Constable is heading back to New Delhi.

'It is an AMAZING story!' she shouts above the noise.

While most of us are only now arriving, Pamela has already been in Gujarat a couple of days and is returning to New Delhi to get clothes, money and sleeping gear. As soon as she heard about the earthquake, she left with nothing but her laptop, a pad and a pen. She has not slept since then.

'I am coming back FOR SURE!' She grins, clearly exhausted.

Pamela is one of my professional heroes: a journalistic veteran with breathtaking energy, she is the most tenacious, passionate reporter I have ever met. She will catch the last flight out tonight and be back on the dawn service. I feel tired just looking at her. She has been in Bhuj, a city of one hundred and fifty thousand in the west of Gujarat and near the epicentre of the earthquake. I try to grab her for information but she has to rush to the plane.

'Go to Bhuj, that's the story. AND HEY!' she shouts, disappearing into the throng, 'TAKE FOOD! AND WATER! AND . . . EVERYTHING!'

First things first. Monday is dawning in Australia and I need to feed the breakfast radio beast before I can even think about Bhuj. I head into Ahmadabad in a taxi, to find families sleeping in the streets for fear of aftershocks. I'd imagined Gujarat's main city would be pulverised, but much of it is still standing – until I get to the wealthy high-rise suburbs. Teams of men claw through apartments reduced to piles of rubble no taller than I am. These crumpled towers were the very symbol of middle-class success, the real estate moguls who built them envied as princes of prosperity. Now, the towers are graveyards and their makers are on the run. It's the same story in prosperous cities all over India – as cities have swelled with people from smaller towns, land prices have soared and shoddy apartments have sprung up to accommodate the influx. Before me, well-built blocks stand proudly next to the ruins of bad ones; a gruesome warning of the cost of corruption and cutting corners. Such building abandon is high risk in a country that sits on great tectonic stress, with the Indian Ocean plate pushing up the Himalayas by a few centimetres every year.

As bad as it is in parts of Ahmadabad, the story is not here. I need to get to Bhuj, so I buy water, food and a ticket for a special flight that's being put on. The big British and US networks are hiring vans and fitting them with everything including the kitchen sink before making the eight-hour drive west. My eyes boggle at the money they're spending and the huge size of the crews – complete with producers, editors and technical operators. For someone who films and fixes everything himself, it's a stark reminder that, in the global media world, the ABC and I make for small and poor players. We can only do our best to punch above our weight.

Bhuj is like being back in Kabul. Entire streets in the old part of the city look like they've been bombed. Measuring 7.9 on the Richter scale, the earthquake struck with the force of three hundred Hiroshima-sized bombs. Clocks are stopped at 8.50; the time when chaos struck. Marches and parades were underway as India marked its national day. In the town of Anjar, buildings on either side of a narrow laneway collapsed on four hundred children as they proudly marched. About three hundred and fifty were killed. In the desert Kutch region – now known as the desert of death – snakes and scorpions spewed from the ground as it shuddered, and the sky turned black from debris. When the rubble is finally cleared, India's worst modern disaster will have claimed around thirty thousand lives.

Four days after 'Black Friday', there is an unsettling quiet. Reminders of life jut from the ruins. The corner of a wedding sari, its gold thread glistening in the sun; a finely carved idol; the limp hand of a child. However, the world is already bored with Bhuj and I need to head for the untold stories of remote towns and villages. But there's not a taxi in sight – those drivers who are not dead are otherwise occupied. Journalists desperate for transport are jumping on the back of trucks to move around. A colleague convinces a local man to drive a few of us around – persuading him with the two hundred US dollars we promise to pay.

He speaks a little English.

'Where is it very bad?' we ask, ludicrously.

'Bhuj very bad,' he replies, incredulously.

'Yes, yes, of course,' we answer in chorus, impatient but straining not to be rude. It's not the time to explain that the world media's brief attention span has moved on from the immense suffering of his city. 'Where *else* is it bad? Which towns?'

'Everywhere bad. All Gujarat very bad.'

The three of us journalists exchange a knowing look tinged with frustration and awkwardness.

'Bhachau,' he adds, as if to fill the silence. 'Bhachau *very* bad.'

'Okay!' we sing. 'Bhachau! *Jaldee! Jaldee!*' Quickly! Quickly!

The hour-long drive to Bhachau is mind-numbing. Families sit in the midst of their flattened villages, dazed and paralysed, waiting for help that may never arrive.

Relief efforts are random: men toss bottles of mineral water from the back of a truck as it trundles through towns. Children laugh as if scrambling for presents. It's the only sign of levity since leaving the Kumbh Mela. The entire landscape is shaken of human habitation: bus shelters, barns, temples are destroyed. When it seems it can get no worse, we get to Bhachau.

Driving into the main street, the only thing that appears to be intact is a three-storey block of flats – until I realise it was previously four storeys. Incredibly, the top of the block held together as the ground floor crumpled beneath it. Only one wall of the town's cinema still stands, the torn silver screen flaps in the breeze. Homes tilt at impossible angles, rooms open to the elements, looking like discarded doll houses tossed onto a rubbish tip. A town of thirty-five thousand has been razed, a third of its people are dead.

Bhachau is a ghost town. The few still living are putting the dead to rest. Amid the rubble, a fire has been lit, and as

I approach, I see this is not just a fire but a pyre. A man is circling the flames, sobbing inconsolably. His harrowing cries swing between shriek and moan, and slice into my stomach like a knife. It's so intense I feel nauseous. I long for the days when I could switch off India's suffering by changing channels. Not that I ever did. In fascination, I always watched the images on the TV – just as I keep watching now. Slowly, shamefully, I step forward and stick my radio microphone next to his wet cheek to record his mourning.

So much for my New Year's resolution to take greater care with the people I meet.

I've not even met him and I am invading what must be his life's most intimate and painful moment. Not that he seems to notice – as I learned with Gladys Staines, privacy does not exist in India. A crowd of locals share my sombre stare as the man throws broken kitchen chairs and the remains of a table onto the pyre. Cremation wood ran out days ago and the wreckage that claimed so many lives is being burnt to escort souls to the next life. Yesterday, I was basking in the spiritual bliss of mass happiness. Today, I am staring at unspeakable mass suffering.

This job is heaven. This job is hell.

With his tears drying in the warmth of the now roaring pyre, the man sits on a pile of bricks and introduces himself as Hasmukh. The remains of his mother burn behind him – Hasmukh's fifth cremation in as many days. He has also pulled from the rubble his wife, two daughters and father. Now, his work is done.

'I feel completely alone,' he moans, 'I don't know what to do or where to go. I can't think straight but I do know I must go. I can't stay here.'

He seems to want to talk, which makes me feel slightly less ashamed, but the nausea is still with me. All that Hasmukh has is his six-year-old son, who is in hospital recovering from head injuries – his only hope in all this horror. When his son is well again they'll join the exodus from this broken place. The sense of total helplessness is overwhelming; there is nothing I can do to help. Welfare groups from the larger towns and cities are pouring into Gujarat in an impressive if uncoordinated relief effort, bringing blankets, water and food. Hasmukh will need those things, but right now all he wants is the impossible. He wants his family back.

I leave Hasmukh to his mother's pyre and wander aimlessly down the main street. I have my story for today, so I try to view this devastation as a person rather than as a reporter. I must make a strange sight strolling down this shattered street, as though on a relaxing afternoon walk. The only sounds are the grinding of bulldozers, or the snorts of pigs and dogs sniffing through the ruins. A woman walks out from behind one pile and asks if I could help look for her two-and-a-half-year-old daughter. The girl was playing in the street when the quake struck and has not been seen since. I turn around in a circle to survey this wasteland, wondering where to start. This mother does not really want my help, she wants me to work a miracle.

Performing no miracles and providing no comfort, I wander back to the car where my colleagues are waiting. We all have deadlines, so head back to Bhuj. The journey is light on conversation but my head is hosting a screaming argument. I can't reconcile doing this job and invading the lives of distraught and vulnerable people. But as ashamed as I am to have preyed on Hasmukh's prayers and tears, I am sure such stories must be told if we are not to get lost in our own small, safe world. It is a grim duty to deliver bad news. I have always been dismissive of Indians talking about 'doing their duty', whether as employees, children or parents. However, for the first time I see, painfully, that I have a duty to bear witness to this tragedy and to convey it to Australians. For better or worse, that means shoving a microphone next to a weeping man cremating his mother. I am a reluctant messenger.

The Kumbh Mela is the best of what I dreamt this job would be – an exotic romp through a mystical land, making for a happy blend of work and enlightenment. I'd envisioned an Indian cliché combined with professional fantasy. The reality is proving very different. As the nation lurches from mass ecstasy to agony, I lurch with it.

One of the parks in Bhuj is sprouting a ramshackle media city. The only hotel still open has patchy power and water, is already full with journalists, and swings with the force of aftershocks. So, most of the media is following the rest of Gujarat and sleeping outside. The park is quickly becoming a busy village of tents and generators alongside satellite phones and dishes. Only now do I realise how ill-prepared I am. I have a sleeping bag but no tent, a box of water, some dried fruit and bananas, but no generator or lighting. As the sun goes down, what has been a warm winter's day becomes a freezing winter's night. I pile on every jumper and shirt in my bag, set up beneath a tree and start tapping my laptop against the cold. A bunch of colleagues huddle around a bottle of scotch – indifferent to the ban on alcohol in the state where Mahatma Gandhi was born. A few metres away, someone squats by the park fence and shits. There are no toilets or running water and it's clear this park will be a cesspool by the time the media caravan moves on.

Finished filing, I climb into my sleeping bag beneath the tree and stare up through a sparkling clear night to stars dancing in blackness – the sort of sky I've not seen since being in the Australian bush. I zip my sleeping bag over my head, and for the first time since sunset, I am warm.

So it goes for days. The cries of survivors beneath the rubble trail into silence, efforts turn from rescue to relief, the story follows the same cycle of all natural calamities. Our media camp slides into a stinking mess of excrement and rubbish. It confirms what I have long suspected: for all the mess and mayhem in India, if a billion westerners tried to live here, the country would completely collapse in a week.

It takes me less than a week to collapse. The cold nights take their toll and a throat infection takes hold. I lose my voice and am unable to broadcast a word. I'm furious with myself: I can't work without a voice and the ABC flies in a replacement. I am not used to getting sick and have become quietly proud of being able to work hard without complaining or collapsing. Now my voice is gone and my ego is dented. Like a lot of blokes, I think of myself as invincible and I'm angry with my body for failing in a time of need. All my resolutions are failing as well. I am apart from my wife, showing no greater care for people and am feeling neither cool nor in control.

Welcome back to India.

CHAPTER 17

STORIES DON'T GET ANY BIGGER (MATE)

Redemption comes at four in the morning. The phone intrudes on my first comfortable sleep in weeks. I swear before I pick up. Only the foreign desk would call at this hour and, still feeling guilty about my sickness in Gujarat, I try to sound as though I'm wide awake and rearing to go.

'Helloooo, ABC.'

'SORRY TO WAKE YA, MATE,' roars a voice so excited it's almost a scream, 'BUT STORIES DON'T GET ANY BIGGER THAN THIS, MATE!'

My head swirls in a storm of fears: Are India and Pakistan at war? Is it a nuclear conflict? Do we have just minutes to live? Will I have time to file before I die? Through the back of my brain I feel Sarah's eyes snap open. She's heard every word panted down the phone. In that moment, when anything seems possible, we blink at each other through the darkness, terrified.

'MATE, MATE, MATE!' The voice yelps.

'WHAT???' I yell, unable to handle the suspense any longer.

The voice calms a little to deliver the momentous news and our fate.

'Don Bradman is dead.'

The words hang in the quiet as we wonder if we've heard correctly.

'The Don is dead?'

'That's right,' replies the hyperventilator. 'You need to file straight away. We need Indian reaction. The place will be in chaos.'

'The place is always in chaos. And it's four in the morning.'

'Is that the time? Shit, sorry, mate. Gotta go. Hear from ya soon.'

The phone crunches in my ear.

Sarah cannot contain her incredulity.

'Stories don't get any bigger than this?' She chokes on the words. I suggest that her cricket-loving father would probably agree, though not if his daughter was caught in the middle of a war between two nuclear-capable nations. I stumble upstairs to the office, where Sarah brings some heart-starting *chai* before heading back to bed.

'What are you going to write?' she asks, walking out of the office.

'That India will be in chaos,' I reply, wearily.

'It's always in chaos. And it's asleep.'

I'm already typing. She shuffles away.

I bat out a few predictable radio paragraphs, anticipating India's grief for the man it has granted god-like status. That's the easy part. Harder will be getting to Bombay, where the Australian cricket team is preparing for its tour. I have about five hours to get pictures of Steve Waugh and his boys giving their tribute to the Don. The ABC evening news bulletin needs the greats of today lamenting the great man of the past. With fifteen test wins under its belt, Steve Waugh's side has already made cricketing history, but there remains a 'final frontier' – a win that would make Bradman smile from the grave: a series win on Indian soil. India's squad may be no great shakes but any touring team knows that to beat India in India – well, to borrow a phrase, stories don't get any bigger.

Except the death of the Don.

I grab my gear, still caked with the dust of Gujarat, and brace for a monumental bun-fight as Abraham drives me to the airport. The dawn flights to Bombay are always packed with businessmen. And at the counter, the prim attendant is polite but unhelpful.

'Sir, there are no seats to Bombay,' she says. 'Even the waiting list is closed.'

I really need to keep cool.

'Could I see the manager, please?' I try to stay polite.

'Sir, he cannot help you. The flight is completely booked.'

'Please.'

'I will get the manager for you, sir.'

After a few minutes, a man fitted in signature moustache and pressed blue blazer strides to the counter.

'Yes, sir?'

'Sir, good morning. My name is Jonathan Harley from ABC TV, Australia.'

'Australia?'

'Yes, that's right.'

'Ah, Channel Nine!'

'Well, no . . . but never mind that for now.'

'How can I help, Mr Jonathan?'

'I'm not quite sure how to put this except to say there has been a death in the family.'

'Mr Jonathan, I am very sorry . . .'

'I need to get to Bombay immediately.'

'. . . I am sorry but the flight is completely booked.'

'Sir, you don't understand,' I plead, desperate and shameless.

He turns his back.

'Sir, sir.'

He walks away.

'Sir, Donald Bradman is dead.'

The airport manager halts. His legs buckle at the knees, his shoulders sag and he turns back towards me, arms stretched as if to hug me to his chest. His face is ashen, his moustache quivers. The silence hangs between us, seeming to last all day. Then, with a stirring squaring of the shoulders and life-saving resolve, he delivers my salvation.

'Mr Jonathan, India's thoughts and wishes are with you and your country. We will get you to Bombay. Please, come this way. We have no time to lose.'

Before I can say Sachin Tendulkar, I am in the air, on my way to Bombay. India has risen to the occasion.

Two hours later I'm crawling through peak-hour Bombay in the first taxi I saw at the airport scrum. I might just make it. Down side streets and back lanes the morning cricket matches are well underway. It's not so much the thwack of leather on willow as the wallop of worn tennis balls on old planks as young boys in rags, men in *dhotis* and teenagers in private school uniforms improve their form before the full heat of the day. India's addiction to cricket is one of the exquisite ironies of British colonial rule: what began as an exclusive pastime for men of means has become the passion of one of the poorest countries on the planet. Indians have made it theirs because the most basic tools of the game can be fashioned for free. The Bowral boy who began with a cricket stump and golf ball would be proud.

As my taxi cruises past Parli Beach, the driver breaks my daze.

'What is your good name, *sahib*?'

'Jonathan. And yours?'

'I am Ahmed. Where from, *sahib*?'

'Australia,' I reply, squinting through steaming morning sun.

'Oh *sahib*, verrrry sorry. The king is dead.'

The news of Bradman's death has clearly arrived.

'Bradman verrrry great man, verrrry sad day for Australia, for India, for cricket. Never another Bradman. Grrrrreat cricketer, grrrrreat gentleman.'

That an Australian hero could be so loved here, underlines Indians' intoxicating generosity of spirit. Against the millions of blind eyes turned to beggars every day, I am constantly amazed by the genuine gestures of pity exchanged between strangers or the ecstasy they may share over the arrival of a child. India's squalid stereotype ignores its glory. For all its problems and contradictions, India is a celebration of life. It is a land sticking out its tongue to Anglo-Saxon reserve and Australia's notions of normality. However, it's not just their inherent enthusiasm that makes Indians mourn Bradman. For a country crushed by a year of fresh match-fixing and gambling scandals, he symbolises a simpler time in cricketing history. Today's cricketing stars are adored and even revered, but Bradman is canonised.

India's traffic is not being generous, though. We are crawling through a city as large as Sydney but as populated as Australia. About three kilometres from the hotel housing the Aussie cricket team we hit gridlock. So close but so far. I'm infuriated; just when I thought things were going right; India defeats me yet again. I throw Ahmed some money, grab my bag, get out and run through the steaming streets. The morning parade of beggars, office workers, shopkeepers, hoods and housewives stop and stare. Nobody runs in India; it's undignified, silly and dangerous. Sweating, stumbling over potholes and dodging man, beast, bike and car, I arrive at the city's most flamboyant hotel looking like a red-faced madman.

I'm too late.

While I sat in the taxi, biting my nails and sweating, Steve Waugh and a few players emerged from their airconditioned suites and briefly spoke to the waiting cameras. They paid tribute to Don Bradman and then sat down for breakfast. Thankfully, before hopping on the plane, I'd expected this disaster and rung a local cameraman, promising him cash if he went to 'the Taj' to film any comments. Manesh meets me in the foyer, hands me the tape and suggests I 'refresh'. There's no time. I push him and his crew outside, pull a comb through my sticky hair and film a piece to camera to ensure that Australia knows I'm in the same city as our cricket team and that the ABC doesn't regret paying the airfare. I watch the tribute tape in his van as we hot-tail it across town to a satellite feed point. I meet my deadline. Just.

Prayers are said, tributes are read and by midday it's as if India has moved on. This whirlwind of a nation never stays in one emotional place for long, but I can sense reserve and sorrow as Australia's three-test tour of India approaches. It's as if Indians are also mourning the loss of innocence – of the times when the game was for gentlemen.

In April last year, New Delhi police charged disgraced South African captain Hanse Cronje with match-fixing. India smirked as the committed Christian admitted his sins, but then wept as some of its own biggest stars fell and the game's image was torn to shreds. I remember the day the country's own Don Bradman went down. I was in my office with a computer fix-it friend, Ashok. As he sat trying to rid my PC of a virilent worm, a news flash came on the TV.

The newsreader looked teary as he announced that Kapil Dev, India's former captain and current coach, had been accused of trying to bribe players to play badly in Sri Lanka in 1994. Ashok put his head in his hands. He was obsessed by cricket. Since he was five, he'd followed every knock of the game, every high and every low, and at times every ball. He even had a video of the 1983 World Cup in which Kapil Dev led his team to triumph. Ashok and his friends had watched that video so many times that he begged me to dub it to a new tape before it broke.

But after he left my office that day last year, he threw the tape out and he hasn't watched cricket since.

At the time, I remember thinking it was a big story but I see now in hindsight that the fall of Kapil Dev rocked India with a force as powerful as the Gujarat earthquake. After Ashok left my office that day, I bolted to the five-star hotel where Dev was to hold a press conference. As allegations engulfed him, I watched a legend fall.

'I don't have to clear my name,' he declared. 'That's what I'm going to tell you again and again. When I play twenty years I don't have to clear. When my conscience dies I don't have to clear my name.'

It was a classic Kapil performance: passionate and theatrical.

He was asked if he attempted to bribe his accuser – player Manoj Prabhakar.

'Do you think I ever had a cup of tea with Manoj Prabhakar?' he pleaded with bloodshot eyes.

The Indian media seemed frozen in shock and unable to question the legend it loved. So, huddled at the front of the packed press conference, I played the bad guy.

'Personal tensions aside, don't you have the problem that he's making specific allegations and your defence is "well, I've played twenty years of excellent cricket". Is that a specific enough response?'

Kapil Dev looked perplexed by my question. 'This is good enough for everybody who I've seen in twenty years,' he replied.

I knew it wasn't good enough for Australian listeners or

for many of his Indian fans but I felt for him. As he stood to leave, Kapil Dev placed his hand on my shoulder, his touch patronising but gentle. He was tired but defiant; not out but badly bruised. As if exchanging a glance with a combatant, his look said: well played but it's still a draw.

Kapil Dev's fall from grace appeared to have had less to do with corruption than bitter rivalries within India's machiavellian cricketing establishment. After endless televised debates among pundits, newspaper editorials, even tax raids on his home, and the efforts of the top investigative body in the land, Kapil Dev's name was cleared. But by then the legend had taken his bat and ball and gone home. Twelve months before his two-year contract was due to finish, Kapil Dev resigned as coach of India's national cricket team and withdrew from public life. The once ubiquitous Dev all but disappeared.

I think of him now as they bury the Don and I wonder if he'd like to pay tribute as well. Having checked in to Bombay's best hotel (I've argued that I need to be near the cricket team), I dial Kapil Dev's office. The man himself politely takes the call.

'I don't care about cricket any more, Jonathan. I want nothing to do with it.'

I'm shocked by the transformation in his voice. The personable man of the people is gone; Dev sounds dejected and poisoned by bitterness.

'You will know more about the game than I do. I am finished with the game. Forever.'

He softly hangs up. The soul of India would never be the same again.

But India can't blame Kapil Dev for cricket's fall from grace. Just as Bombay is India's commercial capital, it's also the greedy underbelly of the gentleman's game. From the mafia bosses to the small-time bookies, cricket gambling weaves a billion-dollar web across Bombay and the whole country. I fall asleep ensconced in the luxury of the Taj, dreaming of cash, corruption and tomorrow's first test of the Australian tour.

Bombay's Wankhede Stadium feels a long way from watching the soccer in Kabul. There are real windows with glass, not shonky sheets of plastic. Rather than a few tiers of shell-scared seating, stands climb high into the sky. They don't have the elegance of the Sydney Cricket Ground Members' Pavilion, but they seem impregnated with a cricketing passion distinctly Indian. It's still mostly a male crowd, but there are some women. And unlike *any* match I have seen anywhere, the fans are incurably expressive. Cricket may be on the nose but India still cares deeply about the game. It's only the morning of the first day, but the spectators roar, cheer and clap every ball. There is no greater show of India's boundless enthusiasm than in its passion for cricket, and perhaps that can never be beaten by dishonour or greed. I am beginning to see why Australia has not won a test series in India since its 1969–70 tour – the fans will shout any visiting side into submission.

But India's excitement will soon turn to anguish. An Indian collapse gives Australia its first win of the series and its sixteenth consecutive test triumph by just the third day. It appears Steve Waugh will conquer his final frontier in the second test in Calcutta.

I ask to be sent to the story: I'm no cricket tragic, but I do love a good game and I'm fascinated to see if this Australian team can keep making history. Of course news editors love stories about winners, and my expenses are approved.

One of India's many wonders is that a state called West Bengal sits in the east of the country. At its heaving heart sits Calcutta, the former capital of the British Raj, and as I fly into this legendary city, I am expecting colonial splendour. By now I should have learned to stop expecting anything.

Calcutta is a cage – a grid of traffic, crap and filtered sun that makes Delhi look clean and spacious. Once magnificent buildings are thick with diesel excrement, windows are frosted with layers of crud. Industry – in all its mechanical and human forms – has colonised every spare inch. Cars, buses and auto-rickshaws seem too big in these crowded streets; as though they've taken a wrong turn into a world half their size. I don't feel larger than life: I am overwhelmed and overheated, basting in a blend of sweat and petrol. My only comfort is that everyone else seems to be covered in the same subcontinental sauce. The heat does not discriminate between caste, class and colour – it is India's universal embrace.

I head straight for the embrace of Calcutta's legendary Eden Gardens Stadium. From my hotel, I make the ten-minute walk across a dustpan park towards a dull roar and above the stench of sweat and petrol, I can smell the faintest whiff of victory. Not ours – theirs. India is staging arguably the greatest comeback in cricketing history. Having been forced to follow on, they pulled off a Lazarus-like resurrection thanks to a swashbuckling knock by V.V.S. Laxman, who has notched up the highest ever individual test match score by an Indian. Now, on the fifth day, India is poised to end Australia's astounding winning streak. I am flanked by thousands leaving work and heading for Calcutta's sanctum sanctorum. Together we pass clusters of men huddling around televisions in *chai* stalls, sweating over the outcome of every ball. A massive roar pours out of the stadium as I approach the security check, where a policeman is sternly waving his finger at the paper under my arm.

'*Sahib*, no newspaper!' he announces.

'What do you mean no newspaper?'

'NO NEWSPAPER!'

I'm not sure if he's angry or just yelling to be heard above the crowd.

'But I'm a JOURNALIST!'

'NO NEWSPAPER!'

'WHY NOT?'

'NO NEWSPAPER!'

You can't argue with logic like that, so, bemused, I surrender my paper and plunge into a human cauldron. If I felt small in the streets of this city, I feel microscopic in its stadium. Only the Melbourne Cricket Ground rivals the size of Eden Gardens. The massive structure heaves as sixty-five thousand fans jump and thump on the wooden benches; and the high cyclone fences which divide the bays tremble against the crowds. I claw up to the media room, a glass box high in the heavens, airconditioned and far removed from the mayhem. It offers a great view of the game but is a million miles from the fans – and, for me, they're the story. I need 'atmos', radio slang for atmosphere, so I dive back into the public gallery.

As I take up a bench in a screaming bay, I feel a hint of fear. I am one very white Australian face in a sea of Indian fans, and they're not so much cheering as jeering. In Calcutta, cricket passions are felt most keenly and expressed most aggressively, especially when their own *maharaja*, Saurav Ganguly, is captain. Nervously, I pull out my radio recorder.

'WHERE YOU FROM?' a young guy screams above the roar. He's so excited, spit flares from his mouth. As I wipe his saliva from my eye, I figure this would be a prudent time to lie: 'England' or even 'New Zealand' would be safe responses. But my mouth is working ahead of my brain.

'AUSTRALIA!' I scream back.

Like a burst of wind stirring a bushfire, a circle of young men bristle with excitement. They have an enemy in their midst. There's a jostle and a push against me, the hint of a challenge. Testosterone is in the air – the smell of battle on and off the pitch. It all seems more gladiatorial blood sport than gentleman's game. I am no brawler and, while I understand the tribalism of team loyalty, I've certainly never understood getting into a fight over your team winning or losing. I glance up to the airconditioned press boxes above me. My colleagues, comfortably cool, served tea and biscuits by silent waiters in white jackets, are hermetically sealed from the frenzy engulfing the stands below. I consider for a moment – all too brief a moment – returning to the safety of the box. But it would seem a dishonourable retreat.

I was always taught that discretion is the better part of valour but my mouth has other ideas.

'C'MON AUSSIE!'

The words launch from my throat, shrill like a man without wits.

Did I say that? My brain is shouting at my mouth to shut up, while around me is stunned silence. The Indian fans cannot believe my disregard for their strength in numbers. My screaming could be suicide. The crowd roars as another Australian wicket falls. The ground is vibrating, and the smell of pure adrenalin is making my muscles twitch. The men on either side of me are pressing against me, jostling, shaking their fists and showing the whites of their eyes. Fight or flight? I consider the exit options. I see only a wall of high cyclone fences and I pray that India wins.

I am more afraid now than I have ever been. This is more frightening than Kashmir, or an angry pro-Osama rally in Peshawar. Those places seemed to have an order of sorts. This feels totally unpredictable. So why not leave? It's as easy as walking back up to the media box. But my male pride gets the better of me: just as it's a test of testosterone that will decide who wins out in the middle, it is my own test of strength to hold my ground in the stand. It may be a pathetic test but I need to purge myself of the frustration

I felt at getting sick in Gujarat and regain a sense of invincibility.

My team is slain but, thankfully, not me. India has levelled the series one-one and ended the greatest winning streak in test cricket. The crowd is exploding, the fans around me scream into my microphone. I press record and hope for the best.

'AUSTRALIA'S COMING TO AN END!!!' shouts a teenager whose eyes are about to pop out of their sockets. 'I CAN'T EXPLAIN IN WORDS. I AM JUST ENTHUSI-ASTIC ABOUT OUR PERFORMANCE. AUSTRALIA'S BAT WAS FULL OF GLORY BUT IT HAS NOW COME TO AN END.'

Screams swirl around the stadium as men and boys hug and bounce like they're on trampolines. It's a roar echoed in stalls and offices across the city and the country. It's the most spectacular Indian win since Kapil Dev held the World Cup aloft in 1983.

Amid this total chaos, I breathe a sigh of relief. But soon I can barely breathe at all. Flames and smoke fill the air. Everyone is lighting sheets of newspaper and tossing them to the rafters; and it seems Eden Gardens will burn in a blaze of glory. *Now* I see why the policeman confiscated my paper as I entered. It appears the only person who had his newspaper taken was the only one not wanting to set it ablaze.

Still, we survive. I should have deeper faith in Indians' ability to get overcharged without exploding into violence. I am in awe of India's ability to venture to the edge of anarchy, only to step back from the precipice. And as I watch, boggle-eyed at this outpouring of pride and passion, I see a nation united. For all India's diversity and division, cricket is the country's one common religion. Across bound-aries of class, caste, religion and language, everyone can pray in the temple of cricket. It is glue, binding a country that seems to teeter on the verge of disintegration, offering a shared purpose, playfulness and identity.

And I'm reminded how the squeals of HOWZAT!, long Dennis Lillee-like-run-ups and the crash of neighbours' windows smashed by wayward hook-shots provided the rhythms of my young suburban summers. Backyard cricket matches were where my brothers and friends would conquer or conk-out, forging memories of sun and sweat and friendship. Such memories are stitched into my Australian character but lie mostly unseen, revealing themselves at the most surprising times, in the most distant places, and in the company of sixty-five thousand screaming strangers.

CHAPTER 18

WHODUNIT IN KATHMANDU

India's ecstasy knows no bounds. With its win in the third and final test in Chennai, sealing the series for India, disillusioned fans have fallen back in love with cricket and country. The nation is awash with renewed self-adoration, and to be Australian is to be a loser; I've not been this embarrassed since we voted against becoming a republic. Adding to my discontent is the return of the Indian summer.

It's taken nearly three years but I have finally worked out how to combat the great Indian baste – other than following the country's wealthy to Europe or America from May through August. The answer is to shower. Regularly. Four or five times a day. One to wash off the sweat accrued through the thirty-three degree nights. One after the mid-morning trip to do an interview. Another to freshen up for lunch. The fourth on return from an afternoon errand, and the fifth, final soak is to gain some sense of sanity before sleep. All are cold. On the odd occasions when I foolishly try to cook, I take a quick dunk between serving and eating: with no kitchen airconditioning, simply boiling water drenches your shirt with sweat.

Despite the discomforts of the season, I want to throw a lavish party for Sarah. Apart from it being her birthday, I need to make up for the fact I've spent the first half of our first year of marriage almost entirely on the road. So, I book waiters and tables, buy boxes of mangoes and wine, order dozens of roses and rolls of satin for decoration. Diplomatic friends lend me their ritzy glassware, and, most importantly, the work front looks clear: I can see no big stories on the horizon.

How blind I must be.

Four o'clock, Saturday morning, the phone rings. Again. It's the foreign desk. Again. This time, I don't even try to sound awake.

'Ugghhhh?' My mouth and brain are jammed in neutral.

'I'm reaaaaally sorry to wake you,' the voice begins, 'but there's been a big shoot-up in Nepal.' The voice is far too chirpy for both the hour and the horrible subject matter.

'Ugghhhh . . . Nepal?' It's the first time I've been woken by anything to do with the tiny, Himalayan kingdom that usually makes the news only when there's a mountaineering triumph or tragedy.

'It looks like the King's been killed.'

My eyes are still glued shut and my brain remains asleep.

'I think you'd better get there.'

'Get there?' My brain crunches into gear. Kathmandu? Today? 'I'll call you back.'

Sarah's more concerned about the story than I am.

'You've gotta go,' she says. 'Nepal will be freaking out if the King's dead.'

'Really?' I'm in denial but, having trekked there a decade ago, Sarah remembers Nepal's mass reverence for its royalty.

'*Really*,' she replies. '*Go!*'

I sit on the edge of the bed, hold my head in my hands and groan. 'No! No! NO! Not TODAY!' I grudgingly throw some clothes in my bag, hurriedly explain tonight's catering arrangements for the party at which Sarah must be both guest of honour and host, grab the dog-eared copy of Lonely Planet's *Nepal* from the office bookshelf and kiss Sarah goodbye. As the car heads down the road, she cuts a forlorn figure in her dressing gown at the front gate.

I am greeted at the Royal Nepal Airlines office by a long queue of Indian and foreign journalists already camped on its doorstep. It doesn't open for several hours but nobody will risk losing a seat on what may be the only flight all weekend. This is not the day to be stuck in Delhi. Half of me hopes there are no seats so I can stay for Sarah's birthday, but fate puts me on the plane – by which time I've forgotten that I was supposed to do anything other than work this weekend. The ageing cabin looks like something from a 1960s James Bond film – the décor has not changed since the aircraft was built. The food looks like it's also from the sixties, so I pass on lunch and pour over my back-packers' bible on Nepal. I grimace at my hypocrisy. I have seen countless journalists come to India on assignment for a week or two, having only read the *Lonely Planet*, and it always struck me as intellectually lazy. Now, as we bounce through the clouds into Kathmandu, I, too, am nothing but a Lonely Planet pundit.

But no book could prepare me for the Elizabethan tragedy that has befallen Nepal. The plot could be by Shakespeare, the screenplay by Quentin Tarantino. In an exotic mountain kingdom, a popular crown prince falls for a beautiful but forbidden love. A disapproving and scheming queen says he must choose between his girlfriend and the throne. In a tumultuous act of revenge, the gun-loving heir mows down both parents and seven other royal family members in a blaze of automatic gunfire, before shooting himself.

Or is this the story? Somehow I must unravel a tale involving characters veiled in regal secrecy and fiercely contested by countless conspiracy theories. Besides, palace intrigue was never my forte. My only consolation is that I won't be alone: the royal massacre may be devastating for Nepal but for the rest of the world it's intriguing. Journalists are pouring into Kathmandu. Entering the arrivals lounge, I am taken aback by the armies of crews with their mountains of gear. Even though I have all but ignored Nepal, it is part of *my patch* and I'm not used to sharing it. Every sort of reporter – from seasoned news hounds to tabloid gossip writers – has come for the worst mass murder of royals since the slaying of Russia's Romanovs in 1918.

I sprint ahead of the pack to Kathmandu's famous Yak and Yeti Hotel, where I luckily get a room. The Yak and Yeti is what Kabul's InterContinental would look like if not riddled with shell and bullet scars: a refurbished temple to 1960s architecture, in an ancient and exotic city. In fact, Kathmandu offers a flash of what Kabul or Srinagar could have become if tourism rather than terror had taken root – complete with traffic jams, pollution and rip-off merchants. However, this is no time to be thinking about holidays and, as much as I would love to nestle into a pool-side deck chair, a national catastrophe is unfolding. So I grab my radio gear and head out into a Shangri-La that is in shock.

My taxi putters past women weeping before grand garlanded portraits of the slain King Birendra and Queen Aishwarya. Footpaths are piled with hair as men shave their heads in the Hindu symbol of respect and mourning. There is the constant mumble of prayers and the pungent tingle of incense in the air. Crowds are overtaking the streets so I abandon my crawling taxi and join the throng on foot, swept along by a rushing river of emotions – disbelief, despair and suspicion. In a region where rumour and conjecture are the currency of conversation, people can smell a conspiracy.

But before Nepal decides whodunit, the country will put the dead to rest. Hindu religious law demands that cremation be conducted as quickly as possible, and hundreds of thousands are lining the funeral procession route. Brahmin Hindu priests dressed in white *dhotis* carry the slain on biers draped in shrouds and flowers through the rutted and winding streets. Mourners throw flowers and scream in grief.

'It cannot be!' a crinkly old woman wails, the saggy skin beneath her jaw drawn taut by her cries. 'Our King is our god!'

This is mourning tailor-made for television: the world has not seen such scenes since the death of Diana, Princess of Wales. However, there is no polished casket sliding through silent and stunned streets; here the faces of the dead are uncovered for all to see, and emotions are loud and raw. Nepalese believe their king to be the reincarnation of the Hindu god Vishnu, the protector. Their guardian is gone. This is a cosmic calamity.

Unable to carry my camera gear around town, I've left it at the hotel and will rely on pool footage shot by the agencies. It leaves me free to observe everything with new intimacy. As much as I have come to love filming, for once I can concentrate just on the journalism and it's strangely liberating. The human river of mourning spits me out at the cremation site called Arya Ghat or 'best place', in front of Nepal's most important Hindu temple – dedicated to Lord Shiva, destroyer of worlds. Reserved for the cremation of royalty, the Arya Ghat lies on the sacred Bagmati River and is framed by gracious timber pagodas. The Bagmati may be sacred but it looks to me like a fetid sewage stream. Thousands are already sitting along steep terraces and some have climbed high into the crowns of surrounding trees looking over this narrow amphitheatre where pyres of stacked sandalwood are draped in marigolds and jasmine. They look like giant four-poster beds, with a sapling at each corner holding a light canopy of saffron-coloured fabric.

As the crowd waits for the bodies, people exchange

condolences and conspiracy theories, allowing me to piece together the 'who's who' of royal Kathmandu. The central character in this romantic tragedy is Crown Prince Dipendra, an affable twenty-nine-year-old demigod who is surrounded by sycophants, captive to protocol and mad about guns. Nepal's most eligible bachelor loves the intelligent and independent Deviyani Rana, the daughter of a prominent Nepalese politician. Standing between them is the haughty and manipulative Queen Aishwarya – widely dubbed the 'wicked queen' for her scheming ways – and the adored King Birendra. Then there's the dysfunctional extended family. The slain King's less popular younger brother, Gyandendra, was briefly a three-year-old boy king during a 1950–51 palace crisis but has spent most of his adult life quietly concentrating on his business empire. The people are ambivalent about Gyanendra but they hate his son, twenty-nine-year-old brawling playboy Paras Shah. He has a dark reputation for hard living and lawlessness – including accusations he has killed two people and beaten up several police officers, never to be punished. His most notorious incident involves the death of a popular musician whom many Nepalese believe Paras intentionally ran down in his jeep. The idea of him becoming Crown Prince is too much for most Nepalese to stomach.

I wriggle into a group of young Nepalese convinced of Crown Prince Dipendra's innocence. 'He's a very nice person,' one guy says. 'He's very honest,' adds another. 'He couldn't do it himself. It's not true. We don't believe it at all.'

As night falls and I lap up the gossip, some people clutch transistor radios in the hope that state-run Radio Nepal will sort fact from chatter. They get only banalities that stoke the intrigue. None of the statements read on radio says the King has been killed, only that he has 'ascended to heaven'; the deaths are described as an 'unanticipated incident' occurring during a happy family gathering; and the first official statement by the man who would be king, Gyanendra, says members of the royal family were 'seriously injured in an accidental firing from an automatic weapon'. It's a public relations farce performed by a panicked palace.

The conspiracy theories are no less ludicrous but much more entertaining. There are many variations, involving Indian interference in the kingdom, CIA collusion and machiavellian manoeuvres, but the most popular explanations accuse the hated Prince Paras of trying to blast his way to the throne. One account suggests the royal bad boy paraded as his cousin Dipendra, sporting a mask that fooled his own family, and gunned them down in cold blood. There are stories Dipendra had already secretly married Deviyani in a Hindu ceremony, while others claim astrologers warned the King that his son should not marry or have children until he was thirty-five. My ears tingle with the fantastic chit-chat.

Members of the government sit glum-faced on the ghats, including Prime Minister Girija Prasad Koirala – who is also being accused of masterminding the massacre. A soft rain begins to fall as the bodies arrive, but rather than respectful silence, people scream 'Prime Minister, resign!' and 'Leave the country!' Centuries of tradition roll on oblivious to the heckling as the bier-bearers place the bodies on the pyres and, in observance of ancient Vedic funeral rites, a cousin of the King circles then sets alight the late monarch's body, finally placing the flaming torch across his face. As he moves on to the corpse of the Queen, a military band blurts out the national anthem followed by the last post. It's a discordant soundtrack to a haunting Hindu ritual.

As flames lick the sandalwood logs and climb into the night sky, the crowd grudgingly disperses, while television reporters film their pieces to camera in front of the spectacular pyres. With the influx of media 'outsiders', I can't find any familiar New Delhi cameramen from whom I could bludge a quick five minutes of filming. The new arrivals are too hurried to be bothered with some stranger who hasn't got his own crew. I am jealous of these proper teams with professional gear, who don't have to beg, borrow and steal in order to do their stories. Frustrated, I rejoin the mob and return to the hotel soaked in this city's sullen mood, a very long way from Sarah's party, which I should be hosting in New Delhi.

With the new day, the reality of Nepal's loss is setting in. Grief shifts to confusion and resentment, so I set out to measure the mood. The Narayanhiti Palace is only a few minutes' walk from the hotel and, although it's still early in the morning, thousands are already queueing to pay their respects. Mountains of flowers are piled at the gates as grievers file past portraits of the slain King and Queen. Notes stuck to the gates ask, 'Who am I now?' Unlike last night, there is no weeping – just bewilderment. For TV, the incredible pictures speak for themselves, but I need to paint the picture for radio, so I press record and stick my microphone into people's mourning.

'I think it's not true,' insists a young woman with an American accent copied straight from Ally McBeal. 'For me it's like losing my own parents. It is I think for everybody. Our only hope and our only base was the King and they are killed.' Her friend offers an expressionless nod and adds, 'There is some secret, whatever. There is something behind it.'

I don't bother to note down people's names – I just need good, short 'grabs' to pepper my pieces, not life stories. The voxpop – as in vox populi, or voice of the people – brings public opinion from afar straight into the homes of Australians.

Peering through the metal palace gates, I try to imagine the billiard room where the killings took place and wonder if the lakes of blood have been mopped up from the elegant marble floors. The palace reveals none of its secrets, and offers only a lonely spokesman to recite a ridiculous official line. Chiran Thapur, the dapper Palace Master of Ceremonies who speaks with the clipped accent of an exclusive British education, steps out into the throng of media and mourners. I pull this finely suited gentleman to one side for what turns out to be the most bizarre interview of my life, beginning by my asking what happened on Friday night.

'It was a burst of automatic weapon fire,' he states matter-of-factly, 'and then there are these people who are killed accidentally.' He's memorised a press release it seems only he believes.

'And whose hand was the gun in?' I ask.

'This I don't know and it would be presumptuous on my part to tell you.' Seeing my skepticism he adds an after-thought: 'It's the truth.'

'Do you think that will satisfy twenty-two million Nepalese who want their King back?'

'You know,' he resumes, his expression impenetrable, 'they've shown their great love and respect for King Birendra; he was one of the greatest of all men. But we have to accept the fact that he is no more.'

'In a country where conspiracy theories and rumours blossom every day?' I try hard not to sound scathing.

'These conspiracy theories and rumours occur every-where.' He pauses for a moment. 'I can give you so many examples of what happens in your countries. Where are you from?'

'Australia.'

Without so much as a blink or breath, he fires straight back.

'Australia. You find out what happened to Harold Holt and you let me know.'

In the twinkling of an eye, this Master of Ceremonies has shown he is the master of the one-liner. I am silenced by his lightning switch from slain Himalayan monarch to mysteriously drowned Australian Prime Minister, and Chiran Thapur excuses himself with a satisfied smile, moving on to flabbergast the next journalist.

I bump into the *Washington Post*'s Pamela Constable and Stephen Farrell from the *Times* of London, a quick-witted, quick-tempered workhorse based in New Delhi. They've teamed up for the story and between them is more journalistic drive than the total of most newsrooms. I've not seen Pamela since the Gujarat earthquake – now, as then, she is tired but buzzing in journalistic heaven. Unburdened of my camera, I tag along to see how reporters from two of the world's greatest papers operate. If I thought I was an energetic worker, these two are manic – constantly working the phone, scrambling for contacts, seeking out sources. Their focus is as simple as it is impressive: to be the first to publish whodunit. It's a sobering lesson in the difference between my work and theirs: where I will do as many as ten stories a day, they will do one. But theirs must be groundbreaking. I report on events and try to second-guess what will happen; they delve deeper into the who, the how and the why of a story. Where they investigate, I mostly reiterate. In a world of glitterati, literati and paparazzi, electronic media are mostly reiterati.

I leave Pamela, Stephen and their furious search for a scoop, walking back to the Yak and Yeti to churn out material for Monday morning in Australia. Tapping on my laptop, thinking through my fingers, I see afresh how this story is swinging from the tragic to the ridiculous. In one of the many postscripts to the massacre, Crown Prince Dipendra is not quite dead – he is lying on life support in

Kathmandu's military hospital and, incredibly, protocol
dictates a brain dead Crown Prince be duly proclaimed
King. Incapacitated, he will be assisted by the slain King's
brother, Prince Gyanendra, who rushed back to Kathmandu
from a jungle retreat on Friday night. Gyanendra's absence
from the fatal party only fuels the conspiracy theories but
one thing is certain: he faces an unenviable dilemma –
whether to pull the plug on Dipendra's life support system.
And, if he does, who will become King?

Dipendra is King for just two days. Announcement of his
death and that Gyanendra will be monarch ratchets
up the tension in a city already set to explode. I set out on
this grey Monday morning for Gyanendra's coronation ceremony, walking so as to absorb the atmosphere of a city in
crisis. Police are out in force, gangs of young men skulk
around the streets on motorbikes, and all the while small
shrines stage countless acts of devotion. I pass a family
offering prayers and lighting incense before portraits of the
King and Queen at a makeshift mourning platform. While
their rituals of piety and humility verge on the poetic, I can't
help but think Nepal would be better off without its royalty.
Monarchies have long struck me as a medieval abomination
best left to history.

And Nepal's royals are no different.

They're a second-rate elite lording over a third-world
country. If anything, this tragedy has exposed them as an
isolated and self-obsessed court of petty oldies and an
arrogant young jetset generation. For twenty-two million
Nepalese, of whom at least forty per cent live in abject
poverty, the only consolation is their reverence for a
monarch they see as an incarnation of a benevolent Hindu

deity. It strikes me as a cynical scam, sustained by a cloistered elite over a near-feudal society. In 1990 King Birendra relinquished executive power; but a decade of multi-party democracy has disappointed everyone, producing ten governments in as many years and, among some, a nostalgia for the stability of absolute monarchy. Tears over Birendra's death are shed as much in mourning for the man as in fear for the country's future. The only people cheering are Nepal's Maoists, who lead a fierce and burgeoning insurgency and are set to gain from this instability. They demand a republic and already control parts of the impoverished hill districts.

I sidle up to a group of young men heading in the same direction. They are cursing the soon-to-be-King and his only son, shouting as they stride along the rough footpath.

'Kill the murderers! Punish the murderers!'

I butt in to ask if they believe Paras is behind the killings.

'Yes, we believe it,' says the tallest of the three. 'Because we heard that from the history we know that Paras was raping so many girls, trafficking girls and killing so many people and last year he had killed a famous singer, Praveen Gurung.'

Whatever Paras has done, his father will suffer the sins of his son.

'He's really not liked this Prince Paras, is he?' I ask.

'Yeah, he's not likeable.' All three frown in unison.

'But is that a good reason to distrust his father?'

'Maybe it's a good reason.'

Maybe this is all a good excuse for these guys to let off some steam. I turn right towards the old palace; they go straight ahead. 'We'll see you later!' they smile. 'Watch out for us!'

It will not take long to understand what they had in mind. In the meantime, in the old palace courtyard, Nepal's third king in four days takes to the throne. The new King Gyanendra sits impassive beneath his bird of paradise crown as courtiers and government ministers throw coins at his feet in a show of loyalty. It is a sombre ceremony in a rain-soaked courtyard and playboy Paras is nowhere to be seen. When the new King emerges from the palace in his horse-drawn carriage, escorted by brass bands and royal guards, he is greeted with sullen silence. The crowds lining his route to the new palace do not cheer or clap. Some jeer.

'Down with the King!' they shout. 'Hang Paras! Hang Paras!'

I sprint back to the hotel to send my stories for the evening programs and, as I'm filing, Kathmandu explodes. King Gyanendra is barely through the gates of the new palace when grief and frustration boil over into violence. Thousands clash with police as rocks are exchanged for rubber bullets and tear gas. It might be a bit of fun for the three guys I saw on my way to the coronation but at least three people are killed.

And I miss the whole thing.

I am so busy feeding the various radio and TV programs, I can't check what is happening – I'm cloistered in my hotel, cocooned as royalty from the people and the story. By the time I've finished filing, a hasty curfew has been imposed and nobody can leave. Soon, many journalists show signs of cabin fever and flock to the bar, where they swap tall tales and war stories. Alcohol and being a correspondent have long been best friends, and in Hemingway's day it seemed if you weren't drunk, you weren't doing your job. However, in my bi-media world of round-the-clock deadlines, most of the time I don't have time to get drunk. It's a pleasure enjoyed by print journalists.

As I walk past the bar, London's Fleet Street pack are cackling about their inevitable 'Brits in the shit' stories – tales of British backpackers stranded in this turmoil. Indian journalists are intently debating Nepal's constitutional crisis, and Japanese journalists are comparing functions on their Palm Pilots. Thankfully, a handful of Nepalese journalists have been helping us to lobby authorities to get an army escort to Dipendra's cremation this evening. When an army truck pulls into the car park, we swarm out like starving refugees rushing an aid drop. I jump onto the back to find Pamela there, and she's even more animated than usual.

'Have you EVER seen a story like this!?!' she beams. 'I'm tellin' ya, is there any other job you'd rather be doing?! This is the best job in the world. THE BEST!'

I let her words percolate through my brain. I think of all the mistakes and miscalculations, late nights and frustrations – and the constant feeling that you never know enough. I think of the crappy pieces to camera and the maddening bureaucrats – and the testing and satisfying fact that you are always learning. I smile at the excitement of jumping from a crisis in Kashmir to cricket chaos, or a coup in Pakistan, then becoming an overnight 'royal correspondent' in this Himalayan kingdom. Such a relentless road is taking me through unchartered worlds beyond me and within me.

'You're right,' I reply, looking her square in the eye. 'It *is* the best job in the world.' From someone not sure he wanted the job and with no clue of how to do it, I have grown to learn it and love it. At least when things are going right.

Huddled like cattle in the back of this topless truck, we roll through smoking, abandoned streets. Rocks line the road – the footpaths have been reduced to rubble by protestors tearing them up to throw at police. Burning car-tyre barricades smoulder by the side of the road. A few people peer through shutters but no-one dares venture out.

When we arrive at the sacred Bagmati River for Dipendra's cremation, it's immediately clear this will be a very lonely funeral. It is performed with the same ceremony and ritual as for his parents but crowds are kept away by curfew; a pitiful farewell for a tragic figure. Mesmerised by the flames wrapping his body, I can't help but feel some pity for this mass murderer. Dipendra was a prisoner of his privilege, bound by medieval rules and cocooned in a world of aristocracy and taboo. He was educated at Eton, would jetset around the world and skydive for fun, but he could not decide his dinner companions or his bride. He had the best and worst of the old and the new. Deviyani Rana was deemed an unacceptable future queen even though she was the grand-daughter of one of India's wealthiest *maharajas*. She failed the feudal test of seven generations of 'pure' lineage because her grandmother had been a mistress to the *maharaja*, rather than a legal wife. King Birendra presented a compromise to the Crown Prince: keep Deviyani as a mistress and marry the family's choice of bride. Deviyani was blue blood but not quite blue enough and, as a modern, independent woman, would not be intimidated by an arrogant queen. It was an unshakeable love triangle: the girl implacable, the mother immoveable and the son inconsolable.

However, much of this is still a matter of speculation and extrapolation. We need a witness.

For days, Kathmandu lives under the uneasy combination of curfew and confusion. The palace does not bend from its 'accident' line, although a rushed judicial enquiry is commissioned by the new King. Then, sudden word of a mysterious press conference races through the media grapevine: it's to be held at the military hospital, where the slain were brought on Friday night, and we flock to it. Impatient and intrigued, we squeeze into a small room thick with the smell of hospital disinfectant; I kneel at the front of the pack, below a whiteboard leaning on an easel, unsure what to expect.

Unannounced and unpretentious, in walks a royal witness to the massacre. The god of journalism can be benevolent. Dr Rajiv Raj Shahi, the late King Birendra's nephew by marriage, picks up a whiteboard marker as if he's about to present a university paper and starts to sketch the billiard room where family dinner turned into royal bloodbath.

'Around nine, I heard a burst of gunfire around this area,' the young doctor begins, pointing to his diagram.

What follows is confirmation of what has been dribbling out over the last couple of days – and directly contradicts the palace line that this was all an accident. Some things are vague because Dr Shahi escaped out a window and so could not clearly see what happened; though, in a surprising twist, he praises the bad boy Prince Paras for saving the lives of several royals by shoving them behind the safety of the sofa. The judicial enquiry would later flesh out further details of the night, but for now, before a packed and stunned media, a witness has solved this Himalayan mystery.

Dipendra did it.

An otherwise normal Friday royal family dinner turned to massacre when Dipendra, dressed in combat fatigues and carrying an automatic submachine gun, a rifle and a shotgun, entered the palace billiard room to slaughter his father, his younger sister, three aunts, two uncles, and, finally, outside in the garden, his mother and brother. Then he shot himself in the head. Earlier in the evening, Dipendra had appeared so drunk, he was escorted to his room by Dr Shahi, Prince Paras and another relative. But instead of crashing out, he would crash and burn; and take his family with him.

'What motivated him to do this I'm not sure,' Dr Rajiv

Raj Shahi concludes, providing dramatic flourish befitting this entire saga. 'But it was the then Crown Prince Dipendra who committed this murder. Anybody who touched the King is no more what he used to be. He was just a murderer.'

He marches out of the room, leaving a perfect closing quote for a perfect story. Many Nepalese will not believe this first-hand account, or subsequent official reports, but as far as the media's concerned, the tale is over after a neat week of riots and royal intrigue. We now know whodunit. What we will never really know is why.

It's not the only unfathomable tragedy in the region. Two thousand kilometres west, a human crisis is turning into catastrophe as tens of thousands pour out of Afghanistan, to escape the deadly drought. Aid agencies warn that more than a million people face starvation.

Recently, Afghanistan has been grabbing headlines but not with tales of human suffering. While I was busy covering cricket, Taliban militiamen used rockets, tanks, even spades and hammers to destroy central Afghanistan's ancient Bamiyan Buddhas. It was the biggest story from Afghanistan since US cruise missiles targeted al-Qaeda training camps in 1998 and, despite worldwide outrage, including criticism from its closest ally, Pakistan, the Taliban were unrepentant. Supreme Leader Mullah Mohammed Omar said he was 'proud' to order the destruction of the false idols and dismissed the international outcry as a 'drama'. Apparently, this should be transparent to Muslims with 'common sense'. For a regime starved of recognition, it won a moment of attention, albeit condemnation.

And for those who watch Afghanistan, it was a telling

reminder that the plight of the country's people just doesn't rate as a story any more. Health and social indicators place Afghanistan as the harshest, poorest, sickest and least-educated country in the world and, now, the drought will make bleak even bleaker. Rather than receive help, Afghans will receive indifference. At the western-end of these Himalayan mountains, far from Shangri-La and its perfect royal tragedy, lies the perfect travesty.

CHAPTER 19

ARITHMETIC OF APATHY

The first rays of day throw their magical glow over hell. My hotel hire car, a glistening, airconditioned biosphere, edges into its bowels, and ghostly faces wash past my window. The driver squints through the windscreen as if navigating a furious storm. We are entering Jalozai, in Pakistan's north-west Frontier Province.

'*Sahib*,' the driver grizzles, rocking as if reciting verses from the Koran, 'Jalozai no good place.' He was reluctant to come but could not turn down the work – especially once I'd tipped him in advance. Joining us is Peshawar-based journalist, Ashfaq Yusefzai, a rakish young guy with the annoying habit of ending every other word with 'oh'.

'See, Jonathan-oh,' he grins as we drive in, 'I told-oh you, I could-oh get us-oh into Jalozai.'

It cost me a two hundred dollar bribe to officials but Ashfaq has delivered on his promise. Authorities want this place out of the media gaze, and as we crawl through the dawn haze, it's easy to see why. Eighty thousand Afghans are rising to another morning with nothing but the barest essentials and the will to live – and either of these could give up any moment.

I step out of my comfortable car into a sea of human

sewage. Those chewed up by drought and conflict are spat out at Jalozai and made to live among chunder and shit. My nose stings with the acid stench of sweat and stale piss; somewhere, rotting meat is sweetening the mix. My eyes and mouth want to snap shut against the onslaught of dust. In a blink, the soft glow of dawn has evaporated and Jalozai is glaring at me in a stark white-hot blaze. I pull my camera and tripod out of the boot and brace for a day of filth and filming.

In this makeshift city made of tarpaulin, faces gawp from gaps – the malnourished stare that speaks all languages. Eyes are hollow with hunger. Skin is flaky and blotched. Tongues lie quiet in slackened jaws. But young children also run and play, defiant or ignorant of their circumstance. The soundtrack is a crackling Bollywood whine from a prized transistor radio not yet hocked for food or medicine, backed up by a chorus of wet coughs.

It takes me all of ten seconds to attract a crowd, so I climb onto a parked truck to film an expanse of blue plastic punctuated by squares of charcoal canvas, dumped on a dustbowl thirty-five kilometres south-west of Peshawar. Technically, this is *New* Jalozai. Across the way, I can see the rooflines of *Old* Jalozai, with its established mud huts and bazaars that mushroomed in the wake of the 1979 Soviet invasion. More than two decades later, its fifty thousand residents are here to stay. Having forged their own local economy they supplement it by smuggling timber, semi-precious stones or drugs over the Khyber Pass. For the new arrivals starting their day beneath me, there is no work, water or world concern, and I pan my camera across a scene of endless suffering.

En masse, this place is too much to digest, so I climb down from the truck in search of personal stories. The instant mob trails behind me through this ocean of hovels. Already it's screaming hot, so I pull out my water bottle and take a long swig. But as I lower my head, scores of parched faces stare back at me, desperate for a drink. Ashamed of my insensitivity, I offer the bottle.

'*Paani*?' I ask, pathetically. Water? Someone take it, all of it, just put me out of my privilege. But the gesture is hollow: there is only a piddling amount for each thirsty mouth. Not that they would ever accept, because in their eyes, I am the guest. Inevitably, an invitation for tea is extended.

The offer is made by Nazir Mohammed, a young man parading as a senior citizen, who brushes a boy away to arrange tea. With his wisps of greying hair curling from beneath his multicoloured skullcap, Nazir is crouching on his haunches, his heels flat to the barren ground between his tent and the crude drain running along in front of it. From behind his beard comes a shy smile, offset by diamond eyes.

'I don't usually do this,' he volunteers, waving a pink razor in the air.

Shaving the heads of his son and daughter would be a much smoother job with water but that would be wasteful. Nazir is using a blunt, disposable shaver and above the sounds of the camp rusty razor grinds on scalp. I grimace but the children sit impassive as their father transforms them into mini-Kojaks.

'We don't have the water to wash their hair,' Nazir says as he scrapes. 'For hygiene, I have no choice but to shave their heads. The girl and the boy.'

Nazir and his wife, Nasima, have had one less head to shave since a bitterly cold winter night claimed their three-year-old daughter Masooma. I remember the cold snap that swept across the region – I was huddling against it under the tree in quake-stricken Gujarat, wrapped in a down sleeping bag. These people have only a plastic sheet, and Masooma died of the combined effects of cold, a chest infection and diarrhoea.

'We fled the fighting to save our children,' Nasima

laments, 'but instead this place has killed one of them.' She turns to where her daughter is buried on the hill behind Jalozai, but cannot look there without weeping. From on top of that hill, Nasima can see New Shamshatoo – an under-utilised United Nations' camp with proper tents, blankets and medical facilities that would probably have saved Masooma's life. But the eighty thousand residents of Jalozai are not allowed there, thanks to a criminal bureaucratic row between Pakistan and the United Nations over their registration as refugees.

As tea arrives and Nazir pours it, I look at the face of this thirty-one-year-old. He is my age but his face bears the burdens of a man much older. Between sips of tea and telling his family's story, he ploughs his way across the crown of five-year-old Nafessa, her thick black hair falling off in melancholic folds. Nafessa's six-year-old brother Shaizai is already shorn and looks on blankly as the crowd swells, offering advice on how best to do the job. Nothing is private, nothing is sacred here.

Home for this family is a village in Kapisa Province, around seventy kilometres north of Kabul. In the shadow of the mighty Hindu Kush, on the fertile Shomali Plain, it should be a peaceful, productive place, but civil war put Nazir's family in the firing line. Ever since the Taliban's scorched-earth push north of Kabul in 1999, the predominantly Tajik population of the Shomali Plain has been either cowering or fleeing. Most recently, the regime has been stopping food getting to besieged civilian populations – whether via aid agencies or traders. Nazir's village is near the Panjshir Valley – bolthole of the legendary *mujahideen* commander, anti-Taliban bulwark and Northern Alliance leader, Ahmed Shah Massoud. The Panjshir is a rugged and landmined gateway to the last ten per cent of Afghanistan not controlled by the Taliban.

'I fought with Massoud against the Russians,' Nazir

announces proudly. He took up arms against the infidel invaders at the tender age of fifteen. While I was busy battling acne and wondering whether my coming career as a rock star would be best served playing rhythm or lead guitar, Nazir was waging a freedom struggle. Whatever puerile teenage rebellion I was waging, Nazir has always been a dutiful son. Until now.

'My father said don't leave Afghanistan. Stay with us in spite of the hunger, war and everything,' he mumbles to his torn shoes, staring at the ground. 'I told them I want to save my children. I ignored my father's orders and now I've lost my daughter.'

My twin in age, yet my senior in every other way, Nazir has always been deeply respectful of his father's instructions. Even before my dad died in 1997, I wouldn't have been able to remember the last time I considered obeying him; his authority had been long annulled. But squatting before me, a father of three, one of whom is dead, two of whom are starving and now shaven, still defers to his elders. Patriarchy runs deep round here and obedience lasts long beyond childhood. Nazir's defiance was not inspired by the recklessness of youth but by the forces of war and weather. His family joined the swelling ranks of the mobile. They became the latest among the twelve million refugees around the world – not including the twenty-five million people displaced within their own countries. Nazir pours more tea and tells me about his journey.

It began by squeezing his family into a taxi in the middle of a cold December night. He paid a king's ransom to a local villager to drive them to Charikar, the nearest main town. The journey south to Kabul and then east to Jalalabad was spent huddled in the back of a truck with no cushions and no suspension. They walked the final seventy kilometres from Jalalabad to the border, saving the last of their money to bribe the guards at the Torkham border crossing. They were lucky to get through. Within weeks, Pakistan would lock its gates and hang out a sign: AFGHANS WELCOME NO MORE. Soon, Australia will do much the same.

I leave Nazir, his tea and his shaving, and set off to find what services, if any, are available. My crowd and I walk along deep, dry ditches that will soon be muddy streams when the monsoon comes. Thousands of families peek from beneath their hovels at my strange passing parade – each one of them with a subtly different spin on suffering. Old women fan lilting babies, young girls fan fading old men. I am greedy for their stories, curious to grasp this biblical exodus. This place is a story smorgasbord; every person has a tale of woe worthy of any prime-time news bulletin. Not that Jalozai is big news – the plight of Afghans, at home or on the move, has long been passé. But these thousands of unwilling travellers make me rethink my own journey and wonder what all my fuss has been about. For all my insecurities and discomforts, I have not known hardship. I have only known hard work, and rewarding work at that. I vow to never complain about my circumstances again, though I know my promise will only last until my next insignificant disaster.

The problem for the people of Jalozai – apart from the immediately obvious – is that, officially, this refugee camp does not exist. Pakistan will not allow the likes of Nazir, his family and the other seventy-nine thousand, nine hundred and ninety-five squatters to register as refugees. It insists the problem should be dealt with in Afghanistan itself. Those fleeing have been caught between the bureaucratic empires of Islamabad and the United Nations. Without Pakistan's authority to take down names and question refugees about why they came, the UN will largely withhold help. The standoff plunges Jalozai into suspended animation. No registration, no relief assistance.

I walk towards a clearing in this plastic wasteland, to

find a long line of mostly women, children and the elderly waiting patiently. It's a surprisingly beautiful scene – a pastiche of saris and shrouds in gorgeous greens and flaming reds. The women tug their embroidered veils over their faces at the sight of the camera, while the children smile and giggle. As if to compensate for their caked-on dirt, the kids' clothes are fantastic purples and pinks with patterns of flowers and animals. A young boy proudly marches around the ground in adult gumboots, which come up to his thigh. I film along the snaking queue and eventually discover a makeshift medical centre, run by Médecins Sans Frontières. It's the only clinic of its kind in the whole of Jalozai.

I poke my head around the tent flap and am waved in by Dr Assad Menapal, who looks more exhausted than the refugees he is treating. One by one they enter his yellow clinic with its dirt floor for a few minutes of basic care. Born in Afghanistan's central province of Wadak, Dr Menapal is tall, dark and hamstrung; because of the bureaucratic gridlock, he is one of just four doctors trying to treat these eighty thousand refugees. It's like trying to hold back the tide with a broom.

'You can see that one person per day is dying,' he sighs.

With the young and old most vulnerable, the sign on the wall – scribbled in Pashto and Persian – says it all: EQUIPMENT FOR DIGGING GRAVES AND MAKING COFFINS IS AVAILABLE IN THIS HOSPITAL.

Meanwhile, ten thousand more refugees are heading for Pakistan, the latest wave in more than two decades of bearing the burden of Afghanistan's refugees. When Afghanistan was the 1980s fulcrum of the Cold War, five million Afghans were living in Pakistan. Then, international donor funds poured into refugee camps, but when the Soviet Union withdrew its troops, the world lost interest in Afghanistan's homeless. With around two million still here,

Pakistan wants no more and insists Afghans must be helped in Afghanistan.

I have the guts of a good story and, as I march back through this maze to Nazir's tent, I begin tossing this travesty around my frying mind. Pakistan's seductive logic that the suffering Afghans should be helped in Afghanistan masks a sinister hypocrisy. By pumping the Taliban with arms, Pakistan is helping fuel a deadlocked civil war. All of Afghanistan's neighbours have a mischievous hand in the country's turmoil, but without Pakistan, the Taliban are little more than aspiring emperors with Allah's calling card. The suffering in Jalozai is inextricably tied to Pakistan's own selfish, short-sighted designs in Afghanistan. Jalozai is a symptom of bad men doing dirty deeds and good men doing nothing.

Nazir is as I left him, squatting in the dirt outside his flimsy castle. He smiles like a man battling madness: mouth going through the motions of happiness, hoping his mind will follow. Nasima does not attempt such deception – either for me or, more importantly, for herself. A few rows away, new arrivals are hoisting their plastic wigwams, coming to terms with the fact that their arduous journey has been barely worth it. We chat some more until lunchtime – mine, not theirs. I thank them, shake hands and politely decline another pot of tea.

On the way back to the car, I toss around the clichés of Jalozai, the same phrases used to describe refugee camps the world over, from Rwanda to the Balkans.

Living Graveyard.

Hell on Earth.

The World's Worst Refugee Crisis.

Jalozai is all of those things. And more. But somehow, it has not touched me as I feel it should. It *is* horrible, the stories wrist-slitting, the scale overwhelming, the bureaucratic obduracy infuriating. But the words don't match the pictures. They seem too lame and clichéd.

As the jamboree of refugees fade from outside my window and the fury of Peshawar comes into view, I realise the problem is not in my words but in my heart. My language is filled with emotion but I am not. I could not put myself into Nazir's battered shoes; I went through the motions but was barely affected. My response – to the stench, sights, discomfort – was physical, intellectual, not emotional. Something is hardening, the blisters on my soul forewarning callouses.

I have disappeared from Nazir's life as quickly as I dropped in, one of countless visitors – media, aid workers, dignitaries – to skip through Jalozai. The disaffected get used to well-fed western faces, the well-dressed and neatly pressed, affecting empathy, urging action.

Another visitor, sympathetic, ineffective.

He came.

He filmed.

And nothing changed.

After wrestling with my conscience, I resolve to push myself harder. I need to go back to see Afghanistan and its humanitarian disaster first hand – not just via a morning's easy drive to Jalozai. The ABC is supportive of the story and a UN friend hooks me up with two Afghan aid workers returning to Kabul. Together we take a taxi back to Taliban territory but their sparse English and my pathetic Pashto make for light conversation, so our pothole roller coasting is spent gasping at Afghanistan's devastating drought. Last year's half-full lakes are now parchment, the Kabul River is an even tamer trickle and trucks full of refugees pass us for a closed Pakistani border. But water still flows at the Hotel InterContinental and it's even hot. I shower away the day's blanket of dirt, which flows down the drain in rust-coloured rivers, and with thick, wet snorts, I flush out the oily black snot congealed in my nose. Clean and pleased to be in Kabul, I slide into sleep.

In the morning I go straight to the Foreign Ministry to register. They feign a warm welcome and send me to Hanafi, a one-time Afghan TV cameraman whose job now is to enforce the Taliban's ban on filming any form of life. He looks like a confused cartoon character, with the foolish face of a bearded Homer Simpson and a voice like Speedy Gonzalez.

'Ah, MEEEESTER JON-U-THUN!' Hanafi is sitting self-importantly behind his desk. 'Welcome back to Kaaaabul.'

I fill out my forms as he reminds me of the law of the land.

'Meeeester Jon-u-thun, you will be knowing the rules for journalists in the Islamic Emirate of Afghanistan?' I try not to roll my eyes. 'Noooo filming living things. Noooo filming at the soccer stadium. Noooo disobeying your official trans-lator.' Clearly, they remember my last visit. In fact, in light of the soccer stadium debacle, I am amazed they have given me a visa.

'Is there anything I *can* do, Hanafi?'

'Of course. Yoooo doooo as yooo are told.' Hanafi slaps his tummy and wobbles with laughter. When he has calmed down, he gets back to business. 'Tell me, what is your program?'

'I want to see the suffering of the Afghan people,' I begin in my best concerned tone. 'I want to see the effects of the drought and urge the world not to ignore this problem.' He nods solemnly as I try to appeal to the Taliban's deep sense of suffering international victimisation. 'I want to go to Hazarajat.'

Hanafi's face freezes. This will not go down well with his Taliban bosses. Over the centuries, the ethnic Hazaras have been Afghanistan's most deprived people but the Taliban have waged a bitter campaign against them that has verged on ethnic cleansing. The only recent media visit to the remote, mountainous region was a carefully controlled fly in and out to the destroyed Bamiyan Buddhas, proving to the world that they really had been blasted into oblivion. I am asking the impossible.

Hanafi looks down at my completed form, scribbles something across it and stands to go. 'Come back tomorrow.'

I come back tomorrow. And the next tomorrow. And the tomorrow after that. A week of tomorrows is not a lot in Taliban time but in news time, with deadlines ticking over hourly, it's an eternity. My bosses are patient and continue to support the story but soon I will have to revert to Plan B – hitching a ride on one of the big agency flying aid drops. It's a sure enough way to get a story, and the agencies are hungry for publicity to help raise funds and political support, but it's likely to be a short, formulaic exercise in media management. The likes of the UN and the International Committee of the Red Cross have kept Afghanistan alive through its darkest years but it's not the best story to do.

A small Afghan aid organisation saves the day. A friend at the UN suggests I contact a journalist-cum-aid worker by the name of Hamed Eqbal, who helps run Development and Humanitarian Assistance Afghanistan. His office is hard to find, squatting at the end of a muddy lane with the smallest of signs, and inside it's just as hard to find anyone around. I tentatively walk upstairs, towards the sound of fingers rapping on a laptop, where sits an Afghan Robert De Niro. Hamed is intense and intelligent, lives on a diet of Marlboros and Nescafé and has an ego the size of southern Afghanistan. I immediately like him and when he pulls some Foreign Ministry strings to secure permission for a trip to a nearby corner of Hazarajat, I like him even more. It's a big win but the regime is not giving too much away: I can leave Kabul for just one night and, of course, must take an official translator. That would be Hanafi. Hamed needs to look at some of his projects in the area so we agree to depart at dawn – Hamed De Niro, Homer Simpson Hanafi and Meeeester Jon-u-thun.

We farewell the upright cargo containers acting as an inglorious city gateway and climb into the Hindu Kush. The journey is slow but hypnotically beautiful. Bubbling streams weave through ageing orchards of apple and peach, crumbling mud fortresses hide behind eddies of dust, shades of aubergine and green turn to sepia and rust. We feast on a breakfast of fresh kebabs, lounging on a fire-warmed floor, and for lunch sit cross-legged on a carpet in the sun by the banks of a snowy river. A turn off to the right will take you to the blasted Bamiyan Buddhas, while on the left, an abandoned Soviet tank sits still stocked with live shells. Afghanistan is not for everyone, but those bound by its spell never get it out of their system. Its spell is cast on me.

The road levels and we arrive on the roof of the world in the district of Behsud. It's as far as we're allowed to go but much further than any journalist has been down this road recently. I am amazed to have come this far – and that any job could be so thrilling. I am in journalistic heaven, exploring a story largely untold, and intoxicated with exotica.

First stop: the local Taliban boss. Commander Bazil is an ethnic Hazara who fought the Taliban before joining them in 1998. He boasts the handsome, refined Mongolian features of the Hazaras, a proud people supposed to be descendants of Genghis Khan. His feline eyes are cruel and kind and Bazil rations smiles strategically. After tea and niceties, we pile into his war wagon four-wheel drive for a sightseeing tour of his drought-ravaged kingdom, driving at breakneck speed across moonscape mountaintops golden with afternoon sun. I pull out my camera, waiting to be banished; only to be encouraged.

'Film this area because it's beautiful,' Bazil barks, fancying himself as the Taliban's first ever film director. 'But the ground is all barren and the situation is very bad.'

I can't believe how film-friendly he is: the only thing getting in my way is his 'Allah' ornament – the Taliban's answer to Australia's fluffy dice – that swings from his rear vision mirror, an Arabic swirl flashing silver.

We visit villages inhabited only by those too old to move or too young to look for work in the towns or cities. Set amid tall poplar trees, they seem like rural retirement villages staffed by five-year-olds. Worm-infested water trickles from springs, more likely to bring sickness than health. There is no food, no seed, no stock. People have only themselves and Allah for survival.

'The Islamic Emirate of Afghanistan and its offices can only ensure security of the area,' Bazil tells me over tea, 'but financially it's got no money to solve the problems of the people.'

That job belongs to the outside world; and it stopped caring long ago. At least Bazil is honest – the veteran *mujahid* is concerned with fighting, not feeding. The shifting front line lies down the road in neighbouring Bamiyan district, though the victims of war can be seen right here in Behsud. We drive to a family compound deserted by its owners who have fled the drought, only to be occupied by war refugees from the nearby Faladi Valley where the Taliban are waging fresh offensives.

Pulling up in a screech of rubber that coughs out clouds of dust, Bazil sends me and Hamed in while, to my shock, he stays outside to press the flesh with the local men. He keeps Hanafi with him, leaving me to talk and film freely with those inside. I step into a darkened room half the size of a single car garage, to find nine families. Three scrappy half-eaten loaves of bread sit as the centre of attention: tonight's dinner, tomorrow's lunch and probably tomorrow's dinner also. The women and children sit pressed against the walls, as if to get as far as possible from the loaves' temptation; they stare like couch potatoes stare at a television. A toddler nibbles on grass roots. In a corner, a boy, perhaps twelve years old, squats with one hand pulling his knees tight to his chest, the other clasped across his mouth. Whatever he has seen should not be seen by anyone, certainly not a child. His silent trauma is harrowing.

I am drawn to an upstairs room by mumbles and rasping coughs. On the floor lies a young mother shrouded in rugs of brilliant colours, after walking for days through snow, nine months' pregnant. She survived the journey; her baby did not. It was stillborn shortly after she stumbled through these doors. Her seven-year-old daughter fans flies from her face; snot streams from her four-year-old son's nose like a faulty tap. They have stories of war, terror and Taliban abuses – all told with the slow, efficient speech of the malnourished. They watch me with exhaustion and suspicion. I watch them with media greed, charged with adrenalin, salted with sympathy. I must work quickly: Bazil could tell me to stop any moment. After a week in Kabul hustling and waiting, and what will end up being two days' driving, I film the story in twenty minutes.

I leave feeling shocked by the deadly nexus of war and drought and excited by what I have on film. Hamed's organisation has a small compound where we will spend the night and he suggests the ABC put on dinner for the commander and his cronies. I don't understand how a plump lamb can be found in the middle of a devastating drought, but in Afghanistan, it can, and apparently with ease. It is slaughtered and stewed, the men of the district descend and, without writing invitations or making calls, I am having the Taliban to dinner.

Twenty men. Five bowls. And a lot of bread. We sit around the edge of a rectangular room, scooping greasy gruel with chunks of *naan*, several men slurping from the same bowl. Sharing is everything – even if it means disease. But I've been lucky so far and surrendered long ago to whatever intestinal fate awaits me. There are smaller bowls also, with a hoof or two swimming in stew, draped in leathery flesh. It's a delicious scene of men and meat, beards and turbans. I've never seen a dinner party like it, let alone hosted one. And there is no relaxed lingering or conversation with food. It's time to shovel – perhaps in an effort to eat as much from your shared bowl as possible. Talk can come later.

I have been sharing my bowl with a wispy-bearded Hazara with terrible teeth and a tall, handsome Pashtun named Khurram, who works with Hamed. Khurram has been overseeing the trucking of wheat to remote villages in preparation for winter, and, unlike our other dining companion, he has a glorious set of teeth shown off regularly with a broad and gentle smile.

'Actually, everyone calls me "Happy",' he says, smiling, as if to prove the point. However, the nickname brings responsibility in this cheerless land. 'It's not easy,' he admits sheepishly, 'to be happy all the time. But I try. I try my best. On the outside we're smiling. On the inside we're crying.'

Khurram is an architect by training and a poet by nature. In a land where buildings are bombed, not built, he trucks relief wheat while, in the backyard of his mind, drafting plans for glorious homes in the Kabul of his dreams. War doesn't just kill and crumble, it crushes dreams, it collapses the imagination. We talk about war and peace, Afghanistan and apathy.

'Tell me,' Khurram asks, 'why does the world care more about the destruction of the Bamiyan Buddhas than the destruction of our people? What the Taliban did to the

Buddhas was very, *very* bad. We are all ashamed. But the world cares more about statues than starving people?'

I have only glib comments about the shocking symbolism of blasting the Buddhas, and Afghanistan being just one of many humanitarian disasters competing for the media's attention.

'Ah yes, that is life in the west, everyone is competing, everyone moves so fast. I lived in America once. You see,' he frowns, wiping the last globules of grease from his fingers, 'a man's soul travels only as fast as a camel can walk. No faster. In the west, everyone moves too fast to care about anything.'

Khurram's camel-riding enlightenment is interrupted by Commander Bazil unceremoniously standing to leave, taking his entourage with him. His exit abruptly ends our little dinner party and we retire to the sleeping room. Seven of us lie around the *Bukhari*, a wood-burning stove, though I'm the only one who tries to rest. The other men spend most of the night smoking Marlboros, drinking tea and telling jokes in Pashto. I fall asleep choking on thick clouds of smoke, with the sound of hoarse chuckles in my ears and the gentle pad of camels' feet in my dreams.

The next morning, our car tumbles back down the mountain to Kabul, the driver hiding my camera tapes in the floor cavity beneath the gear stick in case we get searched at the Taliban checkpoints. We do, but the tapes stay hidden and the story goes to air, capturing Afghanistan's worsening burden, making me feel better but, ultimately, helping no-one. Khurram is right: the world doesn't care about Afghanistan. Maybe I should stop bothering and go back to New Delhi to see my wife. It's not as if anyone would notice that I *hadn't* done the story; nobody else is. Besides, Australia seems to care less and less. When four hundred and thirty-eight asylum seekers, rescued by the Norwegian ship *The Tampa*, are refused entry into Australia, signs of any public protest and compassion are eclipsed during an election campaign fanned by fears of 'illegal immigrants' and 'queue jumpers'. The majority of them are Afghans, of whom most are ethnic Hazaras.

It's not the suffering of Afghans – or how the west receives those who try to flee – that soon brings the world's media back to Afghanistan. It's the threat of the death penalty being handed down to eight foreign Christian aid workers, including two Australians, who are accused of using their charity work as a front for proselytising. Trying to convert Afghans to Christianity sits high among prohibitions governing the conduct of foreign aid workers, which also forbid them from eating pork in public, playing loud music, and 'walking nude'. Along with the Australians, four Germans, two Americans and sixteen of their Afghan colleagues have been arrested – and fears for the Afghans' future are even greater.

The story causes a media rush and by August Kabul's two hundred-room InterContinental Hotel is crammed with all of a dozen journalists. I've rarely seen another guest in the hotel and, with journalists from the *New York Times* and Germany's ZDF TV network, it feels as close to fun as you'll get under the Taliban. This unscheduled peak season is also a bonanza for hotel staff, who compete for our favour and tips, racing to carry our notebooks and pens or filling our rooms with flowers till they resemble hothouses. Apart from the comedy of staff antics, there is little relief from the daily drudgery of treading from the Foreign Ministry to the UN guesthouse where Australian, German and American diplomats endure a humiliating waiting game. One of the world's most isolated and sanctioned regimes suddenly has an audience and it's in no hurry to send it home. This will be a clash of civilisations fought on Taliban terms.

The further the regime slides into international isolation, the greater its appetite for symbols of legitimacy. The Foreign Ministry has been given a makeover: new white curtains flutter across tall French doors; a computer sits grandly in the reception room, though no-one seems to know how to use it; on the walls hang intricate carvings reinforcing the Taliban's ultimate legitimacy:

'THERE IS NO DEITY BUT ALLAH. MOHAMMED IS THE APOSTLE OF ALLAH.'

The regime marks the anniversary of Afghanistan's independence, won from Britain in 1919, with its most pretentious show of authority since taking power nearly five years earlier. Tanks and armoured trucks, scores of war wagons packed with fighters in flowing turbans, stinger missiles and rocket-propelled grenades are paraded before tens of thousands of Kabulis. Crowds clamber onto battered buildings to catch the best view of this extraordinary display of ragtag totalitarianism. There are songs of triumph (without musical accompaniment, of course), banners announce 'AFGHANISTAN IS THE GRAVEYARD OF INVADERS AND COLONIALISTS', and the Taliban official party display the arrogance of men who believe they will rule forever.

The Taliban wait for no man. Except CNN. After weeks of stalling, the TV-shy regime fires up its infamous justice process once CNN's Nic Robertson arrives to take the scoop of the self-described world news leader, and on a shining autumn morning, we are summoned to the Kabul Supreme Court to see the eight foreign detainees appear. In a small room with a rich red carpet and intimidating swords on the wall, thick texts in glass bookcases and about a dozen senior judges thumbing worry beads, Taliban-style justice gets underway. The eight foreigners are led in and sit on chairs at the front of the room, and if they held any hopes for a fair trial, they are dissolved when Chief Justice Noor Mohammed Saqib opens his mouth.

'This court shall prove your guilt,' he declares from behind his imposing desk as the other dozen judges nod and stroke their grey beards.

Over the next half hour, the words 'show trial' bounce around everybody's brain. The scene would be laughable if the stakes weren't so serious, and as the detainees are led out of the room, Diana Thomas, the bolshier of the two Australians, hisses: 'Pathetic! Just pathetic!'

The verdict may be certain but the sentence and the timing of the trial are in the lap of Allah. When I return to the hotel, some journalists have already decided to leave, figuring that any verdict is at least a fortnight away. I decide to stay for another week, until my visa runs out. I am working on a people-smuggling story, tying in with the ongoing *Tampa* crisis, and, besides, who cares about a couple more days? I finish my posting in three months and this will be my last story in Afghanistan. Perhaps the last time I will ever be in this magical, maddening land.

The Taliban make its media guests feel all the more welcome by placing us under hotel arrest for a night and detaining our official translators. The Chief Justice has decided he doesn't like cameras outside his court and, just to show the regime is serious, a few rounds of artillery punch into the hill just behind the hotel. We are later told it is just routine artillery practice but I've never seen it before and the timing seems strangely coincidental.

Once released from our hotel straitjacket, I return to the daily tedium of office visits, tea and talk. Stepping out of the

Foreign Ministry into its garden still damp with morning dew, I realise this has become a mainstay of my world. In fact, I'm losing touch with the world. Sarah is travelling in southern India with friends and we've not spoken in weeks. There is no TV – my only links beyond this place are my shortwave radio and colleagues in Sydney. I don't even know what day it is. Shit! My mum's birthday!? I glance at my watch with relief. Thank God, I've got ten days to go. Who knows what could happen in ten days? The trial might be over and I might even be back in New Delhi.

There's nothing to worry about.

Today is September 11.

CHAPTER 20

SEPTEMBER 11 FROM THE OTHER SIDE

September 11
Midday

It's often unsettling when Taliban officials smile. At the Foreign Ministry they're grinning and hugging each other as though they'd just won the football final. What could possibly be making these usually stern-faced rulers so joyous? Death – or rumours of one, at least. And not just any loss of life. Kabul is abuzz with talk that the legendary Lion of Panjshir, Ahmed Shah Massoud, has been assassinated; that two Arabs posing as journalists detonated a bomb disguised in their camera. If true, it would remove the one man whose charisma and military genius unites the loosely allied anti-Taliban forces. Without Massoud standing in their way, the Taliban could finally seize control of the last, defiant ten per cent of Afghanistan. They have already launched a major offensive against the front north of Kabul in Takhar Province, to capitalise on a leaderless Northern Alliance – though reports of Massoud's death, while firming, are inconclusive. So, I spend the afternoon working contacts around Kabul before heading back to the hotel to write my stories for the morning radio programs. A totally Taliban Afghanistan may be about to be born.

5.29 pm

The hotel lift is broken and I am leaping up the stairs, three at a time, panting and sweating, in order to catch the BBC *World News* with the latest on Massoud. I rush straight through to my balcony and turn on my scratchy shortwave radio as the news theme begins:

Coming up – a passenger aircraft has crashed into the World Trade Center building in New York City. Black smoke and flames are bellowing from the tower.

A court in Australia has ruled illegal that country's policy of turning away boat people trying to find asylum. The government is fighting the ruling . . .

And mystery in the chess world: is an anonymous internet player Bobby Fisher?

First the world news . . .

Reports are coming in from the United States that a passenger aircraft has crashed . . .

5.45 pm

The BBC is reporting that a second plane has hit the south tower. I rush across the hall to the CNN room, where Nic Robertson has the CNN website up on his laptop through his satellite phone. He is gasping as I walk into his room. The site is jammed with traffic, the screen frozen on a far-off photo of a flaming north tower; a candle over a glistening autumn Manhattan morning. A handful of journalists huddle with an ear to the radio and an eye on the website. I can't believe that this is the most dramatic event of my life and I am stuck in the most media-unfriendly corner of the planet. There must be a better place to see what's happening; I am of the television generation and need to see this to believe it. I know where to go.

'Where are you off to?' they ask, as I walk out the door.

'To the UN staff house!' I shout, charging down the hall. It's the only place in Kabul allowed a TV.

6.00 pm

It's a beautiful autumn evening. The air is clear but there's just enough dust to give the setting sun a syrupy glow as it slumps behind the mountains. Kabul is oblivious to the drama in America: the ban on TV slows things from spreading and, besides, it's still preoccupied with the fate of Massoud. There is something strangely fitting about Kabul's ignorance. The world has been oblivious to the suffering of these people for years. Their despondent faces have been all but absent from US televisions – and now, as American anguish stares out at the world, Afghans will miss the show. For a moment, the world seems bizarrely in balance.

6.10 pm

I tumble into the UN, where a tight horseshoe of people is hunched around the TV, stunned and silent. The news presenter's voice greets me as I enter.

'And there are reports that a plane has also flown into the Pentagon . . .'

Now the world feels very out of balance. Everything seems possible and none of it is good. As an act of despair or good sense, somebody has opened the only bar in the country and is serving whisky and gin. They're settling into a Tuesday night of TV viewing like no other. I drink coffee.

It is hard to see what is happening. The UN satellite only gets the BBC and its New York camera position is far away on a highrise office block in the north of Manhattan. The south tower is completely obscured by its twin. We are locked into the one shot, which makes it look all too remote and silent to be real. I cannot see or hear the shower of boiling debris, the blast of fuel and fire. For once in my life, all I want is American news.

Ian MacKinnon, my Irish freelance colleague, flaps through the doors, his jaw hitting the floor as he swivels towards the TV and absorbs the picture. The Americans in this room are ashen. The US diplomat and the parents here for the arrested aid workers are not only wondering what is happening to their homeland but what will happen to their children. They drink Coke.

Ian breaks the silence.

'We're in the second most dangerous place in the world.' It's the first thing he says – the first thing *anyone* has said. It's what we've all been thinking but could not find the courage to voice. Already, everyone is assuming this gruesome carnage is the work of America's most wanted man. Osama bin Laden. He lives here in Afghanistan. And here we are. We all know Washington will want his blood and once again Afghan blood will be shed.

6.30 pm

An eruption of smoke billows from behind the north tower. The BBC has still got only the one, distant camera and we can't see the cause of the plume.

'What is *that*?!?!' we gasp in chorus.

It appears as though a massive bomb has exploded in central Manhattan. Nothing seems impossible.

I've got to ring Sydney. It's still hours from the dawn bulletin but I need to know what they want from me. I also need some contact with the outside world. Walking out of the UN, I'm shocked to see it's dark. I'd been so glued to the TV I did not notice the day disappear. Driving through Kabul, the streets are deserted, but for the begging widows and their children – blue ghosts in the night.

8.00 pm

I try calling Sydney but the phone won't connect. The satphone is so temperamental; it's driving me nuts. I turn on the radio to find out that that horrid Manhattan pall billowing as I left the UN was the south tower collapsing. And in the meantime, the north tower has also imploded.

The whole world seems to be tumbling down. And here I am, in a city that has long turned to dust, with only a radio and a sat-phone that won't connect. I leave my door open and steadily my room fills with journalists coming to listen to the radio. Hotel staff also stick their heads in the door. There is nothing to do but sit on the bed and listen. And listen. I feel like a character in one of those old black and white photos of families leaning into the wireless, listening intently as World War II begins. For millions around the world, September 11 will be tattooed on their minds as a defining television moment; for me it will be a radio memory.

9.00 pm

The White House says it's too early to say who's responsible but Osama bin Laden is fast becoming the centre of attention. Al-Qaeda and bin Laden are invariably described as 'shadowy' and 'secretive'; adjectives that will soon become very worn. But as Washington tries to grasp just who is the enemy, it is already clear the mighty, wounded empire will respond with force and fury.

Copies of Ahmed Rashid's *Taliban* are flying around the room. Every journalist is thumbing through, cramming everything they can about the al-Qaeda leader. There is unspoken regret about having not paid him more attention earlier – not that he's been inviting the media to his bunker for a beer and a briefing. I keep dialling Sydney, and when I eventually get through, I am whisked straight to the TV studio for a live phone cross. It is 2.30 in Sydney and the ABC is streaming CNN, interspersed with some of our correspondents. Ahead of me, Tim Palmer reports from Jerusalem, where some Palestinians have been celebrating the attacks.

9.30 pm

The Taliban move to make a preemptive media strike. On word that the Foreign Minister, Mullah Wakil Ahmed Mutawakil, will hold a press conference, we gather downstairs in the dining room. He strolls in, as impenetrable as when I met him in Kandahar nearly two years ago; his soft facial features, flowing beard and neat, white turban are apparently unflustered by the bedlam of the last few hours. He condemns the attacks, asserts that the Taliban have nothing to do with them and that Osama bin Laden could not design such an audacious and sophisticated operation from a country as isolated and impoverished as Afghanistan. There must be clear evidence against bin Laden before the Taliban will hand him over. Well, that's what my reports say, anyway. I have to condense the long-winded rhetoric of the Foreign Minister; this maligner of the modern media is no master of the short, sharp grab.

'Our policy was very clear, even from the beginning,' he drones in measured tones. 'We have criticised and will now criticise terrorism in all its forms. It has not been proven that Arabs are behind such incidents and even now it has not been proven that Arabs are behind them.'

Incredibly, there are hardly any questions – the modern media seems too stunned to try. I attempt to fill the void but my head is noisy and scrambling for clarity, so my questions are clumsy. I'm glad this is not live, I think to myself. But, unknown to me, CNN is sending out the press conference live via video-phone and my very rambling questions are getting very global coverage. Not a great way to impress the folks back home.

10.00 pm

The curfew falls and, with nowhere to go till dawn, I order tea and sit down to write a stream of radio reports for the morning bulletins. I want to call Sarah but she is uncontactable, still travelling somewhere in southern India. It feels like ages since we saw each other. I wonder if she knows.

September 12
Midnight

Spring dawn is breaking in Sydney. I imagine my mum, waking up, hearing the news, worrying. I wonder what is happening in New York; try to picture the desperate scramble by people with missing husbands, wives, children, lovers inside the towers. How can two towers, each one hundred and ten storeys, just collapse? How do they fall? Straight down like a sandcastle? Sideways? What does it look like? My mind is mangled with thoughts of what must be happening in Manhattan. I fear for friends who live in New York and I fear for friends in Afghanistan. Already, there is talk of retaliation.

2.15 am

In stark contrast to New York, there is nothing more to report here. I've fed the breakfast radio beast and it is suddenly surprisingly quiet. Sydney says I should get some sleep, rest while I can; before the war begins. But I don't want to. I am wired, firing with the possibilities of the coming days and weeks. My beloved drug adrenalin has been on free flow all night and I will need a lot more where it came from; a marathon is about to unfold before me. Sleep seems like the strangest idea in the world, so I shower to slow down and listen to the radio, which only winds me back up. I turn it off, and climb under the covers.

BANG! BANG! BANG!

A thick fist is thumping on my door. It's attached to a panicked voice.

'IT'S STARTED! THEY'VE STARTED!'

I swing open the door to a red-faced, shaking Ian and I have no idea what he's talking about.

'THEY'VE STARTED BOMBING ALREADY!' he shouts as he bounces off the walls down the hall, swearing along the way. 'FUCK! FUCK! FUCK!'

I run across the hall to the CNN room, which faces east over Kabul, to see the sky exploding with flashes and flares. It looks like Sydney on New Year's Eve. Two aircraft are thundering missiles across the sky, hitting what looks like the airport and a major ammunition depot. The depot takes on a tortured, flaming life all its own.

It's almost beautiful and certainly exciting. Our make-shift media family stands on CNN's balcony, looking at the explosions, then at each other, the explosions, each other, the explosions, each other. We scramble for answers, feeding off our ignorance. CNN's Kamal Haider is the most confident voice, and reckons the aircraft are too high to be Northern Alliance helicopters. It must be American aircraft making an immediate retaliatory attack. I reckon he knows more about this stuff than I do.

2.30 am

It's 8 am in Sydney. I race to my room and phone the *AM* studio. Miraculously, the sat-phone connects and I'm put straight onto air. The presenter, Linda Mottram, sounds strong and clear in my headphones; my voice sounds weak and faint in my head. I don't feel scared – just a fresh thrust of adrenalin. Everything seems to be moving in slow motion and at a thousand miles an hour. I start by painting a picture of the explosions for listeners, then I hear an odd knock. At first I think it's someone at the door but it's closer than that. Much closer. As I talk, I glance down to see my legs shaking like twigs. My knees are striking a hollow, involuntary rhythm: bony castanets in syncopation with the sound of blood pumping through my brain. Now I am scared, my mind following the lead of my body. My mind and mouth divorce each other, and I start sprouting the uneducated guesswork we all formulated on the balcony:

'It is possible that it is related to the civil war. But you have to see it in the circumstances of the last few hours. You'd have to put your money on the fact that this may well be some form of retaliatory strike from Washington, in particular because of what seems to be the magnitude of it, the high altitude of the plane, and what seems to be extremely closely targeted firing as well at this stage.'

The sat-phone drops out. It's divine intervention – the god of journalism preventing me from speculating any further. My fingers dial frantically to get back on air but I can't get through.

2.57 am

Three minutes to the end of the program, I'm back on air for a brief update. I've had time to reconsider, and now I choose my words more carefully. Soon, the Pentagon will deny any hand in the attacks. It is Northern Alliance vengeance for the assassination of Massoud – though his death is yet to be confirmed. I need to keep calm and measured and get my facts straight. At home, I might have had a drink but there's no chance of that here, and through clenched teeth I steal some fretful sleep. The bombing stops but I can still hear it in my dreams.

5.00 am

The sound of the alarm clock drills into my head and I sit bolt upright in bed, trying to piece together events from the last twelve hours. I'm not sure if it was real or a nightmare. I reach over and turn on the radio, which confirms I am imagining nothing. I ring Sydney and start working on the lunchtime and evening bulletins.

6.30 am

At breakfast, all the journalists are talking exit strategies; they've been told to leave by their bosses. Last night's bombing may be over but the US could start retaliating any minute. By the time my tea and toast arrive, I learn the only ones not told to go are CNN, the *New York Times* – and me. The United Nations is putting on special flights to evacuate non-Afghan staff tomorrow and there will be room for journalists. I throw down breakfast, and jam to the back of my mind the question of whether I will stay or go, then I head into Kabul to sample the rumour mill.

Driving downtown, I wonder how many people in this city have spent the night huddled over their radios, swinging on every word from the BBC or Voice of America. Perhaps some have even seen the television images on clandestine sets with satellite dishes. It's an irony that one of television's defining moments has been orchestrated by a movement sheltered by a regime that despises TV.

I head straight for Chicken Street, Kabul's main commercial strip, where carpet traders, trinket sellers, jewellery merchants and conmen are clustered in doorways, chatting animatedly. It's the easiest place to measure opinion as most of the men here speak English, so I nudge into a group, my recorder rolling. They're bracing for another war.

'Of course everybody are afraid from this attacks,' moans a man with sheepish eyes and a crooked frown. 'It's so dangerous!' His friend picks up the theme: 'We're all concerned because, you know, we have been in our fighting circumstance for twenty years and we are afraid of this . . .' his voice peters out as he contemplates what the wrath of the world's superpower might mean. A pregnant pause hangs among us, as we wonder whether Kabul could be bombed to whatever existed before the Stone Age. I ask if they know much about Osama bin Laden. 'Afghanistan people know him,' sheep eyes replies, 'but don't like him.'

Amid the nervousness, there is real empathy for the people of America. Afghans know all too well what it means to lose loved ones to senseless violence. They've been living with terror for years.

8.30 am

I leave the chatter of Chicken Street to do my usual circuit of Kabul contacts, though it's a total waste of time. Nobody is at the Foreign Ministry – perhaps Taliban officials have already fled to take refuge in Pakistan. Colleagues I visit know little more than I do. As I head back to the hotel to write my story for the evening bulletin, I am fatalistic; nothing is in my control.

10.00 am

The Sydney newsroom sounds like it's in meltdown; I can hear the mayhem down the phone. Because my camera has died, I don't have a single fresh frame of footage for one of the biggest news nights ever, and I am completely dependent on the CNN material. My story has 'CNN exclusive' blazoned across it and the only way we can prove I am really in Kabul is with a piece to camera. Mercifully, Germany's ZDF TV cameraman lends me his digicam and I film a very rough-looking piece with the sun high in the sky and casting shade across my face that makes me look like Dracula with a five o'clock shadow. My kingdom for a cameraman. Now I just need to file the story.

11.30 am

I bang on the iron gates of the Arabic news network, Al-Jazeera's, Kabul office. There is no answer for what seems to be an eternity, thanks to the world's slowest watchman. Finally, they let me in and I race through to the control room to feed the tape via satellite.

'Shoes!' The Al-Jazeera technician is yelling at me to take mine off. I race back to the front door, remove my shoes and run back into the control room, pulling the digicam tape out of my pocket.

'We can't play that,' the technician sneers.

'What do you mean?' I sneer back.

'We do not play out DV. Only Beta – SP or SX but only Beta!'

I can't believe the biggest news story in contemporary television is being reduced to an argument over video-tape formats. The ABC has already booked a twenty-minute satellite feed at exorbitant expense. Al-Jazeera's standard rates out of Kabul are ridiculous and they've hiked them even further overnight. So, faced with the prospect of sending nothing at all, I am close to overload.

'Can't we dub it to Beta?' I ask.

'No problem! We will just invoice you.'

'Invoice me? What for?'

'Editing.'

I am about to flip out. 'We're dubbing a twenty-second piece to camera!'

But blessed with a monopoly, they've got me over a barrel and bill for the minimum: one hour. After bickering and bartering we finally feed the most expensive piece to camera in ABC history; I have just spent all of the organisation's international coverage budget for the next week.

I step out to the main office to prepare for a live cross to follow the story. Apart from an opportunity to provide the latest information, it will hopefully reinforce that I really am in Kabul and don't work for CNN. As I scribble some notes, I'm distracted by a couple of young staff who sit glued to the TV, playing and then replaying something on video.

'Play it again!' one of them squeals.

'Ooooooofffff!' they gasp.

At first, I catch just a flash in the corner of my eye. Then, I see in full horror what the world has been watching:

United Flight 175 charging into the south tower, swallowed in a wall of glass, and then exploding into an inferno. It is far worse than the picture my mind had been painting.

The guys replay it – who knows how many times.

It's already playing in high rotation in my mind.

1.30 pm

Ideally, a live cross from Kabul would feature an expansive vista of the city as backdrop. However, Al-Jazeera has as its neighbour a tsar in the Department of the Promotion of Virtue and Prevention of Vice who has prohibited live crosses on the Al-Jazeera roof. It's offensive for him to have to watch such infidel activity, so I must stand behind a high fence, in front of an anonymous wall. I could be out the back of the ABC in Sydney.

As I stare down the camera, my mind is numbed, shocked, sleep-deprived and adrenalin-sozzled. In another baptism of fire, this is my first live cross for TV. I have little idea what to do. The image of the second plane ploughing into the south tower is flashing behind my eyes.

There's a problem with the satellite booking – it's on, it's off, on, off. IT'S ON! Thirty seconds and YOU'RE ON! Sydney's news bulletin crackles into my ear, faint and scratchy. I can hear President Bush down the line:

'The deliberate and deadly attacks which were carried out yesterday against our country, were more than acts of terror,' he declares. 'They were acts of war.'

Tony Eastley, the presenter, crosses to me:

'Jonathan, already the US has said anyone sheltering a terrorist will be treated as a terrorist themselves. There must be a lot of tension in Kabul at the moment.'

I'm skydiving – and don't know if the parachute works. I'm talking, breathing, talking, not screaming:

'Quiet nervousness, Tony, is probably the best way to describe it . . .'

That is, nervousness in Kabul, not just in my gut. I finish my answer, then silence. My earpiece is dead. I don't know if I am on air or off. Did they hear me? Has Tony gone to the next story? My brain crashes. What should I do? I really would rather have had a lesser story for my first live cross. Are there any more surprises to come? Reboot. Brain is back. I'm guessing the time it takes for my brain to reconnect is as long as it would take Tony to ask a second question, so I speak into the void, and hope that I am still on air.

'Tony, I'm having a little trouble hearing you but I think I should add that the United Nations has been mentioning that it will be evacuating all of its non-essential staff . . .'

The parachute does work. The producer tells me I was still on and that the timing worked. The viewers would be none the wiser to my having been unable to hear a thing. Perhaps it's beginner's luck.

However, I can't get cocky – there is no room in my head for self-congratulation right now. All I can think about is whether or not I should leave, or if I'll be made to leave. I don't want to go, but quickly chat to my boss, who is understandably concerned that the UN is leaving and that I might stay. I suggest we take it day by day.

2.00 pm

I head to the UN staff house to check on the parents of the detained Americans and find them looking more glum than ever before. They face the harrowing prospect of joining the diplomats on the UN flight tomorrow. One father is angrily ignoring the advice to leave.

'I'm not leaving this place without my daughter!' he shouts. 'If we bomb this place and my daughter is bombed, I want to be bombed too.'

Their desperate faces are just more pieces in the surreal, insane jigsaw of the last twenty-four hours. Yesterday, the trial of their children was the story; today, their plight is barely a sentence.

4.00 pm

I call the ABC's *Lateline* studio for a phone cross.

'You're on soon,' they tell me.

'I've only got a little bit of battery left in my phone,' I tell them. 'Shall I call you back?'

'No! You're on in a minute!'

Twenty minutes later, I'm still on hold and I feel like throwing the phone against a wall. Clearly Sydney is in disarray but my conditions here are not exactly a breeze. As if by miracle or to prove me paranoid, my battery holds out better than I expected. They cross to me.

The battery dies and my cross dies with it. My fury is phenomenal. I know it's only a story and I know the story is not me but I can't control my outrage. I scream into the sandy sky, which makes a spectacle of me but fixes nothing.

Cut off and worn out, I take the long route back to the hotel, travelling aimlessly through the late afternoon streets, soaking up the city's haunting beauty and perhaps the last days of that bizarre social experiment that has been the Taliban. Along the banks of the Kabul River, women do laundry, their *burqas* thrown back above their heads, billowing behind them as they go about their domestic duty in the same way as their mothers and grandmothers before them. It seems many things in Afghanistan are destined to never change; then, in a tectonic shudder, some things change with shocking force. The more things change, the more they stay the same. My eyes greedily drink up this empty, exhausted city; I am filing Kabul in my mind, so that at least I will never forget it.

5.30 pm

The elevator is still not working. I climb the stairs and open my door to find a ringing sat-phone. It's Sarah. She sounds drained and distressed at the end of a line that is scratchy thanks to India and wobbly care of the satellite. She's read about last night's bombings and has seen the ABC website.

'How are you?' I can hear the exhaustion wrought of worry in her question.

'Oh, I'm *fine*!' I try to sound as though I've been sitting by the pool all day; if there was one.

Her tired tone switches swiftly to fear. 'Jonathan, when are you *getting out of there*?'

'The attacks weren't that bad,' I offer. 'It was just the Northern Alliance.' The distinction will offer her no comfort. I realise we're having the same incongruous conversation we had when I was near Kargil in Kashmir. The circumstances are different but the themes are the same. Danger. Fear. Torn loyalties.

'Pleease,' she pleads. 'You . . .'

Silence. Another connection dies on me. It's the fourth crucial call to collapse on me since last night but this time I'm thankful.

Sarah was calling from a public phone and won't call back. It's a relief: partly because I don't know how to say I might stay and partly because I don't need her anxiety. An impossible sense of dilemma is rising in my throat and in my ears, The Clash is back – should I stay or should I go? I want to do right; but by whom? I love the trust my bosses place in me to make decisions but I also envy those colleagues who have been ordered to leave. For them, there is no dilemma. In three years I have gone from option overload to just plain overload.

I am too tired, too wired to think clearly. And I'm torn by conflicting emotions and desires. Ambition, duty, fear and ego are churning throughout me. In search of some sort of structure, I formulate a rough plan: as long as I can be fifty per cent confident of getting out safely, then I'll stay. I file my stories and fall asleep.

September 13
1.30 am

The sat-phone screams into my dreams. I flip out of bed. 'Putting you through to the studio,' the Sydney voice says. Suddenly, the presenter, Richard Morecroft is in my ear and I'm on air, being asked questions about which I know nothing. A special breakfast news program has been hastily set up and nobody bothered to tell me. I answer the questions, hang up the handset and fall back down on the bed. I crash back to sleep, not sure I was really awake.

6.00 am

I rise to the noise of colleagues packing bags and wheeling gear down the hall. 'I'll stay,' I tell myself, 'take it day by day.' I stick my head out the door as CNN's Kamal Haider walks past.

'Hey, Jonathan!' he grins. 'Are you staying or going?'

'I'm staying.'

'That's the way!' He slaps me on the back. 'Hang out with us, and have some fun.'

Fun is not quite the word I would use . . . but whatever. I walk down to breakfast to find a foyer full of people arguing over bills and realise I've been here for weeks and not paid a single Afghani. After breakfast I clear my account, which leaves me with just two hundred and twenty dollars. That will last me a couple more days in Kabul or it will pay for a seat on the UN flight.

I embrace journalists who have become close friends in this bizarre hothouse, then head back to my room, contemplating the wisdom of my staying. Peter calls from New Delhi and gets straight to the point.

'Please, *sahib*,' his voice is imploring like I have never heard before. 'You *must* leave. It is not safe. Please, *sahib*, we *very* worried.' His appeal cuts through me like a knife.

Peter is honest, hardworking and honourable but he never, ever, *ever* tells me what to do. In caste, class and corporate-ladder conscious India, the hierarchy is everything – and that means not telling the correspondent when or where he should stay and go. His audacity born of anxiety thumps me like a punch. I have been too busy and consumed by events to appreciate what may soon happen to Afghanistan. I have been unmoved by the world's fears of war. Is this suicide? Maybe I'm being a cowboy.

'Peter,' I finally reply, 'I'll think about it.'

I hang up and sit on the edge of the bed, assessing my situation. I have no camera, no money, no flak jacket and nobody.

7.30 am

I grab my wallet and passport and race to the UN flight office. It's a scene of organised chaos; as though the whole western world is trying to flee Kabul. Journalists, aid workers, the three visiting diplomats and parents of the detainees, are all scrambling with bags as the staff carefully weigh and tag every item of luggage. The guy at the weighing scales gives me a confused look.

'My bags are at the hotel,' I explain. 'Are there any seats left?'

'Just one,' he says, 'but hurry!'

I step into the office and approach the bookings' desk. The last seat. Stay or go? Courage or cowardice? Hero or zero?

As if in slow motion, I watch my hand pass my last dollars over, then fill out the form and sign on the dotted line. I can't believe these fingers are making this decision, apparently oblivious to the ruckus going on in my conscience.

Over my shoulder, the Al-Jazeera correspondent Taysir Alouni is trying to buy tickets for his family. He is staying but they are going. As Taysir walks out the door, an Afghan UN staff member glares after him.

'Fucking Arabs,' he hisses. 'They have fucked this country right up.'

I race back to the hotel, packing bags with an abandon I'll no doubt regret. Clothes are crammed into the camera bag, cords are stuffed into my suitcase. As I tumble through the foyer, tossing my room key on the bench, the staff are incredulous.

'You're leaving, Mr Jonathan?' they ask. 'Pray for us. We don't know what will happen, when the bombs will fall or where. We miss you. You are one of us, you are Afghan. We thought you would stay forever, through good and bad.'

So did I.

Midday

After filing my last-minute report from the tarmac at Kabul airport, I board a plane I don't want to catch. My stomach is a tangle of thick, twisted knots as I watch the debris of planes sprayed around the skirt of the runway disappear beneath me, and, climbing above this rusty, dusty city, my conscience is as battered as the rocketed remains of the mud homes below.

I am abandoning a people, a story, a place in a time of need. I feel like a coward and a cop-out; no correspondent has built a career out of fleeing the action.

I tell myself I have no option.

I don't believe it.

CHAPTER 21

SEND IN THE CLOWNS

When the sputtering taxi drops me off at my Pakistan hotel, I am greeted by a storm of fishing vests, pressed chinos and glistening hiking boots. It looks like a fly-fishing convention. It's the international media circus. As I weave through the foyer of Islamabad's Marriott Hotel, there is gruff, tough talk of weapons and war. Testosterone hangs so thick you could cut the air with the Swiss army knives holstered onto every bloke's belt.

I stand gobsmacked in the midst of this cyclone. Even in normal circumstances Islamabad seems like a first-world metropolis after Kabul, but now I am aghast at the frenzy before me. I feel as if I've been hauled from the Taliban *Mad Max* set to a Hollywood press call. It doesn't feel right. I resented the world's journalists invading *my patch* in Kathmandu, but now I feel completely conquered. This humdrum hotel in this sterile city is being overrun by a TV tribe that's migrated from New York, Tokyo, Moscow, Santiago, and in the less than forty-eight hours since the attacks in the United States, it has moved with breathtaking speed and force. This is not a mere media pack, this is a complete nation; and I'm about to become part of it.

I sidestep the stacks of flight cases and camera gear as I head for the reception desk, where the attendant seems relieved to see a familiar face.

'Yes, of course, Mr Harley,' he smiles, 'we can always find a room for a regular guest.'

'I'll take three,' I reply, 'two colleagues are on their way.' My mobile rang on the way from the airport: the ABC is flying in a cameraman and correspondent. And there'll be even more to come.

'Sir, I can only give you two.' The American networks, worldwide agencies and BBC have already claimed scores of rooms and driven prices through the roof. As he hands me the form to sign, I choke at the hyped-up room rate.

'There must be a mistake,' I splutter, 'the ABC gets a much cheaper rate.'

'Sir, these are our rates.'

'Since when?'

'Since September 11, sir.'

I sign on the dotted line but know we won't be staying long: the Marriott will keep hiking its prices and already the accountants can be heard screaming from Sydney. War, before it even begins, is good for business. And bad for the shrinking ABC budget.

Not ready for this throbbing throng, I head for my room, dump my bags and switch on the TV. I've still only seen two images since the Tuesday attacks, still circling in my mind. Mesmerised, I catch up with the world, watching Manhattan's conversion from commercial zone to war zone, and, like everyone, my understanding silently shifts. Planes become bombs, skyscrapers become dust. New Yorkers covered in the pall from the downed World Trade Center towers are eerily reminiscent of the refugees at Jalozai – dust-covered and dazed. I sit and stare for hours.

Now caught up, I feel strong enough to face the circus. Marvelling at a hotel elevator that actually works, I head to the foyer café. It's thick with cigarette smoke hanging in asthmatic clouds; old comrades reunite with the thwack of manly backslaps and porters groan under the weight of equipment worth millions of dollars, only to receive a few rupees in tips for their effort. At a table in the corner, a gaggle of South African journalists, identical in their stern expressions, are studying CNN; furiously scribbling details to regurgitate in their stories.

From the sober seclusion of Kabul, this is as exciting as it is intimidating. And after more than a month of teetotalling, I seek solace in the hotel's new bar (which brings Islamabad's official drinking spots to a grand total of three). The Bassment is half full, mostly with foreigners, but there's a smattering of Pakistani men and several nubile young women in midriff tops and heavy make-up – despite the edict that it's for foreigners only. Two ageing reporters slouch on the bar, their skinny legs cocked on stools, ruddy complexions pointing to eons of alcohol. On approach, I vaguely recognise the ruddier of the two: a magazine writer I met while covering Pervez Musharraf's coup nearly two years ago.

'Welcome to the war!' he smirks, reaching across his beer to shake my hand.

'Well, it's not started, yet,' I reply, gulping greedily at my beer.

'It will, don't you worry. America's getting ready for a big one. And you know what I'm going to do as soon as this is over?'

'Go home?'

'Nuh!' He slurps his beer for effect. 'First stop, the lovely ladies of Bangkok for a scrub and tug. Always end a big story with a stopover in Bangers.'

The expression on my face must hang somewhere between revulsion and bemusement, so his mate reinforces the point.

'You know!' he hurls above the rising din. 'A steam and cream!'

'I tell ya,' ruddy man resumes, 'we can send you to the best places.'

'Ummmm, no thanks.' They look at me like I'm a wimp. 'I'm married.'

'So? I was married once. Twice, actually. Or was that three times?'

They both wheeze with laughter. I smile awkwardly – half wanting companionship and to be part of a gang, half wanting to run back to my room. I'm staring at that most clichéd image of the war correspondent: alcoholic, over-weight and divorced. I have looked up to older Australian journalists who inspired me and I know many are not clichés, but is this where I'm heading? Is the road to war littered with lonely, ageing reporters? Is it too late for me to bail out? But I can't not be thrilled by the buzz and soak up the excitement of this deliciously rugged and ridiculous scene. It drips with the bravado of Hemingway and the absurdity of Seinfeld. War seems inevitable and every player from journalist to aid worker, UN staffer to CIA operative is descending on Islamabad. It is not just a big story, it is *the* story. Some will simply be 'doing a job', while others will claim to be serving a cause. Some, like me, will be hoping to make their name. Yet, we share one common cause: we all want a walk on the wild side, beyond suburbia and super-markets. I am a member, for better or worse, of a circus that is highly competitive and quasi-courageous. It is the circus of swinging dicks. It's largely, but not only, a male performance: some of the women seem to swing with as much bravado as the men. In this show, what counts is the size of your ego and your audience.

If ever I wanted to fill the stereotypical shoes of the hard-drinking correspondent, I now fail dismally. After a couple of beers I am a write-off, thanks to the combined impact of tiredness and the prohibitions of the Taliban. So I return to my room, and sink into sleep with a mix of relief and regret for being out of Kabul. Mostly, it is regret; I vow to return as soon as possible and brace for the long haul ahead of me.

Thankfully, help is on the way. The ABC's China correspondent, Tom O'Byrne arrives, along with a freelance cameraman, Paul Sutton, who also lives in Beijing. Their familiar banter makes me realise I have spent most of the year isolated from anything or anyone Australian, including Sarah. Their long vowels and quick wit open a window in me that has been slowly closing, but there's no time to reminisce. General-now-self-appointed-President Musharraf is on the verge of a foreign policy backflip: the Taliban that Pakistan has coddled for a decade will be abandoned. Peshawar's pro-Taliban, anti-American extremists will be taking to the frontier city's narrow alleys and crooked lanes to vent their rage. Television loves an extremist, so in the morning Paul and I head west.

With strong sun bouncing through the taxi's back window, I get to know Paul as we weave along the Grand Trunk Road. Paul is tall, funny, randy and ramshackle – charismatic verging on goofy. Best of all, he has gear, tapes and seems to know what he is doing. I feel more at ease than I can remember: after three years of crash-learning television, I have finally got a cameraman and an Australian colleague with whom to talk, work and laugh. As we bounce past the pink grandeur of the Moghul Attock Fort, I wonder if I've become something of a robot – a self-contained media machine who has come to rely solely on himself.

Peshawar greets us with its usual assault of clutter and sputter, the smell of meat and mayhem. But this time satellite dishes litter the lawn of the Pearl Continental Hotel and, in a city where a week ago it would have been a struggle just to make an international phone call, now you can rush pictures anywhere in the world immediately. With the media here, the Islamists of Peshawar have a captive audience and they'll waste no time.

A rally is planned for this afternoon, so we rush to the old part of town where the tangled web of overhead power and phone lines seem to be the only things stopping the crumbling buildings from collapsing. Even in the quietest moments, these crowded streets feel claustrophobic, and as the ranks of the outraged gather, they become a massive Muslim mosh pit – far larger and more focused than the pro-bin Laden rally in these same streets two years ago. Still, Islam's instant rent-a-crowd follows a familiar script.

'*OSAMA ZINDABAD*! LONG LIVE OSAMA!'
'DEATH TO AMERICA!'
'*TALIBAN ZINDABAD*!'

Zealous teenagers scream and shout with the fervour of adolescent girls crying out for their favourite boy band. Banners shout 'AFGHANISTAN = AMERICAN GRAVEYARD', courteously written in large, clear English for American audiences. A crudely made effigy is raised to throaty cheers. For those (like me) who don't recognise the likeness to George W. Bush, someone has kindly scrawled 'Bush Dog' across the torso. Unfortunately, someone has forgotten to dowse the effigy in petrol and it fails to flare. Then someone liberally splashes petrol all over it and, throughout this tightly knit crowd, I can envisage much more than 'Bush Dog' going up in flames. I glance nervously at the guy smoking next to me and wonder if it might be time for a quick exit. Miraculously, we are not burnt to a cinder and the mob surges in a human tsunami of screams and predictable slogans.

'*ALLAH-O-AKBAR! ALLAH-O-AKBAR!*'

As we race along these crusty streets it is hard to tell who is running this show. We need the protestors as much as they need us and, through the coming crisis, the media circus will repeat this ritual too many times to remember. And, though much of the anger here is real, our cameras will not capture the complexity of the scene.

'Photo?! Photo?!' shout many of the boys bouncing before the lens. They are laughing, jumping, sticking out their tongues. I suspect most are simply letting off steam – the politics a perfunctory concern. Our cameras fix on the angry-looking ones; the fun-lovers are filtered out of frame.

A photographer falls over in the rush, a flaying mess of swinging limbs, cameras and straps. He grabs his head tight to his chest, bracing against the stampede. But he need not worry. A posse of protestors surge forward, gently pick him up and politely dust him off.

As we roll forward again, a young beard runs up and screams straight in my face.

'You American dogs tell your President: attack Afghanistan and he will die!!'

He is so in my face I can feel his hot breath in my nostrils.

'I'm not American!' I scream back. 'I'm Australian!'

'Australia?!?' His anger shifts to surprise, then delight. 'Oh!! Steve Waugh first-class captain! Very good! Welcome to Pakistan!' He turns and dissolves into the crowd.

The world will not see these moments of humour and humanity. As Americans stare at the smouldering ruins in New York and Washington, then switch to these scenes of protests and ask, 'Why do they all hate us?', one answer is that not all of them do. Quite a few rally out of boredom. For all the talk and marketing of a global village, many of these young men feel excluded from a party they'd love to attend. But they cannot be dismissed as thousands of mere frustrated party-goers. At the fore is a hard core of idealists – highly motivated, devout foot soldiers ready to die for a pan-Islamic ideology nurtured by Pakistan's crucial network of *madrassas*. I need to get away from the slogans and update myself with this talk of *jihad*.

The next morning, we head for Peshawar's tranquil out-skirts. Framed by fields of corn, Maulana Rahat Gul's *madrassa* is a picture of serene, rote learning. It is a small seminary, much more modest than the sprawling complex at Lahore where talk of *jihad* was focused on Kashmir. The young men here all attended yesterday's rally but without their sweat and slogans they look like bored high school students. The only noise is the rhythmic mutter of boys reciting verses from the Koran, rocking on their crossed legs as their forefathers have done for centuries, repeating holy words and marking mental paths – lessons for life and death, war and peace.

Maulana Rahat Gul is a slight man in his sixties with refined, wrinkly hands reflecting a life of texts, not toil, and he proudly gives me a tour of his school, as we talk of the newest addition to Islam's antique syllabus. 'Osama bin Laden is popular because of US propaganda,' he tells me, stroking his wiry white beard. 'He is the hero of the people, an Islamic symbol against America. My students will fight the US. We can't force them but nor will we stop these boys from taking up arms against America.'

Such talk of 'voluntarism' is disingenuous. For the Taliban, Pakistan's *madrassas* have been an ideological and military umbilical cord. Now, the test will be how many of the at least eighty thousand Pakistanis who trained and fought with the Taliban through the 1990s will again take up arms, this time against the world's hyperpower.

The *maulana* resumes, warning that America may be targeting bin Laden but that's not how it will be seen here: 'If they attack, it won't be against Osama but against the people of Afghanistan and the Muslim movement.'

Pakistan's Islamic corps is being called to duty. The dovetailing of *madrassas* with groups in the North West Frontier Province and Baluchistan has created a lethal marriage of tribal, religious and political ties. Their vow to implement Sharia law directly threatens the already shaky Pakistani state and suggests a future for Taliban-style governance even if the regime falls. An increasingly aggressive pro-Taliban, ethnic Pashtun belt stretches from Peshawar to Quetta, where groups have purged women from public view, torched cinemas and even shot video shop owners. The ways of the west are not welcome and Washington's new friend, President Musharraf, is in Islamists' sights.

As is to be expected, the conspiracy theories flow thick and fast – and are of a grander scale than those that followed Nepal's royal massacre. The *maulana*'s interpreter for our interview, Sayedul Arifin, seems a bright and curious young guy but when he shows me this morning's newspaper and translates the curling Urdu words, I am reminded that not everyone is getting the same 'news'.

'See here?' he stabs the page with his finger, 'four thousand Jews stayed away from the World Trade Center on the day of the attacks!' Sayedul Arifin is reciting a theory borne of paranoia, and it is one I will hear many times, even repeated privately by high-ranking Pakistani officials.

'It is not the work of Osama bin Laden!' he continues. 'Show us the proof he has done this thing. It is the work of Israel. They want to use the American power against the Muslim.'

I am fast learning that in the 'war on terror' there are going to be few conversions across the ever-widening divide between Washington and a disenfranchised Muslim world. In this battle, people will believe whatever reinforces their existing convictions. About bin Laden, America, oil and religion.

Paul is starting to look stunned and I am feeling frustrated. The battle lines in the coming conflict have been long drawn; September 11 has merely entrenched them. As fearful as I am for the future of Pakistan, I don't want to portray it as a nation of one hundred and forty million fundamentalists itching for a fight with the west. Hoping for some conciliatory views, we head for the leafy environs of Peshawar University. When I first visited here, the campus was being applauded for its scheme giving young Afghan women a tertiary education. I'm hoping that that liberal spirit has survived September 11.

We find a circle of young men sharing jugs of tea the colour of Mars bars and talking about – what else – Afghanistan. Unfortunately, I won't find the moderation I am looking for; talk here is also of taking up arms for the Taliban.

'Most definitely,' insists Syed Imran, a Caucasian-looking agriculture student with emerald eyes and a thick lisp. He is a good middle-class boy – which right now means preparing, if need be, to die. 'People say that it's not death for Afghanistan, it's death by Islam. They are implementing the true spirit of Islam there in Afghanistan. That's why they're so popular in the Muslim world.'

A dozen friends, all in their early twenties, nod sternly while I choke on my tea, just as I did in Kabul with Masood and his Thursday night mates when we talked of girls. I wonder what *they* would say to these peers about the Taliban's 'true spirit of Islam'. I offer some accounts of life under the regime but am dismissed as a mouthpiece for western propaganda.

'How many of you have visited Afghanistan?' I ask.

Not one. They've digested an ideological diet that celebrates the Taliban, idealises Osama and demonises America. Afghanistan is once again a mythical symbol of foreign resistance and piety. To fight for Afghanistan is to be brave and a believer. To be a man. For these lads, to be Afghan is an ideal to which all men should aspire – especially since Pakistan is lacking its own meaningful mythology. I am getting oddly used to talk of *jihad* and sacrifice, and consider how much is hot air: it's hard to see these polite guys taking up arms against the greatest power in history. My only consolation is the wide divide between words and action: reciting the script is one thing, acting it out another altogether. In this part of the world, there is a lot of room for bluster. There are many paper tigers.

Back at the hotel, as I write and send my story, I fear I'm not giving a full picture of Pakistan. Peshawar feels set to explode but this is not a nation of hardliners. Many Pakistanis don't like the Taliban but nor do they want to be in the pocket of Washington. However, in the miles of newspaper reports and days of TV stories from this country, 'moderate' Pakistan will be overlooked or made a mere footnote. The reasonable are not as dramatic as the screamers and shouters – or as dangerous. There seems little room in this war on terror for moderation.

As Washington gathers its weapons and global coalition, my circus settles into a routine of rallies, refugee stories and rhetoric. President George W. Bush is promising to 'rid the world of evil-doers'. British Prime Minister Tony Blair vows the world 'will not walk away' from Afghanistan. The Taliban are 'ready to take steps' to release the arrested aid workers if the US drops its 'threats' against Afghans, and the Northern Alliance must fight without its assassinated leader, Ahmed Shah Massoud. Food and medicine will fall along with the bombs. Taking nobody on their word, Afghans are fleeing and another million refugees are expected in Pakistan. Aid agencies are frantically ordering tents but fear there is simply not enough canvas in the world to accommodate them. And Afghanistan is more shut down than ever before. The Taliban expelled the few remaining foreigners the day after I left, so we rely on refugees and Afghan aid workers to be our eyes and ears in the country. The only window on the Taliban is its embassy in Islamabad, where, at daily press conferences, Ambassador Mullah Abdul Salam Zaeef has become an unlikely media celebrity with his stormy warnings to the west.

After weeks of reporting from Peshawar and Quetta, I return to the capital to find the ABC has moved out of the hotel and rented a house to save money. On my way from the airport I swing by the Marriott to see who is still around and to catch any gossip. As a precaution against car bombs, our taxi is searched. Bag inspectors and metal scanners greet us at the front door. Inside, the foyer seems more claustrophobic than ever – the sea of stubbled chins and Old Spice has grown and the media circus is going stir crazy with waiting. As I pass the reception desk on the way to the café, a sweaty, middle-aged man in sports shorts strides to the counter.

'Excuse me!' His manner is arrogant, his accent thick American. 'Excuse me!'

'Yes, sir?' An attractive woman behind the desk is polite and smiling.

'I have just been told by the gym instructor this hotel has no tennis courts!'

'I'm sorry, sir, that's right.'

'How can you call yourself a five-star hotel and not have tennis courts?' His arrogance is shifting to anger.

'I'm sorry, sir, but . . .'

'Well, it's NOT GOOD ENOUGH!'

'Sir, we can arrange a court for you, but we would need to avail you of a car.'

'I can't BELIEVE this! I come all this way, waiting for what's supposed to be the biggest war since 'Nam, if it ever gets going, and all I want is a game of tennis and I have to LEAVE THE HOTEL!? It's a DISGRACE!'

He storms off, a black cloud in shorts and sneakers. For some, it seems the war can't come soon enough. Convinced I am missing nothing at the Marriott, I catch a taxi to the Taliban Embassy to submit a fresh visa application. I'd put in a form before leaving Islamabad, to which I and the other thousand media applicants had received the stock reply: come back in two weeks. In other words, you're dreaming. There is talk some journalists will be allowed into Kabul, but in the swirling rumour mill that is Islamabad, I don't take it too seriously. I slide past the frustrated media mob at the embassy's front gate and go down the side lane to the visa section. A handful of reporters are sitting on benches despondently filling out forms and I sit down to also perform this pointless ritual.

'Do you think this is worth the effort?' a good-looking American man sitting next to me grins.

'Probably not,' I shrug.

'I guess not,' he sniffs, standing up with his finished form. 'I'm Daniel, by the way.' He extends his hand to shake mine before turning to leave. 'See you round.' It is Daniel Pearl of the *Wall Street Journal*. I've never met him before and we'll never meet again, but long after this is all over I will remember him.

The only problem with returning to Afghanistan is that I still don't have my flak jacket. Okay, it's not the only problem but it's a big one. Mercifully, my flak jacket arrives from New Delhi and, with it, so does Sarah. Acting as armour courier may not be the most romantic reason for a visit but we're desperate to reconnect and I'm too obsessed with the story to go back to New Delhi. As I wait for her to emerge from Islamabad airport, I am a knot of nervousness: for much of this year we've again been living and loving down clunky phone lines, in a melee of misunderstandings, longing and worry.

When Sarah appears, I'm right to be nervous. India is again taking its toll on her health – she looks tired and drawn. Who knows how I look. I want to hold her but Pakistan's conservatism means we can't embrace in this public place. Driving through the cool autumn night, we're speaking different languages. I want to talk about the war and the Islamabad circus; Sarah doesn't want to hear I'll be in danger again. Our lives seem more removed than they've ever been and our conversation is constipated. We are together but planets apart.

Sarah stays for ten days, silences stay awkward and my workload remains relentless. My head is too crammed with military minutiae to either allow her in or give anything in return. We steal a few evenings at the UN and French clubs – the only places where you can eat and drink at the same time – and the alcohol loosens me up. Like the drunken older correspondents I met when I first returned from Kabul, booze is becoming my social lubricant. Right now, we are supposed to be in Kerala – a first and final Indian holiday before my posting ends at Christmas. Not only are we not in Kerala but, after September 11, my boss asked if I would stay on an extra six months. Torn between love of the story and Sarah, I agreed to an extra three.

To save her health and her sanity, Sarah returns to Delhi

and will soon go to Sydney for the summer. With the familiar mix of relief and regret, I wave goodbye as her taxi disappears; for once, she is the one waving through the back window and I am left looking forlorn. As the black and yellow bug of a cab putts away, I begin to feel this war is leaving bruises we can't yet see or understand. They are grinding into us and I am too blinkered by events and ego to care.

Finally, the moment we've been waiting for.

The war begins as a spray of flashes on snowy TV screens. Ropey night camera images televised live via videophones from northern Afghanistan announce Operation Enduring Freedom has gone into battle mode and Islamabad's circus goes into hyper-drive. The war may be a thousand kilometres away but the media front line is the roof of the Marriott Hotel, where satellite dishes and camera positions have been mushrooming. Through the night, the chatter of correspondents fills the air, pontificating to presenters ten time zones away. These are the dish-monkeys, reporters who make their living atop hotel roofs providing the latest 'spots' on a story while enjoying five-star comforts. In a world of round-the-clock coverage, the dish-monkey is increasingly the backbone of TV news.

Reporting on a conflict I can't see, smell or hear is infuriating; it is impossible to reliably assess civilian or military casualties, or gauge the impact and progress of combat. As the American-led air campaign rolls on, I am dependent on agency pictures and copy, punctuated by comments from Islamabad press conferences. For weeks, I churn out material from six in the morning till midnight. Desperate to return to Kabul, I lobby every contact I can to try to get a visa.

The Taliban Embassy clams up, creating a gold mine for Pakistani journalists close to the regime. When I call a local reporter who has previously helped smooth my path to the Taliban, he politely explains he's tied up with American and Japanese networks. In other words: the ABC can't afford him. The best paid fixers in Islamabad are earning up to four hundred US dollars a day. The only chance at a breakthrough is to pool our efforts, so I join forces with the *Times*' Stephen Farrell to push for an audience with the Taliban Ambassador. We don't so much want an interview as to lobby for visas, and after days of waiting and calling, we are given an appointment for nine the next morning.

Paul has returned to Beijing and ABC cameraman Michael Cox has arrived from Sydney. Michael is an imposing figure with a gentle manner who has so far only seen the Islamabad waiting game, so he's relieved to at least have an interview to film, even if I'm expecting no surprises. We arrive at the embassy to find England's Sky News is also included, and we crowd into a bland drawing room with too few chairs. By the time I return from reception with a stool, the Ambassador is slumped in the sofa and taking questions. When he turns to me, I ask how the regime's *jihad* policy works and why Australia appears to be exempt, even though Australian forces are fighting alongside British and American soldiers. When asked in press conferences whether Australia is included, he's said no; so his reply surprises everyone.

'Any person, any military, any people. They come into Afghanistan for a reason, for fighting with the people of Afghanistan, and we are ready for *jihad*,' Mullah Abdul Salam Zaeef begins. 'Any people, when they join with the Americans, they are American for us.'

I'm not sure I've heard correctly through his accent so I try to clarify whether he is only talking about Australian troops on the ground or in Afghanistan.

'And what about Australians in Australia?' I ask.

'Any, any, any person.'

'So the *jihad* could be extended to Australia?'

'Yes, yes, yes.'

He turns to take more questions from the others, then, almost as soon as the interview begins, it is over. The Ambassador stands to leave and we all jump up with our carefully prepared visa applications and examples of our less Taliban-hostile reports intended to show we are 'friends' of the regime. It's a hopelessly hypocritical moment: having slammed the regime for its tyranny and terror, we now try to ingratiate ourselves. His Excellency accepts the applications with a look that says 'forget about it' and glides out of the room.

'Well, that was a waste of time,' Stephen moans as we walk out the gate. 'Except for you, Jonathan. You've got a shit hot story!'

The story becomes much hotter than I could have possibly imagined or wanted. Michael and I drive back to the new ABC house, a cold castle looking out to the Margalla Hills that ring Islamabad. I play the tape to confirm the Ambassador really said what I thought he did, then start to write the story. I don't want to reduce his remarks to a crudely edited grab so I leave in my questions to preserve the context. I juggle crosses for radio, do my piece to camera and Michael races off to the Marriott to feed the TV story to Sydney. I dictate a lead down the phone: 'The Taliban have declared a *jihad* on Australia . . .'

The story sparks a storm of controversy. The next morning, Sydney's tabloid *Daily Telegraph* shouts 'Jihad Declared on Australia' on its front page, talkback radio goes ballistic and I cop a wave of condemnation. 'Aunty's reporter puts the Boot into holy war' headlines *Sun-Herald* columnist Miranda Devine, in a reference to Evelyn Waugh's William Boot in *Scoop* – a bumbling incompetent masquerading as a correspondent. In a display of family unity, Devine's columnist father, Frank, in the *Australian*, dismisses me as 'a morose ABC youth in Islamabad'. I am accused of eliciting a Taliban *jihad* – as though an Australian reporter could make the only spokesman of one of the most uncompromising regimes in the world say anything.

Unwittingly, I have become the story. What I thought was the most honest way to cover an issue has backfired and I am accused of the worst thing I could imagine: making a beat up. I am angry and amazed, and wonder if my own journalistic judgement is starting to waver.

Suddenly, I feel very, very tired. Momentum is everything. After flowing freely all year, the adrenalin has stopped. But I don't feel the job is done or that I can take a break: I still want to return to Kabul and am sure the Taliban will fall from the capital before the winter.

It seems my Taliban lobbying has worked, getting the ABC on a list of twenty news organisations allowed into Kabul. My bosses in Sydney are more measured than I am and insist on my returning to Delhi for a break. There is no shortage of ABC reporters in Islamabad and many believe the war could get bogged down by the winter and run well into next year.

Reluctantly, I return to New Delhi, then spend the weekend with Sarah and friends at Neemrana Palace, laughing, drinking, sleeping and, as much as my mind will allow, ignoring the war. When we get back to Delhi, I am met by Sarah's sisterly friend, Aarzoo, who has comforted her with laughter, gossip and retail therapy in my long absence. Aarzoo takes me for a walk to issue some stern Indian retail advice to me.

'My brother, I have to tell you,' she begins with a grave tone, 'you have failed in your first year of marriage, you are way beyond a one carat diamond now, you are up to a ruby and an emerald.'

She offers to take me shopping but my phone rings. It is Irshad in Islamabad, certain my Taliban visa has come through.

I'm on the first plane back to Islamabad. Jewellery shopping will have to wait.

CHAPTER 22

HARRY

The war moves much more quickly than the Taliban Embassy's visa section. Having dropped more than three thousand bombs on a country already blasted back to the Stone Age, the Americans are punching holes in the Taliban front lines. The battle for Mazar-e-Sharif is gruesome, even by the key northern city's blood-soaked standards. It falls to Northern Alliance forces made strong by US warplanes. Arab fighters threaten their Afghan comrades with execution if they attempt to defect, but the Taliban front line unravels like a hem. From Mazar to Kabul, towns fall from Taliban control. There will be no more visas, because soon there will be no Taliban in the capital.

Then one night, five years after arriving, the medieval militia leave as quickly as they came. A convoy of pick-up trucks snakes south to Kandahar, the exodus only slowed by Taliban stopping to empty the money changers' market of millions of American dollars. The Northern Alliance and the journalists travelling with them are triumphant as they pour into a city waking from its five-year incarceration. Soon, the media in Islamabad will be freed from the frustration of its long-distance coverage and the Pakistani capital echoes with the clack of flight cases snapping shut. The circus wheels west for Peshawar, waiting for Pakistan to open its border with Afghanistan.

In the new power vacuum, the road to Kabul will be dangerous and an experienced fixer is essential. I call Hamed Eqbal, the man who got me into drought-stricken Hazarajat. He is in Peshawar with his family and is even more desperate to see Kabul than I am, so he takes leave from his aid work day job and we arrange to meet tomorrow. Packed with camera gear, generator, food, boxes of water and cartons of coffee, Michael and I will leave first thing in the morning.

But Islamabad won't easily release its grip.

The call comes at dawn: the imprisoned aid workers are free and on their way to Islamabad. I am frustrated by the delay in getting away but pleased to be seeing through this long-running story. And it is an incredible story. After three months in detention, a fleeing Taliban pack the prisoners for Kandahar but abandon them during a fire fight in the city of Ghazni, a few hours south of Kabul. The aid workers are picked up from off a field in the dead of a freezing winter's night by an American military helicopter. To many, they are heroes saved by God.

Finally, after two days' delay, I'm ready to leave – but my beloved laptop has other ideas. Two years of South Asian dust, potholed roads and the indelicate thump of my fingers has caused the hard drive to die. A friend puts me in touch with a young IT boffin he swears by; the guy turns up and takes my laptop, promising to fix the problem by tonight.

'Make sure you backup all the data,' I warn as he walks out the gate of the ABC house.

'No problem, sir!' he chuckles.

Why is it, after three years in South Asia, I always feel nervous when someone tells me 'no problem'?

He returns at eleven o'clock, proudly presenting my laptop, with its brand new hard drive. But there is a problem. A big problem. Most of the data has been wiped. By him. Months of wear and tear boil over.

'WHAT HAVE YOU DONE?' I roar.

'Sir?'

'My data! MY DATA! Where is it?'

'Data is there, sir,' he replies confidently.

'No it's not! Only SOME is there!' My rage is volcanic as I click around the desktop, vainly searching for signs of the last two years of my life. 'My stories are gone! My contacts are gone! My sound files are gone!' In all the rush, I have not backed up my material for months and months.

'YOU'VE COMPLETELY FUCKING WIPED MY DATA!'

Michael nearly needs to restrain me. For the first time since primary school, I am considering throwing a punch, or a kick, or telling the teacher.

That's when I know I'm losing it.

'Sir, I can fix,' he offers, clearly fearful.

'No, mate.' Having frightened myself, I try to calm down. I look to Michael, who knows much more about computers than I do, but he gives me a glance of defeat. There will be no getting the data back.

'Just go,' I moan, as if in mourning. 'Just go.'

'But payment, sir?'

'Excuse me?'

'Sir, payment. For new hard drive. Twelve thousand rupees.'

Now I will kill him.

'You have just destroyed all of my work and you want *me* to pay *you*?'

I must look like a man possessed, because he spins and flees, leaving me to stare at my worthless computer. I can only conclude it's finally time to leave Islamabad, and, after a night of angry sleep, we finally do.

As we abandon Islamabad's suburbia, the morning is a moist autumn glow, the trees are raging red. But I'm in no mood to enjoy the morning's glories. I feel vulnerable; not because we are heading for a fluid war zone but because I have lost the laptop I loved. It was my brain, my backup – my life on call. Now that memory is gone and without it I'm not sure who I am and where I'm going. My life has become a string of stories and with no record of them, I am unsure of my past, my present, my future. My broadcasts have become my being.

The more distance that's put between me and Islamabad, the better I feel, tingling with the thrill of a new journey, that strange blend of ambition and apprehension, rich with possibility – like childhood, new love, Saturday mornings. Everything, even arriving in Kabul tonight, seems possible.

Peshawar smashes through the windscreen, its raw energy a rude reminder of Islamabad's blandness. It is unchanged by the past two months of dramas – other than the proliferation of Osama bin Laden t-shirts selling in the bazaars. The frontier city has absorbed the outrage and cashed in on its big-spending journalistic guests without blinking.

First we need permission to travel through the tribal areas and the Khyber Pass to the Torkham border post. We pull up outside an office heaving with media, as if the whole of Islamabad's circus has crammed into one tiny room. There is the frantic flurry of papers, Pakistani fixers sprint back and forth with photocopies of passports, photographs and letters of assignment supposedly from editors in New York, London and Sydney but mostly faked by journalists without the time or concern to get bosses to fax the real thing. Beneath this fury is the fear of failure. No-one wants to be left behind on the road to Kabul. Most have spent days waiting at this office and, for once, my timing is right; within an hour we have papers in hand.

'Are you going in?' a reporter grins, waving his documents.

'*Insh'allah*,' I smirk.

Nobody simply goes *to* Afghanistan; they go *in* to Afghanistan.

For all the excitement, no-one knows if Pakistan's border guards will open the gates. As Pakistan mourns the fall of its bastard son, the Taliban, and curses a Northern Alliance-controlled Kabul, the gates have been slammed shut all week, opened fitfully to let through dribbles of media. We pick up Hamed, who brings along a sidekick called Humayan – he's nineteen, strikes me as a mummy's boy and seems habitually bored but says he wants to learn about journalism. I don't know Humayan and immediately don't like him but, with all our gear, an extra set of hands might be useful.

We squeeze into the two cars hired to take us as far as the border; there we'll have to hire Afghan cars and drivers. At last, eight hours after leaving Islamabad, we join the caterpillar of journalists, fixers, photographers and thrillseekers wriggling through the Khyber Pass. We have no idea what lies at the border, let alone on the other side. The late afternoon sun casts its fading light and we quietly invest our collective karma in this heartless landscape. In reply, we get a sniff of disdain – after all the failed conquerors and successful smugglers this Pass has seen, we are a tiny blip in the scheme of things. Just as there is only one Kipling, there is only one Khyber Pass, but there are infinite insignificant journalists.

The Torkham border is closed. What did we expect? Even in relatively peaceful times, these grilled gates at the heel of the Khyber Pass swing shut at five o'clock – I learnt that the hard way on my first hurried exit from Kabul. Now, two years later, almost to the day, with the last stubborn glints of light disappearing, I am stuck on the other side desperate to go in. Then, I was alone as a western reporter in Afghanistan; today, the country is being overrun with media. Our cars join the long queue snaking back from the gates. Hamed and Humayan smoke while Michael and I head for the passport office. This nineteenth-century glorified shed, with its high ceilings and once-white walls, is usually packed with Afghans and Pakistanis who wait while we westerners waltz in, present our passports to be stamped ahead of the long queue and waltz out. However, tonight it is wall-to-wall westerners, not a local in sight; there will be no jumping the queue. I throw our passports on the growing pile and, with the scores of other long faces, take up a seat and wait, as powerless as the poorest peasants who endure such frustrations every day of their lives.

The passport officer sits at his Partition-era typewriter, thumping out exit visas two index fingers at a time. It is painfully slow. Our sullen silence is broken by a French cameraman whistling something from my parents' generation. I don't know the name of the tune – only that it's old.

'That's my favourite song!' squeals a woman from the corner. 'That's "Fly Me To The Moon!"' A beaming, bespectacled Pamela Constable leaps from the shadows, sweeps the whistling man off his stool and waltzes him around the passport officer's desk as he clunks on his typewriter, oblivious. We laugh and clap. We go back to waiting.

Our emotions are as diverse as the nations we represent.

There are the fearless and the nervous, the sombre and the excited. We are driven by youthful ambition or long, tiring habit. But our faces reveal little of what we hide inside – we all adopt a rugged frown that will at least mask any fear. The façade is broken by a member of the CNN crew, who walks in wearing a nervous scowl.

'They're getting reports of heavy fighting on the road to Jalalabad,' he says.

'Who?' we ask in chorus.

'They don't know. They just say there's been fighting.' He has just been speaking to his people in Atlanta, who apparently sourced the story from a radio report. We plunge into swearing and speculating. Typewriter man keeps thumping slowly, deaf to the commotion, but right now I want him to take his time till the situation clarifies.

The CNN guy is swamped with questions he can't answer.

'Where were the attacks?'

'I don't know. Along the road.'

'How many men?'

'I don't know.'

'Taliban or al-Qaeda?'

'I DON'T KNOW! OKAY?'

Michael looks at me as if to say 'so what now?' Good question. Some teams of journalists crossed the border two days ago; most are in Jalalabad, while a few have gone all the way to Kabul. But there is not a single solid piece of information on which to make a decision and my head is frying with the rumours and speculation. There are vague radio reports that Jalalabad is under siege as rival factions fight to fill the power vacuum left by the fleeing Taliban. Then there are the rumours that Taliban fighters had been seen beyond the Torkham border gates earlier in the day. If knowledge is the secret to safety then, on the information before us now, we won't be very safe.

Michael shows no fear but his face is written with caution

and concern. He peppers me with reasonable, impossible questions. What will be on the other side? *Who* will be on the other side? Where will we stay? How will we know it's safe? They are totally sane, sensible questions to which I have no answers; only growing excitement to return to a place notorious for betrayal and bloodshed. This gentle bear of a man must be wondering if he's been assigned to accompany a careless fool.

I walk outside to stretch my legs and air my brain. Under the charcoal sky my responsibility is clear: it is no longer just my safety at stake but that of Michael, Hamed and Humayan. As if to prove this is no hypothetical exercise, the first crews are being allowed over the border, disappearing into the blackness beyond the gates. I am hit by a wave of jealousy. Just a few paces and a simple gate separate me from that other world that is Afghanistan. We unpack the gear, thank our drivers and send them back to Peshawar. Hamed and Humayan have Afghan passports, so I send them over the border, laden with barrows of equipment, to organise new cars for Jalalabad. We did not come all this way to turn around.

I stroll slowly back to the passport office, kicking the dirt with my boots, trying to place something in my mind, in my stomach. Somehow, I am missing a feeling that has lived with me for much of these three years in South Asia. It would sit in my stomach, a niggling knot, a relentless brake on recklessness. As much as I hate to admit it, that feeling has been fear. And right now, just when I would expect it most, it's not there. It is a strangely lonely sensation. I'm either getting used to this place or losing my mind.

By half past nine, our passports are stamped and we tread across the border by the light of our torches. Nearly ten weeks after fleeing, I am back in Afghanistan, greeted by armed militiamen, their AK-47 rifles and bulbous rocket launchers slung over shoulders wrapped in shrouds against the cold, their feet in dusty flip flops. They will escort us all to Jalalabad. Like the vast majority of the Taliban, these men and boys are ethnic Pashtun, but instead of the trademark black turbans of the fallen regime, they wear the woollen *pakhool* berets made famous by Massoud. These men tolerate the Northern Alliance but their loyalties belong to local commanders who have been negotiating furiously over carving up power in wealthy and strategically important Nangarhar Province.

'Well-cum Afghanistan!' grins a kid with a Kalashnikov almost as tall as he is. His greeting is as close to an entry visa as we will get tonight: there is no passport control because there is no government. This country is still at war.

A voice comes out of the darkness. '*As'salaam aleikum.*' It is Hamed. 'Come,' he says, 'we have two cars. The last two available. We are lucky to get them.'

We walk a short way past huddles of militiamen to a Toyota Corolla taxi and a Mitsubishi van packed with our gear. Two middle-aged drivers wrapped in shawls sit on the taxi's bonnet and chat, apparently indifferent to any hazards which may lie ahead. From beneath their shawls, they extend hands, toasty warm against mine as we shake, before returning to their conversation.

'Humayan, why don't you travel in the van with the gear?' I suggest. 'You might even be able to get some sleep on the back seat.'

My suggestion of sleep hides a horrible calculation: if robbers want the gear, they can have it, and, of the four of us, I feel least responsible for Humayan. Besides, I've already decided I don't like the guy. It's not my most noble moment.

Waiting for the last people to cross the border, I stroll

through the rows of impatient vehicles; the place looks like a used car yard in the shadow of the Khyber Pass, lit by the sparkle of parking lights. The rich American, Japanese and British networks boast glistening four-wheel drives. The smallest and most mobile of the media, the print reporters, have joined forces to hire clunky old school and tour buses with faded 1970s slogans painted on their sides – 'Keep On Cruisin' and 'Love Bus'. It's as though the Partridge Family has been lost in Afghanistan for the last twenty years.

Beyond this narrow strip of light and apparent security, the desert is black and brooding. The shapes of shrubs and boulders are all that can be seen, though we silently wonder what or who else lies out there. The Khyber Pass is a silhouette against the night sky and this usually bustling border is hauntingly quiet. Traders' cargo containers are padlocked shut; the starving, thirsty refugees who have flooded these gates for the last year have disappeared.

Gaggles of militiamen cluster around radios. The news, broadcast in Pashto, is good. Haji Abdul Qadir, the man who governed Nangarhar Province before the Taliban, has been reappointed governor. Two days of tense negotiations have produced a power-sharing arrangement without bloodshed. It is pure Afghan horse trading – and you can almost hear the hiss of relief, like a balloon deflating. This was an early, crucial test of whether Afghanistan's track record of violent conflict would fill the vacuum left by the Taliban, and, faced with international pressure and a desperate domestic desire for peace, rival leaders have made deals, not war. For now, at least.

One moment, we're standing in the half-dark, listening to radios and bouncing on toes against the cold; the next, everyone is sprinting to their vehicles as if seeking shelter against an air raid. The convoy plunges into the darkness in a cloud of dust and desperation, all the safety concerns of a couple of hours ago abandoned as the instinctive, insane urge to race to Jalalabad takes hold. It's a herd mentality and our impatience is all the more absurd when you remember that other journalists travelling from the north have already beaten us to the provincial capital. As the convoy stretches out, the militia escort grows frustrated and abandons the slowest vehicles at the rear. For any attackers waiting in the shadows, these unguarded stragglers are sitting ducks.

Nevertheless, there is something comforting about our cars; they provide an illusion of a skin, however thin, against the blackness, the uncertainty. I know I should be feeling nervous but can only laugh at this phalanx of smuggled taxis, old buses and even rickety trucks guarded by a ragtag army of teenagers. We, the media, share much with these militiamen: we are all lunging into uncertain circumstances, poorly resourced for battle and even more poorly disciplined. Some are rugged individualists, most merely follow the pack.

We thunder into Jalalabad amid a jumble of jeeps and guns, the militiamen heralding our arrival with shouts and horns as we arrive outside the governor's mansion. Its new tenant, Haji Abdul Qadir, will conduct a midnight press conference. It is to be held in the most spectacular room I have ever seen in Afghanistan. The finely decorated domed ceiling is a mosaic of glistening reds and greens, looking down on a vast carpet of finely stitched crimson. The room oozes authority and indulgence, and I am lost in its divine designs when Haji Adbul Qadir strides in looking handsome and regal, promising a new era for Afghanistan. But this seasoned eastern powerbroker represents many of the dangers of the new Afghanistan. He is one of the country's most powerful warlords. His vast business networks encompass a key hand in the cross-border opium trade and smuggling duty-free imports back to Pakistan. An ethnic Pashtun who had fought with the Northern Alliance against the Taliban, he has powerful friends and many enemies. Abdul Qadir would become one of three vice-presidents in the interim government, as well as Minister for Public Works, and on his first day in the job, eight months from now, outside his new ministry, he will be shot through the head by unidentified gunmen. But tonight is for celebrating.

It's Sunday morning in Australia and I need only file for radio news, so I hurriedly scribble some stories and scream them down a wobbly sat-phone line. Thank God that's all I need to do: my brain has shrunk with tiredness. It's two in the morning and the local hotel is already full with media, so we spread out our sleeping bags on the massive mulberry carpet, lie down amid a chorus of snoring reporters and fall asleep beneath the twinkling ceiling.

'HHHHHHRRRRRRRRRRR-TOOOOH!'

A soggy, grating sound seeps into my dreams.

'HHHHHHRRRRRRRRRRR-TOOOOH!'

It's the anthem of Pakistani fixers performing their morning ritual; the same medley of phlegm you'll hear at dawn across South Asia as men compete to clear throats and noses with the greatest gusto. We slide out of our sleeping bags to escape this orifice orchestra and step into crisp sunshine. Michael filmed last night's border crossing, road rally and press conference so, with some extra material from the streets of Jalalabad this morning, we will have a good story for tonight's bulletin. Providing we can find a way to send it.

We begin here at the governor's residence, where new

symbols of authority are already being installed. Flanking the front door, guards sit stiffly, their white-gloved hands tightly clasped on knees, their feet in even whiter, brand new sneakers. They look like kids on the first day of school, wanting to impress the teacher. Unfortunately, nobody has bothered to pull down the white Taliban flag that is fluttering overhead. Michael gets the shots and we walk out of this manicured compound to see how Jalalabad is dealing with its new rulers. On the way out of the palace gates, a wide, bearded smile framed by a yellow cap strides towards us, camera on the shoulder.

'You guys Aussies?' The smile is attached to an Australian accent. 'G'day. I'm Harry. How ya goin'?' His cap is embroidered with a kangaroo. 'I'm workin' for Reuters. I've got some shots you might like.'

Harry Burton is immediately likeable and impressive. If he were a character in a film, you might even think him a cliché – too straightforward and generous to be believable. I'd heard about him: a one-time horticultural technical manager for Coles Myer who threw in corporate hype and made a name as a talented young cameraman in front-line coverage of East Timor. At thirty-three, energetic and ambitious, he's of my tribe. He arrived in Jalalabad with a small media convoy that crossed the border two days ago. After a chat – about work, plans, places – we agree to meet at the hotel, where a British network has set up a satellite dish for feeding pictures. We have a picture link with the world and it's great news: we can send our story today.

After an hour of hurried filming of Jalalabad's new life, we head for the Spin Ghar Hotel to write and edit. We find Harry on the first-floor landing, editing shots of a Taliban arms store he discovered. The shots are fresh and, rather than wait for them to get to Sydney on the Reuters feed, we cut them straight into our story. I write quickly and record my voice; as Michael edits, Harry and I chat.

Conversation soon turns to Kabul and getting there safely. Some journalists have already gone – some with militia escort, some solo.

'We're all going tomorrow,' Harry says, spooling through more shots. 'We'll go in convoy. Come along.'

'I want to get there today, Harry. Jalalabad is fine but Kabul is better.' I am feeling impatient and maintain that the capital is the main game. It's partly editorial judgement; partly burning desire to see it, to explore it, to talk to friends, and to fulfil the final fantasy of filming. I need to get there before it changes too much – and before the stories dry up.

Harry cuts to my greatest worry. 'Will you get there before nightfall?'

The treacherous Silk Gorge and Mahipar Pass, with its harrowing hairpin bends and plunging drops, make the Khyber Pass seem tame by comparison. A small group of bandits could hold up an entire convoy, and in this power vacuum it will be dangerous by daylight; by night it can only be a death wish. We must climb the pass before nightfall.

'If we leave soon we can get to the top by five,' I think out loud. I'm confident the car can make it in four hours, though don't know about the van. Last night it was much slower than the taxi, and the road ahead is much rougher.

'Come with us tomorrow,' Harry smiles. 'It'll be fun. And there'll be safety in numbers.'

Harry has planted doubts in my mind and I even go down to the reception desk to see if there are any free rooms tonight. There are. Maybe we will stay one more day.

I walk outside into brilliant lunchtime sun, the story is fed to Sydney, the van is packed and we can leave, but my mind ricochets. Is the road safe for us to go alone? Is the van fast enough? It should be fine, I convince myself. Hamed agrees and he's travelled the road hundreds of times.

Michael is still trying to absorb his first day in Afghanistan. The decision is mine and time is ticking.

Chris Kremmer thunders through the car park in a four-wheel drive, having crossed the border this morning. He waves but has no time to chat – he's pressing on to Kabul. It's the last straw: Chris is a friend, but as a reporter for the *Sydney Morning Herald*, he is also a competitor.

'Harry,' I sigh as we shake hands, 'I'll see you in Kabul. We're going today.'

Tomorrow's convoy makes sense but impatience and ambition are speaking more strongly to me.

'See ya there,' he grins.

It will be the last time I speak to Harry.

The journey is slow. The van struggles with the road's deep corrugations and plunging potholes. Our lame two-car caravan limps along, the Kabul River to our right, a desert of rock and ruin to our left. But we're not the slowest travellers today and when we overtake a towering Pakistani truck, I see a story opportunity.

'Stop! Stop! Stop!' I yell at the driver. We hop out and hail down the truck. Michael, Hamed and I then invite ourselves into the driver's spectacular cabin; a painted jumble of geometric shapes and colours, it's like sitting in a giant candy jar. At the wheel is Isa Khan, a rakish, middle-aged workhorse with an enormous nose and road-weary eyes. He's been plying this path for fifteen years and has seen every war and warlord along the way. I ask him about security in the wake of the Taliban.

'It doesn't matter who's in charge and who's fighting,' Isa Khan yells above the truck's clunk and clatter. 'I get paid to drive to Kabul and nothing else matters.'

In fact, what happens along this road matters greatly. In the darkest days of *mujahideen* rule, it was controlled by several rival factions, and making it safe was one of the Taliban's greatest achievements. Keeping it safe will be a major test for Afghanistan's new administration – whoever or whatever that ends up being. Isa Khan wants to chat all day but we've got a good 'grab' and could walk faster than his truck, so we say thanks and leave him in our dusty wake.

In the warm afternoon glow, I am soaking up the scene crawling past my window. Men tend to unyielding fields. Young boys shovel dirt into potholes as we approach, hoping for a few Afghanis from grateful drivers, but the exercise seems as fruitless as the first time I saw it on the road to Kandahar two years ago. Men throw stones at our taxi and yell abuse. These distractions won't hide the sobering reality that we're too slow for the sun. When the van gets a flat tyre, I resign myself to what I've been denying: we have lost the race against the dark. After wasting the best part of an hour changing tyres, our caravan limps into the tiny town of Sarobi beneath an ominous purple sky and the shadow of the Mahipar Pass. The drivers are hungry and grumpy, so we stop for kebabs, tea and *naan*, greedily scooping with our hands from big serving plates on the floor. We are only thirty kilometres from Kabul but it seems impossibly far. I imagine the capital as a safe and secure oasis, though I know this is fantasy; I also know that returning to Jalalabad would be as dangerous as pressing on.

We climb into our vehicles and crawl through the pass at an excruciatingly slow pace. The headlights arc through the dark, playing games with the shadows, and I curse myself for getting into the very situation I'd sworn to avoid. Harry's words ring in my head – 'safety in numbers' – and I now wish we'd waited till tomorrow. Fear may have been noticeably absent last night at the border but now it is very much here. Since leaving Sarobi we've not passed a single vehicle – and in war zones, traffic is welcome. Michael seems calm or exhausted. Hamed maintains his inscrutable Afghan-cum-Robert De Niro cool. I try not to reveal my concerns and think about the lucky mascots kept in my bag – the dusty plastic spider given by a friend, a photo of Sarah and me at the beach, a tiny Japanese doll given to me by a little girl on a plane in Brazil. I pity the damned Russian forces who tried in vain for years to take this pass and Silk Gorge below, their tanks and corpses littering its depths. I imagine the furthest place from these moonlit rocks and come up with dinner at a swank restaurant overlooking Sydney Harbour on one of those balmy summer nights that promise to last forever. Somewhere between the main course and dessert of this meal in my mind, the road flattens and we gather speed before pulling up at the roadblock marking the top of the pass, no longer manned by Taliban but Northern Alliance troops. We've made it.

It's a short sprint into Kabul, which looks as cold and closed as always for nine o'clock – except for the InterContinental Hotel. It is a blazing beacon of electricity, a light-house keeping watch over the city. Every one of its two hundred rooms seems to have the light on – though only a handful of them are habitable. We pull into a packed car park: clearly hundreds of people are staying here. I excitedly jump out of the car and run inside, to be greeted by a giant portrait of Ahmed Shah Massoud in the foyer. I laugh out loud at this most telling transformation. Not only were all photos prohibited just a week ago but this image, above all, was pure heresy. Now, Massoud has returned to the capital, immortalised.

At the reception desk, the staff are frazzled by the foreign influx but clearly pleased by events.

'Ah, Mr Jonathan! *As'salaam aleikum*!' one greets me,

throwing out his hand to shake mine. 'You see, we knew you would be back! You are our brother! And now, like you, we are free.'

'Congratulations,' is all I can say. I am genuinely excited for them but fear their freedom may be shortlived. For me, their warm welcome is bittersweet: I feel like a fair-weather friend, having fled the tough times and returning for the party.

The Bamiyan Brasserie is jamming with chatter; the waiters are overwhelmed. It's the first time I have seen more than a smattering of people in this restaurant – it's like an abandoned ghost town miraculously brought to life. My head is firing with flashbacks to Islamabad in those first days after September 11 and the circus is seething with the same excitement – and even more testosterone. With no heating, people pad against the cold with fat ski jackets or wrap themselves in simple shawls. At a table by the tall wall of windows, I find the ABC's Geoff Thompson battling with a pepper steak and showing the contented glow of someone about to go home. After an arduous but triumphant month in the north and having been among the first reporters to march on the new Kabul, his work is done.

It feels that mine has only just begun. I'll be sharing the load with our Moscow correspondent, Jill Colgan and, later, Eric Campbell who is based in Beijing, but it will be full on for all of us. I climb up to the hotel roof to call Sydney on the sat-phone and file radio material for the morning programs, then I go back to the brasserie for too many pots of green tea, swapping stories with Geoff till three in the morning. Reluctantly, I climb into bed like a child on Christmas Eve, too excited to sleep in this long-suffering city.

Dawn déjà vu: Kabul's sun streams into our room and another green tea hangover burns in my brain. As I squint across the valley crowned by a burnt orange sunrise, I wonder how Masood and his Thursday night fever friends have been celebrating the Taliban's exit. It doesn't take long to find out that Masood will soon be leaving – one of the hotel staff tells me he will move to Sweden to join his new wife. As Michael has breakfast I write my TV news story, marrying agency footage of broader developments with our road trip material. The cut story is fed on the roof where satellite dishes are scattered across its flat expanse, like an instant media city keeping watch over Kabul. The scene is as shocking as it is thrilling; the cameras, lights, satellite dishes hold a collective finger up to the Taliban.

But the media's insolence is shortlived. A rumour races through the hotel like a bad case of dysentery: four foreign journalists have been murdered on the road to Kabul. The foyer is grinding with fretful questions.

'Have you heard?'

'Who is missing?'

'Where?'

And the hardest question of all: 'Why?'

When those who led the convoy – a Philippines TV crew – walk through the door of the hotel, we swamp them for answers. A group of armed men tried to pull them over not far before Sarobi – the town where we stopped and ate last night. Wisely, their driver kept going. The next car in the convoy was Harry's.

My head feels like it's about to explode. Harry can't have been killed. He is too cool, too careful, too gorgeous. His karma is too good. As reports come in from Jalalabad, my hopes shatter. The driver of the car Harry was travelling in escaped and spun back to Jalalabad, warning the rest of the convoy to turn back. Bus passengers travelling the route report seeing the bodies of foreigners by the roadside, and Harry, along with an Afghan-born photographer and two journalists, from Spain and Italy, are confirmed missing. By four o'clock, it's almost certain they've been murdered, but no bodies have been recovered and it's time for me to cross live to *Lateline*. I can hear the presenter, Tony Jones, in my ear.

'Jonathan,' Tony asks, 'it is very early and we don't want to raise unnecessary alarm but do you have any idea who they are and what countries they're from?'

What do I say? Harry's dead? Harry might be dead?

'Look,' I begin, not sure where my answer will go, 'we are getting some, ah, mixed reports, so I really think at this stage . . .'

'All right,' I hear Tony in my earpiece almost physically backing away.

'. . . to, ah, to hold back on that information, Tony.'

All I can think of is Harry's family and the unbearable news they were about to receive. I didn't want them to hear it from me. Not on the TV.

I walk through the rest of the live shoot. As many as nine thousand Taliban fighters, surrounded in their last northern foothold, the city of Kunduz, are negotiating their surrender. British Special Forces say they've pinned down Osama bin Laden to a seventy-eight square kilometre area in southern Afghanistan. I go through the motions, mouthing the right words but my mind is elsewhere – on Harry, lying muddy and dead in a ditch by that bloody road. I sign off from *Lateline*, unclip my lapel mike and look out across Kabul under a dazzling dusk. Michael packs up the camera.

Harry's parting words are ringing in my ears. 'It'll be fun,' he told me. 'It'll be fun.'

CHAPTER 23

RUNNING TO STAND STILL

Men will be arrested for the murders, Afghanistan's new rulers will promise justice and chaotic investigations will be conducted – but the Afghan legal system does not work because it does not exist. We piece together anecdotes and it's most likely Harry and his companions were murdered by bandits who panicked or were just impatient and brutal. Journalists vow never to travel the road again and those in the rest of the convoy who turned back are morooned in Jalalabad. We all ask whether the risks in this work are worth it. Already seven journalists have been killed since the war began; the eighth will fall by the end of the month.

Michael and I hunt down hope and happiness in Kabul's cultural revolution. We head downtown, past booming barber shops adorned with posters of Leonardo DiCaprio. Young men stare misty-eyed as fringes are trimmed and flicked, combed and curled. Vanity is legal again. On the streets, traffic grows thicker by the hour, minute, second, as though every taxi driver from the subcontinent is flooding in for work. Distorted music snorts from speakers. Kabul rejoins South Asia's Bollywood obsession, the sounds of silence are gone and that once most scorned force is back.

Television.

Our car turns into Pashtunistan Street. Under the Taliban I knew it as the eerie and tense strip where religious police would regularly prowl, on the lookout for TVs, stereos or video cameras sold there on the sly. Now, such contraband is out in the open and men excitedly wave their newly bought antennae in the air, while others longingly fondle satellite dishes ingeniously crafted from food tins. These makeshift dishes offer a link to a world of BBC and CNN, *Survivor* and *Friends*. Afghanistan – or at least Kabul – is surging from the seventh century into the twenty-first, reality TV and all.

It feels like an Afghan Manhattan and, while Michael films, I soak up the commercial frenzy as a welcome distraction from Harry's murder. But Afghanistan never lets you linger in joy for long and, as we climb into the car to go, a withered old woman bangs on my window. Her gummy grimace and leathery face press hard against the glass; her claw of a hand thumps it like a drum, syncopating with her raspy voice:

'DOLLLARRRR . . . SIR . . . RUPEEEEEEEEE . . . SIR . . . AFGHANNNIIIIIIII . . . SIR!!! SIRRRRRRRR!!!'

I used to look into beggars' eyes and see the injustice in life, the lottery of my privilege, the stupidity of my selfishness. Now, I neither give nor feel a thing. My callousness is complete; my sympathy shot. The first signs appeared in the Jalozai refugee camp but now apathy has become habit. In the cold commotion of Kabul, my heart is frozen. I can observe and communicate to listeners and viewers; the words hold meaning but little feeling. I have become the distant, dispassionate reporter in the fullest sense. Mourning Harry is easy: he is of my tribe, so it's an extension of selfishness. But the suffering of anonymous millions washes past my window in meaningless waves. I am alive but my humility has died. The car pulls away; the woman's rickety legs struggle to hobble alongside, her plea swallowed by the cacophony of stereos bleating onto the street.

The withering widow at my window may not have touched my heart but she has focused my mind on Afghanistan's frail future. Hundreds may race out to buy TV sets or DVD players but millions wallow at the bottom of every health and welfare indicator. Infant mortality is around twenty-five per cent. Almost half the population is under fifteen. Afghanistan's most notorious warlords and drug lords are resurging, thanks in part to suitcases and bin bags packed with millions of American dollars in bribes for their (rented, never bought) loyalty. Neighbouring states will also try to exert their influence by doing the same. Within two years, Washington's new warlord partners in the 'war on terror' will return Afghanistan to the ignominious title of world's biggest producer of heroin, replacing a failed state with a narco-state. And beyond the International Security Assistance Force-protected streets of Kabul, there will be no security or safety.

Not two minutes from the buzz of Pashtunistan Street, Kabul dissolves into a sobering blur of the enormous task ahead. An old man slumped over on a footpath here. A mother begging with child on a street corner there. And the haunting blue ghosts still slide past my window, the *burqa* serving as a hushed reminder of the nervous anticipation. For all the Northern Alliance promises of a new dawn, too many in this town remember their bloody, anarchic and chauvinist rule from 1992 to 1996 and no woman dare risk stepping out from beneath her veil. Afghans are too traumatised to trust anyone any more. And possibly ever again.

As far from Manhattan or Washington as you could imagine, it's easy to forget that the purpose of all this is to end terrorism. Already, President George W. Bush has said 'this crusade, this war on terrorism, is going to take a while', and perhaps the veiled women of Kabul have wise advice: don't be hasty to declare victory. This is their third 'peace' since 1979 and this society knows better than any that winning war is one thing, keeping the peace another altogether. I need some war-weary wisdom and know where to get it.

Khurram the Happy opens his front door with characteristic charm, his perfect teeth glowing inside his newly trimmed beard. His new look makes him seem younger than when we shared our bowl of gruel in the heights of Hazarajat, talking about camels and souls and the carelessness of the west.

'*As'-sal-aam al-eik-um*!' he chortles, stressing each syllable as he sweeps Michael and me inside, achieving in one simple move what has been impossible for five years: welcoming a foreigner into his home. 'Please,' he gestures towards the living room, 'this is your home.' And what a home it is: on the outside, walls crumble for want of repair but inside it's a tenderly cared-for haven. The funky furniture, mothballed stereo and polished glassware were bought three wars and three decades ago, when both Kabul and Khurram were full of promise and prosperity. Taking pride of place are white leather armchairs crowned with space-age arches straight from *Star Trek*. His home is a museum to the seventies, snap frozen in bright, bloodless times.

'I remember peace,' Khurram sighs, easing into his mothership throne and lighting his first cigarette of the day. He savours its flavour, having observed Ramadan's dawn-till-dusk prohibitions on everything but fresh air. 'Peace was very interesting,' he continues as smoke dribbles through his moustache and beard. Khurram talks of peace as if about a book he read many years ago; a work of ficton. His manner is disarmingly gentle and betrays no malice over the decades wasted, the business ruined, the schooling stolen from his three young daughters. I am sure anger lurks beneath Khurram the Happy's placidity, though this may say more about my state of mind than his.

Khurram's wife, Rona, enters the room, a tall, glorious woman with sharp features and sad dark eyes the size of saucers. She is the first Afghan woman I have seen in Afghanistan and I must be the first western man she has spoken with in at least five years. She greets me in Pashto as though I were a long lost friend, before preparing dinner and presenting it to us as we sit on an elegant, plush carpet.

'My wife is very happy,' Khurram tells me, 'because now she is sure in the future her daughters could become doctors, engineers. My daughters are intelligent. Why should they not be engineers or doctors just because they're girls?'

The Taliban have left town just in time for their eldest girl to attend high school and avoid the *burqa*. I desperately want to interview Rona but Khurram warns she will not talk before the camera – she is afraid relatives in Pakistan would scorn her if they saw her face on TV. But as we kneel down to a delicious dinner of *pulao* – a dish of oily rice cooked with meat and vegetables – Rona shows no shyness. She wants to be heard.

'There was no significant problem in my life under the Taliban,' she begins between modest handfuls of food. I wait for a tirade against Taliban oppression; rage over years of house arrest for women; swearing against their chauvinism. To be sure, Rona hates her billowing *burqa* and the headaches caused by squinting through its mesh grill but, like her husband, does not look back in anger. I don't expect Rona's regret for the Taliban's exit.

'When I first heard about the Taliban going, I got upset

because they are also our compatriots.' An ethnic Pashtun and a housewife, Rona is the Taliban's model woman: beautiful, dutiful and devout. Like millions worn down by civil war, she cheered the regime that brought security to her city and now fears the uncertainty that lies ahead. 'On the other hand,' she adds, 'I was happy to see the Taliban leave because there was no education, no entertainment for our children.'

Learning and laughing. Such simple habits of life made difficult by a regime that provided security but strangled the future. Yet, for all the Taliban's misguided, misogynistic and malicious conduct, Khurram and Rona exhibit the Afghans' extraordinary ability to forgive and forget. It's the same flexibility that has underpinned centuries of shifting alliances and it is reserved for fellow countrymen. Taliban foreign fighters – Arabs, Chechens, Pakistanis – are not afforded such forgiveness.

'I do not say that Taliban were bad,' Khurram ponders as he pours tea and lights an after-dinner cigarette, 'they were very nice people.' He must notice me frown, so he repeats himself to be sure I don't miss the point. '*Very* nice people,' he whispers, 'but the system was this way.'

Now, the whole country waits to see what the new system will be and whether it can bring peace.

'These small changes – cinema, music, TV, beard, turban,' he says with his serious smile, 'these things may make a lot of people happy, but I am nervous. We do not have a government yet and when we have a government we will be watching. I am hopeful, but I'm not sure yet.' He stares over my shoulder, as if searching for some distant, peaceful place in the future – or perhaps in the past. 'I'm not sure yet.'

Jonathan Harley

Michael and I step into the damp Kabul night, chastened by Khurram's gentleness of spirit and devotion to his family. Someone once told me 'the meaning of life is children' and tonight I could see what they meant – even if I struggle to imagine my own life ever meaning more than work and war stories. Our car climbs the hill to the hotel, where the subdued mood following our colleagues' murders has already been drowned out by the demands of work. Already a sign-up sheet has been posted for a convoy back to Jalalabad. It has twenty names and is growing. Harry and his travel companions are now a mere media blip.

The InterContinental groans with gossip and gusto – there is not the caged frustration felt in Islamabad but the competition is just as fierce. It's a race to find abandoned al-Qaeda houses or offices and uncover their spoils for stories. Everyone gleans what they can from each other without revealing too much of themselves. There is the familiar hush of whispers in shadowy hallways – secrecy assisted by the clang of tradesmen installing water heaters. The hotel is undergoing a rush renovation, though not by the owners (whoever they are now). Media organisations are taking rooms with no hot water, power or even windows – which is the vast majority of them – and it is left to 'guests' to refit at their own expense. New, small, comfortable guesthouses are sprouting downtown but in the pack mentality of the media, this is still *the* place to stay. It's a comic scene of chaos and construction and many journalists seem busier hauling in heaters, hot water systems or stoves than writing stories. A few crews hire local cooks, bypassing hotel hospitality altogether. Those of us left to endure the Bamiyan Brasserie's menu, now more spartan than ever to cope with demand, are green with jealousy and nausea.

The ABC is relatively lucky – our rooms have hot water and windows. So we need only buy radiators, a kettle and buckets of instant coffee. Caffeine is our staple, occasionally supplemented with sweet biscuits and tinned tuna. My rising coffee intake and the emotional drain of Harry's murder has made me finally face what I've been denying for months: I am exhausted. My eyes feel permanently glazed and the whole world looks grey, even by Afghan standards.

The foyer is buzzing with fresh excitement. Thirty-five kilometres away, around two thousand Taliban are resisting the Northern Alliance in the district of Maiden Shah. It's a battle on Kabul's doorstep and a strangely welcome opportunity to see some 'action'. A BBC crew is going there in the morning and, after a long talk about the risks, Michael and I decide to hitch our caravan to theirs. The 'Beeb' is unsurpassed in the security support it provides to its front-line crews and is usually generous in allowing its much poorer Australian cousin to tag along.

Kabul's sun chips away at the dawn chill as we wait for the BBC in the hotel car park. I bounce on the toes of my boots, half against the cold and half as distraction from the uncertain morning ahead. But I need not worry. Unknown to me, half a world away, family, friends and strangers are praying that I don't end up with the same fate as Harry. My adored ninety-four-year-old aunt, who has seen nearly a century of wars, prays every day; a friend's grandmother bakes a special Greek Orthodox offering, usually reserved for Christmas or Easter; and people I have never met, listeners and viewers, also ask their god that I be safe. Lucky for me, it seems I am the only one losing touch with humanity.

When the BBC crew arrive, we drive south in convoy past Kabul's derelict silos and the old school buses piled high like tin toys, through lifeless fields and rhino-skin mountains to Maiden Shah, the 'Field of the King'. But in this field, there's nothing by way of royalty or battle. In fact, we find only a tiny ghost town, not a war zone. The few stalls and converted cargo containers are boarded up or locked shut. Only the bakery is open, cashing in on the hungry Northern Alliance forces here to flush out the remaining Taliban. Steaming loaves are hauled out of the underground oven as wisps of flour dance on the morning sunrays arcing through the crude chimney hole in the roof.

'What do you want for the future?' I ask the man rolling out sticky strips of dough, and Hamed translates.

'Security,' he replies, then, on the prompting of a Northern Alliance soldier leaning over him, he adds, 'and freedom.'

Whose freedom it will be is anyone's guess.

Outside, the tools of war are being organised. Northern Alliance tanks, rocket launchers and machine guns are dusted off for a morning of war making. The scene is a strange blend of serenity and lethargy, as though combat were nothing more than a hobby for these men. For some, that's what it is. Yesterday's fighting had been light, centring on two tiny, mud villages at the foot of the surrounding hills. Taliban forces hold the smaller village: the larger is disputed by both sides. This may be a desperate last stand by isolated Taliban, but it's also a timely historical reminder to a triumphal Northern Alliance and Washington: controlling Kabul and conquering the whole country are two profoundly different things.

Wrapped in flak jackets and a false sense of security in the morning quiet, Michael and I walk towards one of the villages, hoping to get some close shots. It's a stupid move. We set up behind a building when, almost on the strike of nine o'clock, the Northern Alliance men get down to business. Their rockets whine overhead and crunch into the village mud walls a few hundred metres in front of us.

Ridiculously, I consider edging closer to the Taliban positions, but when an Arab network cameraman – who is either brave or insane – retreats from that very area, we are urged to go no further. Not by him but his driver, a man whose leathery face and grim shake of the head says: get out of here.

We head back to the main road, where a Northern Alliance multiple rocket launcher and tank are perched on a rise with a commanding view of the battle. Below, villages, soldiers and an old Russian tank are laid out like toy models. By now, dozens of journalists and photographers have arrived from Kabul and, for some, the whole exercise seems to be a self-conscious study in cool. Like the tough kids at school who wouldn't wear ties, they reject flak jackets and seem bored by it all. I nickname them the cool kids and wonder if I'm missing something critical – if Taliban rockets try to hit anything it will be these Northern Alliance positions. Common sense would suggest this is a vulnerable place to hang out but what would I know? From the town below, the tank thumps shells into the closest village while, overhead, an American B-52 paints white stripes across a high, clear sky. It drops nothing and, for Northern Alliance commanders seeking assistance, or the media wanting big bang pictures, the only payload is dismay.

The contrast between these two fighting machines and their extraordinary confluence of interests is almost surreal. On this sparkling winter's morning, the world's greatest power has a hi-tech eye so high in the sky as to be barely audible. In its belly sits the means to obliterate every one of us squinting at its path – and who knows how many more. Below, amid the huts of mud and wattle still standing, to the click and whirl of cameras, rusting Cold War relics have been dragged out for what seems a fading form of war involving rockets, tanks, rifles and minefields but with neither side able to strike a decisive blow.

All this might even seem somewhat quaint, if not for a sudden sucking sound whooshing down on us. It's as if God is snorting cocaine across Maiden Shah. What *is* that? God's cocaine nose seems to be heading towards us at a thousand miles a second. Everyone crouches – even the cool kids.

It's an incoming Taliban shell.

Where will it hit? Will it hurt? Reflexively, I dive down in a muddle of limbs and gravel, decidely less cool than the almost nonchalant crouch mastered by most. The snort of the flying shell must last barely a second but feels like an eternity on this exposed hillside; long enough for my mind to run through a long list of panicked questions and . . . WHOMP! It hits about sixty metres away. It's a safe distance but close enough for the Taliban to refine their angles for the next one. I quickly dust myself off in the hope nobody noticed my daggy dive but one of the cool kids laughs at my lack of manliness. I blush.

Taliban rockets edge closer, so I get to practice the art of nonchalant crouching in this ridiculous game of Afghan roulette. Incredibly, nobody seems to be leaving. What are we doing here? Being in harm's way for the story is one thing, hanging around an exposed hillside waiting for Taliban shells to close in is absurd. And we're not even getting great pictures. An unspoken contest of courage appears to be unfolding and I have no interest in competing, so Michael and I happily retreat to the safety of the road where the latest additions to Afghanistan's ever expanding population of internal refugees are fleeing the fighting. They walk towards Kabul: a woman carrying her son; a man, some bags; another leads a cow. All appear oblivious to the belching tank dousing them in thick exhaust as it rumbles along the road. They turn only to see if the latest thud is their home being turned to rubble.

Like many Afghan battles, it stops at lunchtime. As fighters settle down to pray, eat, sleep and negotiate, there will be little more action today and, as it happens, the battle will end in a very Afghan surrender. The Taliban commander Haji Gholam Mohammed Khan and his two thousand men give up some heavy weapons but keep their personal arms and, astoundingly, keep control of the area. In the Field of the King, Gholam Mohammed rules – regardless of who rules in Kabul. In age-old Afghan fashion, he effectively swaps sides, today lending his support to the Northern Alliance and the Americans. Yesterday it was the Taliban and, implicitly, al-Qaeda. Tomorrow, who knows? The perplexing puzzle that is Afghanistan is being put back together in its own inimitable way.

On the drive back to Kabul, miles of bullet-riddled power poles click past my window like a melancholy metronome. War once seemed an abstract oddity of far-off lands but now has become strangely fascinating. I can see how journalists become addicted to its thrill and importance. And the bigger the battle, the greater the rush. Not that I know war – I have only skirted around its edges and would never ever claim to understand it. But since the thundering heights of Kashmir, war has squatted in my life like an uninvited guest, promising to leave but always returning. The lottery of life has brought me here, and I'm grateful, but wonder what it's really made of me.

Perhaps I am just thinking too much. I could always take a leaf from the book of Fox News Channel's war correspondent Geraldo Rivera, with his gun-slinging cheerleading dressed up as reporting. He proudly professes to be armed and, should he stumble across Osama bin Laden, tells viewers, 'I'll kick his head in, then bring it home and bronze it.' Just as the Gulf War helped define CNN, this war in Afghanistan has seen Fox emerge as a fierce media presence with its aggressive barracking for US forces and their allies. Opponents are 'rats', 'terror goons' and 'psycho Arabs' – and Rivera is cheerleader in chief. In a not untypical report, he says:

'We want to be there when they bring Osama bin Laden to justice. We want – I've got a New York City fire department hat I want to put on – on the body of his – you know, the head of his corpse. It's deeply personal, on the one hand. On the other hand, it is my professional calling.'

I think my professional calling is a little different.

Fox News might be out there fighting the war but many media organisations, including the ABC, now won't let their crews travel beyond Kabul. There is understandable management concern in the wake of the murders. I learn too late that our thirty-five kilometre journey to Maiden Shah was beyond bounds, for which I am reprimanded by my bosses. Even without such security edicts, the daily news demands make it difficult to get out of the hotel, let alone the capital. In the coming days and weeks, from six in the morning till four in the afternoon, I am cocooned in my room or pontificating from the roof, writing stories or doing live crosses. Kabul is changing so rapidly and there's a smorgasbord of stories right on our doorstep, but there's barely the time to do them. I love being on air and the thrill of driving coverage but this hotel is starting to feel like a prison.

By my last live cross of the day for *Lateline*, Kabul's early setting winter sun has all but gone and the city is shutting down. Michael and I dash out, scrambling for fresh material to throw into tomorrow's stories. Such encounters seem rushed and superficial. Capturing Kabul's mood of anxious optimism is reduced to fleeting pavement vox-pops. There's certainly no time to build a trusting rapport with women who have been banned from speaking with western men for the last five years. Filming a small riot for food hand-outs ends up being a case of shoot and run. We call it 'value adding' – finding a person or moment to help tell the larger story. What we're adding *to* is the broad story of the day, be it a battle in Mazar-e-Sharif, conflict in Kandahar and anything from everywhere in between.

For our big-picture footage, we rely on a diet of agency material, fed to me by colleagues in Sydney. Frustratingly, I never see many of the pictures that accompany my writing. The world over, 'news' is becoming a drip-feed of agency material, repackaged by journalists from Wadak to Washington who may rarely leave their hotels or offices. On the InterContinental's roof, it's not uncommon for dish-monkeys to be briefed on the phone by a producer in London, Washington or Sydney about events in Afghanistan, only for the reporter to regurgitate the information straight back to viewers moments later. News gathering has become news packaging and the space for critical analysis is shrinking. All media organisations are suffering ever-shrinking budgets and ever-greater demand for immediacy.

Such hermetically sealed reporting dovetails perfectly with my newfound indifference – both encourage viewing the world through a simplified, cynical prism. It's a recipe for not caring and a sure way to bad journalism. And, I suspect, it's the secret path to lasting unhappiness.

This war has helped me build a career but it's time to leave before I forget how to care. Besides, the ABC soon won't have enough money to care. Internatioal interest in Afghanistan is rapidly sliding and the ABC persists in Kabul longer than most.

I get a break over Christmas but early in the new year I am told to return to New Delhi.

Before going, I must buy something for Sarah. Aarzoo's orders about rubies and emeralds are ringing in my ears and Hamed volunteers the same advice. The old me knew money can't buy you love but the new me is desperate enough to try. So, with my pockets packed with cash, Hamed takes me to

Chicken Street where a jeweller produces every precious and not-so-precious stone under the Afghan sun. Luscious, deep blue lapis lazuli roll around the glass counter with iridescent emeralds and unconvincing diamonds.

'How do I know they're real?' I ask, taking a shine to an emerald almost as big as my little finger nail.

'You can taste it!' declares Hamed confidently, popping the rock in his mouth, swirling it around and looking to the ceiling with thoughtful eyes. He pops it out on the end of his tongue. 'It's real. That one is real.'

'Authenticity guarenteed!' the jeweller chimes. 'You get refund, no problem!'

I glare at him, recalling that the last time I was told 'no problem', I lost all my data. After tea and haggling and tea and haggling, I follow the advice of my Indian and Afghan friends and spend six hundred US dollars to buy my wife's forgiveness for my year on the road.

I've never, ever spent that sort of money on a rock before and I never thought I'd become that sort of guy.

The UN flight curls around Kabul, beautiful beneath a fresh dusting of snow. The white blanket hides the rubble and ruin, the reminders of decades wasted and countless mountains this country must climb. To me, Afghanistan will always be beautiful, whether frosted in fresh snow or parched by drought. It is a tragic and magic land that has tested and tantalised every pore in my body. I press my face hard against the cabin window as I did on leaving Australia three years ago. Quietly, I wave goodbye – as much to the place as the me who worked there. That person is as much media marathon man as madman in the making. He may best be left behind.

And Sarah's Afghan emerald? Three years of South Asian scams made me suspicious enough to have it checked by an Australian jeweller friend in Islamabad and, sadly, my skepticism was founded. It was a fake. A good fake – one of the latest Russian jobs – and was still worth about four hundred US dollars. But a fake nonetheless. I returned it and got my money back in cash. Sarah never saw the emerald. I'll tell her the story one day.

Maybe.

CHAPTER 24

SUCH STRONG FEELINGS

Landing in Islamabad is like sinking into quicksand: it feels thick and slippery with dismay and abandonment.

Abandonment because the media circus has left town, taking with it its riches. And dismay because the world's worst fears about *Wall Street Journal* reporter Daniel Pearl are confirmed. The respected, idealistic thirty-eight-year-old was lured into a trap, kidnapped and gruesomely murdered while investigating Karachi *jihadi* groups.

As I step into the Marriott foyer, Daniel's bespectacled face smiles from CNN on the café TV and I grimace that his head is no longer attached to his body, the remains of which lie in a shallow grave somewhere in Karachi yet to be unearthed. The kidnappers not only videoed his decapitation but posted the unspeakable footage on the internet as a crass propaganda exercise. Their premeditated brutality and multi-media savvy has horrified everyone, from world leaders to everyday newspaper readers. Thousands of strangers reach out to his widow, Mariane, who is pregnant with a son who will never know his father. Handmade quilts and booties, offers of financial support and rolled-up five dollar bills pour in, a flood of human kindness in the face of fanatical madness.

I check in at the front desk, then, unusually, head straight for the café. There is no pressing story and so no hurry to race to my room. I just want to stare into the middle distance and despair.

Daniel Pearl did not know it at the time, and nor did Indian authorities, but his fate was effectively sealed two years earlier in the Christmas of 1999. One of the three prisoners India released in exchange for hostages on board the Indian Airlines flight I'd welcomed to Delhi with my incompetent hired crew was Omar Shiekh – the brilliant British-raised Pakistani-cum-Kashmiri *jihadi* who had a penchant for kidnapping. Once freed, Omar Sheikh settled in Pakistan, almost certainly with the knowledge and clearance of the country's intelligence services. He was the mastermind behind Daniel Pearl's abduction.

I order coffee and let the last few weeks percolate through my mind. I am so overloaded even Daniel Pearl's murder could easily wash over me unnoticed; nothing seems strange any more. His killing confirms what I've long suppressed: luck has smiled on me and I don't want to push it any further. Perhaps it's superstition, or cowardice, but my gut says it's time to get off this ride. Well, at least for a while. I drink my coffee and stare across the Marriott's forlorn foyer. A few months ago this hotel was a manic media nerve centre. Now, it and all of Islamabad hold the dejected air of an abandoned lover who'd hoped for more than a fleeting fling. Taxi drivers, fixers and bootleggers are mourning their mini-boom gone by and must return to earning paltry Pakistani rupees instead of fat greenbacks. The resentment is palpable, surpassed only by fresh fears of war with India.

In the last two months, nearly eight hundred thousand troops have amassed along their shared border and the region is again on a war footing. On December 13, five gunmen armed with AK-47s and grenades killed nine people in the Indian legislature before security forces killed them. India felt defiled. The audacious attack hit at the heart of its power and pride, inspiring outrage on a par with, if not exceeding, the 1999 Kargil crisis. Never afraid to hyperbolise, Indian leaders are calling December 13 'India's September 11'. The blame is placed squarely on Pakistan; India accuses its neighbour of backing the insurgents responsible for the attack, and threatens to take direct military action against militant camps in Pakistan if President Musharraf does not. He shuts down two groups, and Washington desperately tries to hose down both sides, but the fear of war is real.

All ties are frozen, diplomats recalled, even the celebrated New Delhi–Lahore bus service, which was supposed to symbolise peace no matter how bad things got, has stopped. Direct flights are cancelled, leaving only the circuitous and expensive route via Dubai – akin to flying from Sydney to Melbourne via Perth. I'd rather drive back to New Delhi, which will at least save the ABC a thousand dollars or so. That's spare change in TV terms but money is running desperately thin. A hotel car is booked to leave at dawn, and Peter arranges a jeep to meet me on the Indian side of the border. I have one final feast of spicy chicken and warm beer with Irshad's family and prepare to put Pakistan behind me.

The day rises slowly over the Punjab Plain as we hurtle through fields dewy green with wheat and rice towards the Wagah border crossing. There is no hint that war with India broods beyond the horizon. Only one unattended artillery gun squats in a paddock, its lone presence seeming more ludicrous than ominous. Real military activity only appears in the final few hundred metres to the Wagah border gates, where soldiers unroll springy coils of razor wire around a paddock. This scorned border is about to achieve a new, notorious milestone. India has vowed to mine the nearly three thousand kilometre length, creating the longest minefield in the world, stretching from the Indian Ocean to the Himalayas and dwarfing the Maginot Line of the Second World War.

I skip up the few stairs into the Pakistani customs house, where officials register my arrival with a slothful shift in their chairs. These men are slovenly at the busiest of times and the past two months have been mind-numbingly slow. Nobody is crossing the border and I may be their only traveller today, but I won't be receiving any special, speedy treatment.

'You want fast service, sir?' a customs officer with piglet ears asks.

'Do I *need* fast service?' I reply, looking around for any other travellers who might slow things down. I am amused by the coming rort, if only because this will be the last time I enjoy the charms of Pakistani officialdom.

'For you, sir,' piglet ears smirks, 'fast service very good. Only one hundred rupees.'

It may be a rort but it's a bargain of a rort. A few dollars is a small price to have a blind eye turned to my satellite phones, generator and the odd Afghan rug – any of which they could use to make my life difficult. I hand over a dog-eared hundred rupee note, my passport is stamped with a thud and a small army of porters sweep up my cargo for India, a hundred metres walk away. As I follow them to the door, piglet ears looks troubled.

'You go India?' he asks.

'Yes, I go India,' I reply, resisting the temptation to ridicule his silly question.

'Will there be war?' His eyes reveal a childlike fear and, this time, it's not a silly question.

'No.' I try to sound reassuring. 'I don't think so. Not right now.'

'Thank you!' he beams, visibly relieved. 'We very worried. Here on border, we very afraid.' Piglet ears and friends stand in the doorway, grinning and waving me away to the land of their would-be enemy.

Wagah's no-man's land is like walking between two patriotic theme parks. I know I am spoiled by the dramatic, natural gateway that is Sydney Harbour but I can't take Wagah seriously. Still, I slow down to savour the gaudy gates and expanded mini-stadiums that seat the nationalistic fans who scream and cheer their goose-stepping soldiers as they fiercely fold away their national flags. Wagah is a concentrated snapshot of South Asia's absurdities. Arranging a humble bus to run between New Delhi and Lahore might have been a logistical and political quagmire but these surly neighbours can coordinate a mutual show of loathing down to the last stomp and scowl. Visiting Wagah's flag-lowering ceremony has become a patriotic duty for Indians and Pakistanis alike, and at times of heightened tension, crowds are larger and louder.

But now, as the Punjab lounges for lunch, I hear only the sizzle of *chapattis* and the chatter of sparrows. The Pakistani porters dump my bags at the feet of India's Luna Park-like entrance and I am back in the land I've come to think of as home. Beyond the soldiers, the driver sent to meet me holds a hand-scrawled sign: 'Mr Jonson'.

'*Nameste*, Jonson-*sahib*,' he giggles with all of India's raw warmth, even in the face of war. Sometimes in India it feels like a billion people want to be your friend. Two smiling strangers, Mr Ashok and Mr Jonson, upon sharing only a few simple words, will be friends for an afternoon drive to Delhi. We jam his jeep with my junk and hurtle through towns packed with cows and *chai* shops, swirling saris and delicious *dhabas*, frying spicy *pakoras* and baking crispy *naan*. After Afghanistan's lunar landscape and Pakistan's shades of grey, India is a vibrant wonderland – the colours, commerce and crud are all amplified. And so is the traffic. Ten hours, two traffic jams and a downpour without windscreen wipers later, the highway gives way and New Delhi sprawls before me in all its crazed glory. Lakhan greets me at the compound gate like a long lost brother. Sarah hugs me like a long lost husband and I am home. Not because it is India but because it is Sarah. She is, we are, home.

I wake late to suburban sounds nearly erased from memory.

'*Aaaaiiiiiyeeeee*!! *Aaaaiiiiiyeeeee*!!' whines the garbage collector, calling residents to hand over the refuse he will turn into riches. Mangy cows clomp down the side lane, chomping their way through garbage even the collector does not want. The water pump grinds into gear, sucking up what's left of New Delhi's rapidly sinking water table to store in giant tanks on our roof. In the kitchen, Rachel and Mary are gossiping as always, and break into wide, delicious smiles when I enter. Rachel makes steamy sweet *chai* and they update me on the health of their daughters, the plots of the hot Hindi soap operas and whether friends from Sydney who visited in my absence were well behaved.

Briefed on domestics, I brace for office life and march upstairs where a mountain of mail awaits me. There are invitations for functions long gone, office accounts long overdue and 'humble requests' for pay raises by staff members.

Dear Sirs (the letter is addressed to both Sarah and me),
   . . . Since the prices of everyday products have gone up this year, I make an earnest request to kindly arrange

to give a suitable financial increment. May I mention I am the lone member in my family who is earning.

I shall always remain highly grateful to you my entire life.

Thanking you,
Yours most obedient servant . . .

I wade through seven months of paperwork to the cheers and thwacks of the local lads' afternoon cricket match; their contest floats from the street through windows open to a glowing February day. Soon home and office will slam shut against the summer scorch, but this year we will miss the sweat-fest.

Our final weeks are a rush of packing boxes and strange goodbyes. Friendships feel so defined by the tumultuous times and region that it's hard to see them lasting far beyond these shores. Most correspondents have drifted back to Delhi after long periods in Pakistan and Afghanistan and a string of spring parties are oddly melancholy. I find myself in huddles with colleagues trying to comprehend our intense experiences. One journalist can't sleep. Another can't wake up. Someone can't stop dreaming about Daniel Pearl. It is hardly happy party talk but at least it makes me feel less freakish about my own sense of overload, and I go home drunk and less despairing.

I feel ashamed for even feeling vulnerable. I grew up with lessons that showed Australian men as hardy, practical types, who were strong and stoic. They went off to war for years in jungles and deserts, and never had the need or time to talk about it when they came home. Strong, silent men who 'got on with it'. I haven't even fought a war; merely skirted around its edges – and then only for a few months. But if Khurram is right and the soul can only travel at a camel's speed, then mine has a lot of catching up to do on the last three years of running. Perhaps mine is a weaker generation of men, or perhaps we're taking better care.

Sarah and I focus on fun and skirt around the hurt. We are bruised by an unimaginable, unromantic first year of marriage. She still aches from the worry of September 11 and resents having been swept up in such a turbulent time. She has experienced it all as a citizen, not a journalist. I can only view it as a journalist; for now, these are the only eyes I have. And since I can make little sense of it myself, I am unable to express it to her. For someone supposed to be a communicator, I am hopelessly lost for words. But amid this alienation and frustration sits a quiet sense of triumph. We have made it through three years of long-distance love and now, slowly, we will rebuild our lives. This time, together.

The last box is packed and shipped, my successor is in place, Rachel cooks one last sublime lunch of *masala dosa* and I hold a final, farcical staff 'coffee and cake' meeting just to savour the awkward pauses. Moolchand sullenly delivers our last laundry load before declaring, 'Siiiirrr, I am verrrrry happy to have you as friend!' He leaves as he arrived: smiling ecstatically. Rachel weeps inconsolably, while Mary tries to touch our feet. For the first time in years, tears well in my eyes but I know my role is to be stoic, to be consoling, to be the *sahib*. Peter brings his perfectly behaved children to say goodbye and gives us a glistening silver tea set, a gift so generous I am embarrassed to accept it. The house echoes with its emptiness, the office is neat and has been brought into the twentieth century. My work is done and it's time to go.

As we step out to the car, the guards are lined up in military formation, proudly displaying recently bought new uniforms. Amar stands stiff and looking serious. Lakhan gives his trademark salute-cum-scratch and then breaks my heart.

'Sir,' he says with tender tears, 'I am having such strong feelings I cannot say.'

I struggle not to lose it and hug both men close to my chest, holding them tight to hold in my own wails. By the time we get into the car my shirt is soaked with staff tears and, as Abraham rolls down the road and we wave through the back window, I can keep it together no longer. We weep all the way to the airport, me much more than Sarah. An ocean of stored and ignored emotions pour onto the car floor. Poor Abraham is frowning like never before, his worried, knotty forehead not sure how to respond to a sobbing *sahib*.

But Abe will have his turn. As we pull into the airport, he starts to falter. He dutifully piles our bags onto trolleys, closes the boot and tries to smile and shake my hand as always with the wish, 'Have a good trip, sir.' He can't get past 'Have . . .' and falls into my soaked shirt and bawls such that I need to hold him up. For several minutes, Abraham clutches me tight, and Sarah and I start to wonder if leaving is such a good idea. Slowly, Abe's crying quietens; he stands on his own, wipes his eyes and returns to his routine.

'Have a good trip, sir.'

With recently tightened airport security, a long queue leads into the departures area and, as we join the line, I look back to see Abraham is bent over the steering wheel weeping inconsolably. After five minutes in line, it's time to go inside. I turn one final time to see Abraham has calmed down and watch as he drives off into the New Delhi night. In his wake, he leaves me with the lasting magic of Indian emotionalism.

'Let's go home,' I whisper in Sarah's ear and she turns to me and smiles with tear-filled eyes. I'd been imagining this moment since the day she came to India and I've been quietly practising this line for months. To finally say it out loud is not quite believable. We'd expected our journey to be as one, but it's been nothing of the sort. If anything, we have travelled in opposite directions. She gave up a job that greatly defined her, came to death's doorstep and then turned those stories of hers into a book about all that she discovered along India's array of spiritual paths, mostly without me. I have become defined by a job that has dominated both our lives and has brought me to the brink of soullessness. Now, a new adventure awaits us.

As our plane climbs over the New Delhi smog line, the capital grinds below in hues of orange and grey and we leave India with much more than we bargained for. We came here as two people. Now, we depart as three. Sarah is growing a baby, a most precious souvenir. I order champagne to toast new beginnings – and I am having such strong feelings I cannot say.

EPILOGUE

THE WAR AT HOME

Bondi Beach stretches in a perfect crescent of baking sand and bubbling sea as Sydney soaks up a shining autumn Sunday. The toned and tanned parade their tits and tattoos; abs and pecs, triceps and biceps ripple in a steroid-sponsored celebration of sex and this city. So very Sydney.

The odd man out in this seductive scene is a lilac-white weed with hairy legs; a modern half-goat, half-man Pan in Speedos and scratched sunglasses. That would be me. But it's not only the physique that sets me apart. Among this fun, I am shocked, even offended by the roasting rows of bodies. Bums wiggle, boobs jiggle as they always have; except now I see with prudish eyes. I am adrift in Bondi's bikini bonanza, and a beach that was once my scene now feels alien and confronting.

My mind is a cinema strobing images from another world – the *burqa*-clad women in the bazaars of Kabul; fly-blown children flopped beneath Jalozai's pathetic plastic shelters; bum-fluffed boys parading as soldiers; a leprous beggar tapping on my ankle. Such lives are far from this city of carefree swims and anxious home renovations. Trying to reconcile these worlds makes my brain feel like it will blow. The first few days in Sydney were ecstasy, embraced in the bosom of family and friends, but now, a week since returning, my body and mind are downloading. My loyal friend, adrenalin, stayed behind in South Asia and it feels like someone has drained my brain and filled it with sump oil.

Only one thing will cut through my mental mayhem, even if only for a moment. After years of righteous ranting, I must turn to my own religion. I walk to the water. Edging into the shallows, my ankles are tickled by cool currents; the tide is out, the sandbank slides for miles, and a teasing undertow quietly, delightfully, threatens. I lean into the surf, lifting my body above the whitewash as droplets spray like shrapnel in the sun. It's friendly fire. I gulp a greedy breath and plunge below. It is bliss. My body is enveloped and my brain is scrubbed of its static. I dive to the floor, as I did on leaving three years ago, stretching stumpy legs to shore, arms reaching for New Zealand, fingers clenching into the sand. I grasp at every grain for truths that mutter through water-filled ears. This salty heaven washes all rubbish away, like a fast-flowing gutter in a summer storm. Above, the waves are small, safe and fabulous fun. I squeal like a child, rapt in this natural high, and gasp at that great Australian congress of strangers sharing the surf – luminescent kids, leathery old men, burdened businessmen. Here, we are all as one and at one with the world. When you're swimming, everything seems possible.

I run up the beach towards Sarah, grinning to the tips of my ears, and the world is more than scorn and suffering. But this beach buzz, like the thrill of a great story, does not last. Slowly, the ecstasy seeps into the sand, fog folds back over my eyes and I surrender to this feeling like I might to a hangover.

Sarah stares to the horizon, salt drying on eyelashes, hand instinctively cupping a baby still too tiny to show. She is shining with the surety of home, the promise of pregnancy and the sensuality of Sydney.

But this city is not all frivolity. When we returned home I was greeted by the news that another friend had killed himself. Talk, dark and gentle Malakai walked out into the pre-dawn morning, never to return, desperate to relieve a mind that would not be quiet. He left behind scores who adored him, a partner devoted to him and their unborn son, who, like Daniel Pearl's, will never know his father. I have filed Malakai's suicide somewhere in the melting pot of my mind, to be emoted at a later date. Mourning Malakai, like many things, will have to take a number and wait.

To the outside observer, the storm in my mind is invisible. In fact, I take a kind of pride in my apparent resilience, an outer air of strength and flexibility. Friends and family expect me to be drawn and exhausted but I am playing the Australian male role after all.

And in many ways I do feel fine; it won't be till the clouds have slowly cleared, one by one, that I'll realise just how stormy things have been. My option overload morphed into plain old overload: too much, too fast, too loud for too long to absorb. In fact, we all have it. Accountants, couriers, teachers, carpenters. We are all moving faster than a camel can walk. It's just that I covered an especially large area at an incredibly tumultuous time. Inevitably, a lot got lost in transmission.

Now, a balding storm in Speedos is covering the length of Bondi, calling as he comes closer:

'JOOOOOONNNNNATHAN HARRRRLLEY!!!!'

My name is being bellowed by a muscly middle-aged man. As he navigates Bondi's patchwork of towels, I struggle to pull a name from my near-defunct memory and consider whether it's too late to get up and run.

'Jonathan! HOW ARE YOU!?' His Harbour Bridge grin is threatening to break free of the confines of his jaw and explode across Bondi. He thrusts out his hand to shake Sarah's.

'Rob Murray!' he declares to her. 'HOW-DO-YOU-DO!'

My memory jolts with a mighty thud: 'Muza'. He was one of a few cool, young teachers from my high school.

How could I not remember him? He was a teenage inspiration, someone who taught me to look beyond my cloistered, comfortable world. Like all great teachers, he taught me to open my eyes and to strive. We'd become friends, only for him to join my long list of neglected friendships. Now in his late forties, Rob looks my age, is twice as fit and glows with an infectious enthusiasm.

'What a journey you've had!' he shrieks. 'My *God* you were *brave!*'

I blush, flattered but embarrassed. If only he knew about the knocking knees on September 11, the panicked dives into Maiden Shah's dirt, the days tied to my laptop, never leaving the hotel, the absurd circus of Islamabad.

'You know,' I begin, 'it wasn't what it looked like. The war was a long way from me.'

'Ooohh, don't be silly!' he gushes. 'You were there, you were RIGHT THERE!'

Was I? The way my head feels, perhaps it was all a dream. And any suggestion of bravery makes me feel like a fraud.

'Well,' I go on, squinting into his piercing blue eyes, 'I was *almost* there.' Rob laughs like a frog in rain but I'm not joking. As I start to unravel the whole blurry journey, it seems unreal, like three years of a 3-D South Asian adventure film. It does seem I was only almost there.

Sarah's belly grows, ultrasounds suggest she is carrying a karate-kicking alien, and the prospect of parenthood descends at high speed. I come home one day to find a cot in our bedroom, drawers miraculously filled with baby's clothes, and highchairs and teddy bears dragged out from family garages. And, on a magical summer Sunday, when the sky seems too blue and high to be true, our daughter is born pink and wrinkled and blinking at the world. Three years, eleven months and four days after departing for what I thought would be the ultimate adventure, life's richest journey of all begins.

But on this ride, my world gets smaller, framed by four walls. It will not be had on Afghanistan's parched plateaus or in the thundering stands of Calcutta's cricket ground. And all hitherto ideas of what's 'normal' get turned on their head once again. I think nothing of licking regurgitated food from a giggling chin or being evicted from my bed at three in the morning by a pocket-sized acrobat. I am addicted to her monkey grip around my neck, her gummy grin and twinkling fingers. Life feels raw and gentle – and optimism is the only option.

Friends and family pour in with love and gifts. After being served tea for years by Rachel or waiters, the tables are turned and I have become a nonstop *chaiwallah*. Among the many who shower us with joy, few are as generous and gentle as Muza, who delivers champagne and astrology charts, birthday books and doting looks. He brings Sarah up to speed with the first series of *Kath and Kim* we missed last year and, when it's all getting out of control, he simply declares, 'It's *all* good!'

But Muza would not be staying for long.

A southerly slices the rain parallel with the ground and punches our faces. This day is steely grey, not like Sydney summer should be, and clouds hang so low they seem to sit on your head. Dee Why beach is a washing machine, deserted but for us in our dark suits and dresses, holding flowers and bracing against the gale, ankle-deep in sand. It's here that Rob will rest. Like Matt and Malakai, we didn't see it coming. We never do. Behind the smiles and strength, the hurt is held from view till it is too much to exhibit. His body is found in harbourside bushland. Letters had been written but nothing that Rob could have said would explain to any of us why those most full of life seem to take their own.

Now, Muza is ashes in an urn and his siblings wade, arm in arm, to scatter him in the water he loved. Rob's church was the beach and, of them all, Dee Why was most sacred. A lone bagpiper fights a losing battle against the gale, waves pummel Rob's suited siblings as they deliver their sombre cargo, and an ageing mother watches her son wash out on an angry ocean.

I've returned from a region caught in war and poverty to a land of peace and riches. Away, I'd idealised Australia and smoothed over its flaws but I can ignore them no more. In the last few years, I've had more friends kill themselves here than be killed in war zones, and the place I always thought of as tranquil, even boring, is looking troubled, even tortured. The noise of South Asia is steadily turning to a low hum in my mind and my camel-paced soul is slowly catching up with events. Don't ask me to explain it all: sometimes the most important words in our hearts will never find voice on our tongues. The media will never broadcast the meaning of life.

Sopping and drained from sobbing, old school friends and teachers take shelter at the surf club. They are the faces of my childhood, etched with smile lines and framed by wisps of grey. I want to talk about Muza or my daughter. They want to talk about my work. What was the war like? (I still don't know.) How did you handle the danger? (I didn't.) Did you see many dead men? (One, a pedestrian run over by a bus.) And my favourite: where's Osama bin Laden? (Well, if I knew . . .) It's wonderful to have people interested in what you do but today I'd rather listen than talk.

It's a day that softens everything. When you vow to be gentle forever and a day. Even though you know it won't last: tomorrow, the train will be late, work will make you mad and life's gentle hand will slip from reach. But we must reach and grab it tight.

I lost that grip. If we run too fast, love too much the deadlines and headlines, we lose the touch that makes us human. I replaced it with indifference, wallpapered over with bravado. I thought South Asia might make me tougher. It just made me meaner. Would I do it again? One hundred per cent, first-class, affirmative, sir. No doubt about it. We make mistakes, we learn, we grow and one day, hopefully, we come home.

The clouds are clearing as I climb into my car, where a photo of my daughter sits on the dashboard, a wide-mouthed frog with saucer brown eyes and barely a strand of hair. I edge through afternoon traffic impatient to see her but with all the time in the world. As I cross the Sydney Harbour Bridge, the setting sun finds its gap and blazes up the river in a golden glow of burnt orange and apricot. It's almost a subcontinental sun but without the weariness. Perhaps, like Australia, I am trying to hold out against the weight of the world outside – that other 'bloody universe' I'd been warned about. But, home and abroad, there will always be young men who will die for a cause and others who die for no good reason at all. And, for all of us, sometimes life's gentle touch will be firmly in our grasp; at others, a faint wave in the distance.

I quietly vow never to lose touch with life's gentleness again. No matter how far I travel.

ACKNOWLEDGEMENTS

Heartfelt thanks go to all those who made the making of this book possible – whether directly in its writing or indirectly through your understanding and support. All of you have played an indispensable role.

Special thanks go to my publisher Fiona Henderson, and my editors Kim Swivel, Nadine Davidoff and Sophie Ambrose, who provided perfect doses of patience and persistence.

To the countless people along the road, too numerous to mention, I am forever grateful for the life stories you so generously shared and which were all too often compressed into a few seconds of broadcast. To the many who freely gave background information, advice and guidance, no story could be told without you.

Sincerest thanks to all my colleagues and friends at the ABC in Australia and New Delhi for your inspiration and motivation.

Thanks to the ever-enthusiastic Rafael Epstein for encouraging me to continue through my darkest moments; to Melissa for keeping secrets; and to Christopher Kremmer for your incomparable insights.

Huge love and gratitude to Mum, Hugh and Andrew for your nurturing, timeless lessons and prompting to pursue the road less travelled.

And to all the friends and family for whom I have been hopelessly unavailable in the course of writing this book and roaming around South Asia, a thousand thanks for your understanding.

Last but by no means least, Sarah: your love, laughter and letters have travelled with me from the very start of this journey. I could not, I cannot, do it without you.